CALVINISM AND SCHOLASTICISM
IN VERMIGLI'S DOCTRINE
OF MAN AND GRACE

STUDIES
IN MEDIEVAL AND
REFORMATION THOUGHT

EDITED BY

HEIKO A. OBERMAN, Tübingen

IN COOPERATION WITH

E. JANE DEMPSEY DOUGLASS, Claremont, California
LEIF GRANE, Copenhagen
GUILLAUME H. M. POSTHUMUS MEYJES, Leiden
ANTON G. WEILER, Nijmegen

VOLUME XVIII

LEIDEN
E. J. BRILL
1976

CALVINISM AND SCHOLASTICISM IN VERMIGLI'S DOCTRINE OF MAN AND GRACE

BY

JOHN PATRICK DONNELLY, S.J.

LEIDEN
E. J. BRILL
1976

ISBN   90 04 04482 2

To my Teachers

TABLE OF CONTENTS

PREFACE

Every preface tries to lessen the debt of gratitude which the author has incurred while reading, researching and writing. My debts are particularly numerous and I can mention only the heaviest. My greatest debt for this book is to Professor Robert Kingdon of the University of Wisconsin at Madison who first suggested to me the need for research on Peter Martyr Vermigli in 1968. His suggestion led first to several seminar papers, then to a dissertation under his direction, "Peter Martyr on Fallen Man: A Protestant Scholastic View." First drafts of several chapters in this book underwent challenging and helpful criticism in Professor Kingdon's reformation seminar at the hands of promising reformation scholars, particularly Lynn Martin, Jerome Friedmann, Robert Kolb, Raymond Mentzer, Robert Richgels and Nancy Conradt. Professors William Courtenay and David Herlihy read the complete dissertation and made valuable suggestions. This book is an outgrowth of that dissertation, which I have revised and expanded considerably.

I was able to do most of the primary research in Florence, thanks to a fellowship during 1969-70 at Villa I Tatti, the Harvard University Center for Italian Renaissance Studies. At I Tatti I was especially encouraged by the Director, Professor Myron Gilmore, and by Professor Peter Bietenholz. While in Europe I was able to visit the major places where Peter Martyr lived and worked: Florence, Fiesole, Padua, Naples, Lucca, Strasbourg, Oxford, and Zurich. Even the historian of ideas needs the indefinable stimulus that old streets and monasteries, churches and lecture halls give his research. I am also grateful to Professor Philip McNair and Darwin College, Cambridge, and Doctor Peter Fraenkel and his team at the Musée historique de la Réformation at Geneva for their hospitality during short periods of research.

The unsung heroes of scholarship are librarians the world over. My greatest debts are to those at the Biblioteca Nazionale Centrale and Villa I Tatti, Florence; the Memorial Library, Madison; the Marquette University Memorial Library, Milwaukee; the University Library, Cambridge; the British Museum; the Bibliothèque publique et universitaire, Geneva; Zentralbibliothek, Zurich; and the Universitätsbibliothek, Basel.

Among Vermigli scholars I owe special debts to Professors Philip McNair and Marvin Anderson and Doctor Sergio Corda for suggestions and encouragement. I have greatly profited from conversations with Professors Peter Fraenkel, John Tedeschi, Jill Raitt, John Bray, Brian Armstrong, Anne Jacobson Schutte, Lowell Zuck, and the late Arthur Piepkorn. Among my fellow Jesuits I owe most to the advice and support of Jared Wicks, Michael Morrison, Paul Prucha, John O'Malley, Thomas Caldwell and Paul Bruckner. The last two did much onerous proof reading as well. I am indebted to the history department at Marquette University and particularly its chairman, Professor David Gardinier, for a lighter load in the spring of 1974, which enabled me to revise my research and prepare my manuscript. Special thanks are due my typist, Marie Reynolds, for hard work and great patience.

I am grateful to Professor Heiko Oberman for encouragement and for inclusion of this book in *Studies in Medieval and Reformation Thought*.

Finally, I owe a special debt to the Marquette University Jesuit Associates for their help with the publication subsidy.

Milwaukee, Wisconsin   JOHN PATRICK DONNELLY, S.J.
June, 1974

CHAPTER ONE

INTRODUCTION

This book examines two closely related problems: what was the theological anthropology of Pietro Martire Vermigli [1] and to what extent was Martyr a Protestant scholastic. This introductory chapter will try to define the meaning of these two questions, to indicate their importance, and to suggest their interrelationship.

Christianity has been one of the most decisive influences in shaping western civilization. The Christian Church and its teachings have been among the most stable and constant elements in our culture for the last two thousand years, but like all institutions and ideologies they have been subject to change and development. The pace of institutional and doctrinal change was especially fast during the sixteenth century. The founders of the new Protestant Churches of the sixteenth century justified their actions primarily on theological grounds. Martin Luther, at once creative theologian and battling popular leader, dominated the first generation of Protestantism, but by roughly 1540 the thrust of Lutheranism was blunted and the cutting edge of the Protestant struggle with Catholicism lay with Calvinism. Calvinism followed the main lines of Lutheran doctrine, but differed in emphasis and nuance in many areas and sharply on a few key points, notably the Eucharist, predestination, and church discipline. Popular and introductory histories necessarily tend to center around a few dominating personalities, and the dominating figure of the new movement and the new theology within Protestantism was certainly John Calvin. But to designate this complex movement *Calvinism* obscures almost as much as it illuminates. It implies a series of master-disciple relationships and a unity of doctrine and direction deriving from Calvin that disappear under close examination. The reality was rather a group of like-minded theologians and church leaders linked by personal contact and correspondence, by common ideals and uncommon energy, and

---

[1] The Latinized form of Pietro Martire Vermigli was Petrus Martyr Vermilius. North of the Alps he was generally known as Peter Martyr (or equivalents in Latin, French, and German) or simply as Martyr, a form often used by Vermigli himself. Little wonder then that modern scholars seem pretty evenly divided between calling him Martyr or Vermigli. For the sake of variety this study will use both names indifferently.

above all by a broad doctrinal consensus, though differing in details.[2]
Most of these men spent an important part of their life in present-day
Switzerland, often as exiles. Several of them can be accurately described as disciples of Calvin, but others are senior to Calvin, for instance Farel, Bullinger, and Vermigli. Calvin was clearly the greatest
theologian among them, and all the rest felt his influence, but they
were not without influence on Calvin. Primarily they were a group of
like-minded thinkers and scholars whose theologies developed along
parallel lines during roughly the same period, and many of their
writings continued influential for several generations.[3] Not a little of
the dynamism so marked in Reformed Protestantism during the years
after 1540 comes from this diversity within a broad unity.

   Peter Martyr Vermigli was one of the most influential theologians
within Reformed Protestantism, although well behind Calvin and

   [2] Besides Calvin, any list of these reformed theologians would include Knox,
Bullinger, Beza, Vermigli, Viret, Farel, Musculus, Zanchi, Tremellius, Gualter,
Myconius, à Lasco, Boquin, Haller, Ursinus, and many others. Many prominent
English churchmen could fairly be added. In many ways Zwingli and Oecolampadius were fore-runners. While Bucer and even Melanchthon were perhaps
closer to Calvin than to Luther in their final teaching on the Eucharist, they
must be classed as Lutherans. The distinction between the reformed and the
Lutherans admits of shading and cannot be reduced to an individual's stand on
any single doctrine, not even the Eucharist.
   [3] Calvin's ". . . international influence, though greater than that of any other
Protestant clergyman, was by no means undisputed. . . . Musculus at Berne and
Martyr at Strassburg were others who were by no means entirely overshadowed
by the Genevan. Looking back on the scene, Calvin's figure may appear to tower
over others, but perspectives are sometimes deceiving, because history tends to
concentrate on a few great names." Marshall Knappen, *Tudor Puritanism*, (Chicago:
1939), p. 137. The same point is made by Heinrich Heppe and Ernst Bizer. See
p. xix of Bizer's long historical introduction to his reissue of Heppe's *Die Dogmatik der evangelisch-reformierten Kirche*, (Neukirchen: 1958). It is more fully sub-
stantiated in chapter fifty, "Die reformierte Theologie bis zur Dortrechter
Synode in ihrer vorwiegenden Unabhängigkeit von Calvin," of Otto Ritschl,
Dogmengeschichte des Protestantismus, Band III, (Göttingen: 1926), pp. 243-282.
The most extreme statement on Martyr's relationship to Calvin comes from
the opening page of a five volume attack on them by the Jesuit controversialist
Cornelius Schulting, who asserts that it was disputed whether or not Calvin
borrowed his ideas in large part from Martyr. Martyr's style was less ornate
but clearer than Calvin's. ". . . illud certo constat Martyrem Calvino longe
fuisse doctiorem: erat enim in scholastica theologica apprime versatus . . . in
omnibus colloquiis et conventibus suo seculo religionis causa institutis ex parte
Calvinistarum semper primas tenuit, semper coryphaeus et antesignanus exstitit:
huic omnes plurimum deferebant, semper ei palmam tribuerunt. Calvinus et
Beza in epistolis primam laudum partem semper facile concedunt." *Biblioteca
catholica et orthodoxa . . .*, (Cologne, 1602), I, 1.

probably Bullinger and Beza as well. His eminence was well recognized in the sixteenth and seventeenth centuries, most strikingly in poems written on the occasion of his death by many leading Reformed scholars. In the century from 1550 to 1650 there were about 110 separate printings of his various writings.[4] Modern scholars have also recognized Martyr's importance and the need for further study of his life and especially of his thought.[5]

The reasons why Martyr has been relatively neglected are not hard to surmise. Unlike Calvin, Bullinger, and Beza, Martyr never headed a local church which would have given institutional weight and scope to his activities and to his theology. Martyr left Italy, never to return, in September of 1542. After brief stops in Zurich and Basel, he took up a professorship in Strasbourg late in 1542 and remained at his post there until November, 1547, when he left to take up the Regius professorship of divinity at Oxford. His nearly six years in England were probably the most influential period of his life. The accession of Mary Tudor made his position untenable, and he returned to his professorship at Strasbourg in October, 1553. Disagreement with the strong Lutheran party at Strasbourg lead to Martyr's departure for Zurich in July, 1556. Martyr taught at Zurich with great distinction until his death on November 12, 1562. Even though Martyr flits across the ecclesiastical history of Germany, England, France, and Switzerland, he was an Italian in the last analysis. The Italian Protestant Reformation was largely abortive. There was no strong Italian Protestant church to cultivate his memory as a founding father. Roman Catholic historians easily forget apostate canons. The Italians of the Cantimori

---

[4] The poems are reprinted at the beginning of Martyr's *Loci Communes*, ed. Robert Masson, (London: 1583) and many other editions of Martyr's works. Robert Kingdon and I will shortly publish a scholarly bibliography of all Martyr editions and writings in the *Corpus Reformatorum Italicorum* series. Martyr's stature among the Reformed in his later years is reflected in the correspondence of the period. Stanislaus Sarnicki writes in November, 1562, to Christopher Trecy: "Ad quam rem utere opera D. Petri Martyris cui me, obsecro, commedes velim. Hominem non novi, sed quum eius monumenta revolvo, apparet hominem esse talem qui cum quovis ex antiquioribus illis viris conferri debeat." *Calvini Opera*, XIX, c. 577. The learned Marburger Wigan Orthius describes Martyr as "... vir tantus quantum nunc theologum Germania nullam habet alium." Letter to Girolamo Zanchi, 13 July, 1561. *Zanchii ... Opera Theologica*, (Geneva: 1605), VIII, I, 156.

[5] Philip McNair, *Peter Martyr in Italy: An Anatomy of Apostasy*, (Oxford: 1967) vii; Marvin Anderson, "Word and Spirit in Exile (1542-61): "The Biblical Writings of Peter Martyr Vermigli," *Journal of Ecclesiastical History*, XXI, 1970, 193; Robert Kingdon, reviewing the fourth volume of the Beza correspondence in *Bibliothèque d'Humanisme et Renaissance*, XXX, 1968, 386-87.

4 INTRODUCTION

school, many of them Marxists, have naturally concentrated their
attentions on the radical Reformers. Martyr was a rather staid, orthodox Protestant. Although there is some interest in Martyr, the Italian
Protestant community is too small and too pre-occupied to generate
a base for large scale historical scholarship.[6]

Martyr's life has attracted more interest than has his theology. The
first biography was by Martyr's confidant, disciple, and successor as
professor of Old Testament at Zurich, Josiah Simler, who expanded
and published his funeral oration on Martyr's life.[7] Although
Theodore Beza knew Martyr personally, the account he gives in his
Icones seems derived from Simler.[8] During the nineteenth century there
were two rather poor biographies, then one rather good one.[9] Until
the last twenty years there was nothing except scattered chapters,
encyclopedia articles, a few scholarly notices, and one long, three-part
article.[10] The three major pillars of the recent modest revival of interest in Vermigli are Joseph C. McLelland's study of his sacramental
theology,[11] Philip McNair's meticulous investigation of his life in

---

[6] Luigi Santini has written two articles on Vermigli in the *Bolletino della società
di studi valdesi*, "Appunti sulla ecclesiologia di P. M. Vermigli e la edificazione
della Chiesa," CIV, 1958, 69-75, and " 'Scisma' e 'eresia' nel pensiero di P. M.
Vermigli," CXXV, 1969, 27-43.

[7] "Oratio de vita et obitu viri optimi, praestantissimi Theologi D. Petri
Martyris Vermilii, Sacrarum literarum in Schola Tigurina Professoris." This
was first published at Zurich in 1563 but is more accessible as a preface to many
of Martyr's works. I have used that printed in the edition of the *Loci Communes*
cited above. The reliability of Simler's "Oratio" is thoroughly discussed by
McNair, *Peter Martyr*, xiv-xviii and *passim*.

[8] Theodore Beza, *Icones, id est Verae Imaginis virorum doctrina simul et pietate
illustrium*, (Geneva: 1580).

[9] Friedrich Christoph Schlosser, *Leben des Theodore de Beza und des Peter Martyr
Vermili*, (Heidelberg: 1809); Charles Schmidt, *Vie de Pierre Martyr Vermigli*,
Thèse présentée à la Faculté de Théologie de Strasbourg, (Strasbourg: 1834);
Charles Schmidt, *Peter Martyr Vermigli: Leben und ausgewählte Schriften*, ("Leben
und ausgewählte Schriften der Väter und Begründer der reformirten Kirche"),
(Elberfeld: 1858). This last is far superior to the two earlier works.

[10] The major article is by Benjamin F. Paist, Jr., "Peter Martyr and the Colloquy
of Poissy," *Princeton Theological Review*, XX, 1922, 212-31, 418-47, 616-46; the
same subject is covered by a chapter in André Bouvier's *Henri Bullinger: le
successeur de Zwingli*, (Paris: 1940); Charles H. Smyth devotes a chapter to Martyr's
English period, *Cranmer and the Reformation under Edward VI*, (Cambridge: 1926);
the longest account in English of Martyr's whole life is chapter 10, 397-493, in
M. Young, *The Life and Times of Aonio Paleario*, (London: 1860).

[11] *The Visible Words of God: An Exposition of the Sacramental Theology of Peter
Martyr Vermigli, A.D. 1500-1562*, (Grand Rapids: 1957). This is a work of real
theological insight, but a bit careless on some historical and bibliographical
details. It somewhat over-emphasizes the modern aspects of Martyr's thought
while overlooking his scholastic side. McLelland has also written, "The Reformed

Italy,[12] and Klaus Sturm's survey of his early theology.[13] The great desideratum remains a scholarly analysis of Martyr's voluminous writings. The *Corpus Reformatorum Italicorum* projects a critical edition of Martyr's works that should stimulate and aid further study. McLelland and Gervase Duffield, working with the Sutton-Courtenay Press, are planning to publish several volumes of selected works in English translation. In Lucca, Vermigli proved himself one of the most effective city reformers,[14] though the seeds of Protestantism were planted in the Tuscan city well before his arrival,[15] but once outside Italy he was never more than incidentally engaged in an active ministry and was perforce thrown back largely upon Latin and the audience of students and intellectuals he could reach through Latin. His impact on his age was largely that of the pure intellectual and flowed mainly from his lectures and other writings. Only after scholars have delved into these will Martyr's place in history emerge.

Why study Martyr's doctrine of man? There are several reasons. Two older currents of thought, humanism and scholasticism, contributed to Martyr's doctrine of man. Both the scholastic and the humanist traditions were deeply interested in the problem of man and his

Doctrine of Predestination According to Peter Martyr," *Scottish Journal of Theology*, VIII, 1955, 255-71.

[12] McNair's typology of the Italian reformation in his first chapter is questionable, but the archival research throughout the rest of the book is beyond praise. McNair is now engaged in studying Martyr's years in England.

[13] *Die Theologie Peter Martyr Vermiglis während seines ersten Aufenthalts in Strassburg 1542-1547: Ein Reformkatholik unter den Vätern der reformierten Kirche. (Band XXXI: Beiträge zur Geschichte und Lehre der Reformierten Kirche.)* (Neukirchen: 1971). This work appeared after my book was substantially complete and exercised no influence on it. In some respects it covers the same ground. Sturm is far more alive to the scholastic influence on Martyr's thought than was McLelland, but he sees it as an unfortunate residue and hence underestimates the originality of Martyr's synthesis of scholasticism and Calvinism and its importance for later Reformed thought. Sturm restricts himself to Martyr's earliest, least productive and least mature years as a Protestant theologian. Nevertheless he gives the best overview of Vermigli's whole theology yet available and has mapped out its inter-connections. For a more extended evaluation, see my review in *The Sixteenth Century Journal*, IV, April 1973, 118. Two other studies of Martyr's theology have been recently completed. Sergio Corda has written a dissertation on Martyr's Eucharistics at the University of Zurich, soon to be published as *Veritas Sacramenti: A Study in Vermigli's Doctrine of the Lord's Supper*. Marvin Anderson examines Martyr as exegete in his forthcoming *Peter Martyr: A Reformer in Exile (1542-1562). A Study of Biblical Writings in England and Europe*, (Nieuwkoop: B. De Graaf, 1975). I have not seen these manuscripts.

[14] McNair, 206-38.

[15] Renzo Ristori has studied Protestantism in Lucca before Martyr's arrival, "Le origine della riforma a Lucca," *Rinascimento*, III, 2, 1952, 269-91.

relation to God. The problem of man was no less central to Protestantism, and all mainstream Protestants of the sixteenth century held a
rather common, consistent view. Although consciously appealing
back to Paul and Augustine, Protestantism brought new emphases
and new insights to the age old problem of man. But quite aside from
the centrality of the doctrine of man there is a further reason for
choosing to study Martyr's teaching on fallen man. This book examines whether Martyr was a Protestant scholastic. Scholasticism had a
distinctive philosophical doctrine of man, largely borrowed from
Aristotle. If indeed Martyr was a Protestant scholastic, the doctrine
of man should provide an excellent focal point for examining his
Protestant scholasticism, since his teaching will have a distinctively
Protestant content, largely theological, and a distinctively scholastic
content, largely philosophical and methodological.

Why is it important to examine whether and to what degree Martyr
was a Protestant scholastic? The answer to this question requires
some background.

The Protestant reformation started with Martin Luther. Its early
success was breath-taking and immensely aided by social, economic
and political factors. But the reformation was also the reaction of a
deeply religious and scholarly man, a monk and a professor, to a
religious and intellectual malaise. He was convinced that the corruption of Roman Catholic religious practice by superstition and
moral turpitude flowed from bad theology, especially from Pelagianism and scholasticism. He attacked both with immense vigor. The
Reuchlin controversy and the success of the *Epistolae Obscurorum
Virorum* indicated an immense reservoir of hostility to scholasticism
that was by no means confined to Germany. For over a decade intellectuals had smiled at Erasmus's jibes against scholasticism and had
subscribed to his program of *philosophia Christi* which tried to circum-
vent medieval theology by applying the newly developed tools of
philology and history to a fresh, humanistic understanding of the
Bible and the Fathers of the Church. To many of these intellectuals,
Luther's *"sola scriptura"* seemed very like humanism's *"ad fontes"* as a
substitute for scholasticism.

Luther's reaction to his own nominalistic training was an intrinsic
part of his quest for a gracious God and the reformation of Christendom. His attitude toward scholasticism is well illustrated by his
Disputation against Scholastic Theology (1517) and his *Appeal to the Ruling
Class of the German Nation* (1520). Many of the theses in the *Disputation*

deal with the doctrine of grace and attack William Ockham, Gabriel Biel, and Pierre d'Ailly as Pelagians. Equally important are the statements on theological methodology directed largely against Aristotle:

> It is an error to say no man can become a theologian without Aristotle. Indeed, no one can become a theologian unless he becomes one without Aristotle.
> No syllogistic form is valid when applied to divine terms.
> Briefly, the whole of Aristotle is to theology as darkness is to light.
> It would have been better for the Church if Porphyrus with his universals had not been born for the use of theologians.[16]

In the *Appeal to the Ruling Class* Luther formulates a sweeping program for university reformation, especially regarding training for the ministry. The crux of his program is the exaltation of the Bible text and the discarding of scholastic commentaries on Peter Lombard's *Sentences*. According to Luther, the use of the blind pagan Aristotle has been introduced into the schools by Satan himself. Aristotle's *Physics*, *Metaphysics*, and *De Anima* and especially the *Ethics* must be discarded, although the use of the *Logic*, *Rhetoric*, and *Poetics* can continue.[17] Luther exhausted his rich vocabulary of vituperation on Aristotle.[18] Vermigli took a very different attitude toward the "master of them that know" which will require careful examination.

John Calvin's training was primarily humanistic and included a far more superficial exposure to scholasticism than had Luther's, but Calvin's hostility was almost equally great. Alexandre Ganoczy examined the first edition of the *Institutes* and found that Calvin knew no scholastic theology beyond Gratian's *Decretals* and Lombard's *Sentences*; of sixty-nine references to scholastic theology, sixty-six serve to illustrate Roman error; the other three are presented as confirmations that a point is so obvious that even the Roman sophists recog-

---

[16] *Luther's Works*, ed. H. T. Lehmann, J. Grimm, (Philadelphia: 1957), XXXI, 112-13; For the original text, see D. Martin Luther's *Werke, Kritische Gesamtausgabe*, (Weimar: 1883 ff.), I, 222-28. Henceforward designated *W.A.*

[17] *W.A.* VI, 457-58.

[18] The Weimar editors have gathered together Luther's statements about Aristotle (LVIII, I, 167-170) and Aquinas (295-96). Luther's attitude toward Aristotle, the scholastics, and reason itself, is much more complicated than these often emotional outbursts would indicate. Luther cannot be classified simply as an anti-intellectual, even if isolated statements give that impression. For a thorough treatment of Luther's attitude toward reason and its relation to faith see Brian Gerrish, *Grace and Reason: A Study in the Theology of Luther*, (Oxford: 1962).

nize it. Later in life Calvin's knowledge of scholasticism grew; but in preaching on Job he states:

> And even if there were in the papacy a doctrine not bad and fully false in itself, it would nonetheless be necessary to detest such a style as they have invented, because by this means they have perverted the true and natural use of the word of God.[19]

Given this hostility toward scholasticism by the two greatest theologians of the Reformation, the student of early seventeenth century Protestant theology faces an enigma. Scholasticism is, if anything, even more strongly entrenched than in the early decades of the sixteenth century. A distinctive Protestant scholasticism developed whose origins demand explanation. More an attitude and approach than a set of dogmatic propositions, Protestant scholasticism defies easy characterization, and definitions are seldom attempted.[20] Brian Armstrong finds four characteristics in developed Protestant scholasticism:

> (1) Primarily it will have reference to that theological approach which asserts religious truth on the basis of deductive ratiocination from given assumptions or principles, thus providing a logically coherent and defensible system of belief. Generally this takes the form of syllogistic reasoning. It is an orientation, it seems, invariably based upon an Aristotelian philosophical commitment and so relates to medieval scholasticism. (2) The term will refer to the employment of reason in religious matters, so that reason assumes at least equal standing with faith in theology, thus jettisoning some of the authority of revelation. (3) It will comprehend the sentiment that the scriptural record contains a unified, rationally comprehensible account and thus may be used as a measuring stick to determine one's orthodoxy. (4) It will comprehend a pronounced interest in metaphysical matters, in abstract, speculative thought, particularly with reference to the doctrine of God. The distinctive Protestant position is made to rest on a speculative formulation of the will of God.[21]

---

[19] Alexandre Ganoczy, *Le Jeune Calvin: Genèse et Evolution de sa vocation Réformatrice*, (Wiesbaden: 1966). The Job quotation is cited by Edward A. Dowey, *The Knowledge of God in Calvin's Theology*, (New York: 1952), 27-28. A generation ago Quirinus Breen showed that Calvin's early training was mainly humanistic: *John Calvin: A Study in French Humanism*, (New York: 1968). On the humanistic structure of Calvin's theology, see Gilbert Rist, "Modernité de la Méthode Théologique de Calvin," *Revue de théologie et philosophie*, 1968, 19-33. Also Brian Armstrong, *Calvinism and the Amyraut Heresy: Protestant Scholasticism and Humanism in Seventeenth Century France*, (Madison: 1969), 33-37.

[20] Armstrong, 32. The difficulty of defining Protestant scholasticism is also made clear by Bengt Hagglund, *History of Theology*, (St. Louis: 1968), trans. Gene J. Lund, 299, 300.

[21] Armstrong, 32.

Scholars have studied the development of neo-Aristotelianism and of neo-scholasticism in both the philosophy and theology faculties of the seventeenth century German universities, especially those controlled by the Lutherans.[22] The key figure in the development of this Lutheran scholasticism was undoubtedly Philip Melanchthon. Before becoming a disciple of Luther, Melanchthon had been an Erasmian, but with a philosophical bent. Sensitive to Erasmus' call *"ad fontes,"* he determined to devote his philological and pedagogical skills to cleansing Aristotle from the accretions of medieval commentaries so that a renewed and purified Aristotelianism might find a proper place in a humanistically oriented university curriculum. With this purpose he accepted a chair at Wittenberg in 1518 and thereby came into that close and fruitful contact with Luther which was to be so momentous for the history of Lutheranism. Luther's influence caused Melanchthon to repudiate temporarily his aims regarding Aristotelianism; he lectured on Scripture and worked out the first systematic statement of Lutheran theology in his *Loci Communes.*[23] But later Melanchthon returned to lecturing on Aristotle; he wrote philosophical treatise such as the *Liber de Anima*, the *Erotemata Dialectica* and the *Initia Doctrinae Physicae* whose every page proclaimed a debt to Aristotle.[24] More and more in the later editions of the *Loci Communes* Melanchthon takes up and uses, often without further explanation, terminology and arguments based on Aristotle's doctrine of matter and form, substance and accidents, and the rules for syllogistic thinking. The Wittenberg curriculum for training Lutheran clergymen stressed philosophical studies based on Aristotle.[25]

Melanchthon considered it impossible for the theologian to dispense with Aristotelian philosophy. Aristotle also dominated his ethical and political thought.[26] He believed passionately in the need for an educated clergy and devoted so much skill to the development of curricula and textbooks that he earned the proud title of *praeceptor*

---

[22] Paul Althaus, *Die Prinzipien der deutschen reformierten Dogmatik im Zeitalter der aristotelischen Scholastik*, (Darmstadt: 1967); Max Wundt, *Die deutsche Schulmetaphysik des 17. Jahrhunderts*, (Tubingen: 1939); Peter Petersen, *Geschichte der Aristotelischen Philosophie im Protestantischen Deutschland*, (Leipzig: 1921).

[23] Jaroslav Pelikan, *From Luther to Kierkegaard*, (St. Louis: 1950) 24-31.

[24] Philipi Melanthonis *Opera quae supersunt omnia*, ed. C. G. Bretschneider, (*Corpus Reformatorum*), XIII, (Halle: 1846).

[25] Pelikan, 33-35.

[26] On Melanchthon's use of Aristotle, see Petersen, 19-108.

Germaniae. Melanchthon's program for undergraduate and theological education spread throughout Germany with the spread of Lutheranism. The mind of the undergraduate was subtly conditioned to think in Aristotelian categories. When the student began theology, scholastic theology came easily and naturally.[27]

This Melanchthonian *trahison des clercs* did not go unchallenged, especially by the bitterly anti-philosophical Matthias Flacius Illyricus; indeed, the controversy for and against Melanchthonianism was the dominant theme of internal Lutheran history fron the death of Luther until the *Formula of Concord* in 1580. The *Formula* returned to Luther by sharply repudiating Melanchthon's synergism and ecumenical unionism, but it consecrated the triumph of Melanchthonian Aristotelianism, which bore a rich harvest throughout the coming age of Lutheran orthodoxy.[28]

Only recently have scholars turned much attention to the origins of Protestant scholasticism within the Reformed tradition. The picture is more complicated and less clear than with Lutheranism. No single individual played the central role of Melanchthon. Moreover, Lutheranism was geographically rather centralized in central and northern Germany and in Scandinavia. Conditions were fairly homogeneous; and during the critical years from the Peace of Ausburg until the outbreak of the Thirty-Years War, Lutheranism did not have to struggle for its very existence. During this period Reformed Protestantism was constantly struggling for existence; beyond that, conditions varied enormously in England, Poland, Switzerland, Scotland, France, the Netherlands, and the Palatinate. The development of Reformed theology could not escape the influence of this diversity and this struggle. Nonetheless scholasticism developed throughout Reformed Protestantism almost as strongly as in Lutheranism. This development must be traced and accounted for. Here again purified Aristotelianism played a crucial role.

One of the best introductions to Reformed scholasticism is Brian Armstrong's *Calvinism and the Amyraut Heresy: Protestant Scholasticism and Humanism in Seventeenth Century France.* Armstrong develops the thesis that within the Reformed tradition there were two major

---

[27] Pelikan, 35. Probably the best study of the interaction of Melanchthonian pedagogy and theology is Helmut Liedtke, *Pädagogik der werdenden Orthodoxie: Ein Beitrag zur Bestimmung des Verhältnisses von Reformation und Humanismus,* (Konigsdorf: 1968).

[28] Pelikan, 38-45.

streams, the biblical humanism of John Calvin and the embryonic
Protestant Scholasticism represented chiefly by Peter Martyr, Theodore Beza, and Jerome Zanchi. By the Synod of Dort the scholastic
stream had obtained a dominance that it held throughout the seventeenth century.[29] Armstrong's contention is not unsupported by
previous scholarship. A generation ago Delio Cantimori had pointed
out that, probably due to their monastic training, Vermigli and
Zanchi manifested a scholastic culture only superficially touched by
humanism.[30] It has long been known that Beza refused to allow
Peter Ramus to teach at Geneva because of his attacks on Aristotle.
Certainly Beza gave Aristotle a prominent place in the curriculum at
Geneva. Beyond that, Ernst Bizer has argued Beza's responsibility
for giving reason a far more decisive voice in theological method.[31]
One of Bizer's students, Walter Kickel, has greatly elaborated this
thesis.[32] The Aristotelianism that formed the core of the new Reformed scholasticism was not the traditional medieval understanding
of Aristotle of the northern universities, but rather a transplant of the
new approaches to Aristotle pioneered in Italy, especially at the

---

[29] Armstrong, 31-42.

[30] Delio Cantimori, *Eretici italiani del Cinquecento*, (Florence: 1939), 36.

[31] Ernst Bizer, *Frühorthodoxie und Rationalismus*, (Zurich: 1963), 6-15.

[32] Walter Kickel, *Vernunft und Offenbarung bei Theodor Beza*, (*Beiträge zur Geschichte und Lehre der reformierten Kirche*, vol. 25), (Neukirchen: 1967). Kickel
shows that the study of Beza as a theologian has been neglected, partly because
there is no modern edition of his theological works, partly because he has been
classed as a mere purveyor of Calvin's ideas. Kickel finds much original in Beza,
especially his use of philosophy and reason in theology. Beza's acceptance of
Aristotelianism as a theological tool parallels and depends on that of Melanchthon.
To be sure, Beza subordinates reason to revelation, but reason can reach a knowledge of God's unicity, immutability, and omnipotence. Beza's thought centers
on the certitude of theology as a science and the sureness of its principles and
methods, whereas Calvin underlined the certitude of Scripture and of faith.
Kickel's thesis found some support from Henri Meylan, Alain Dufour, and
Arnaud Tripet, the editors of the *Correspondance de Théodore de Bèze*, (Geneva:
1965), IV, 9, 182-83, who make much of a request from Beza to G. Grataroli
for a copy "illum tuum Pomponatium." This probably refers to Pietro Pomponazzi's *De Incantationibus* but possibly to his *Libri Quinque de Fato, de Libro Arbitrio*,
et de Praedestinatione, since Beza already possessed a copy of the *De Incantationibus*,
first published from manuscripts by Grataroli, and knew from its preface that
Grataroli owned and planned to publish the manuscript of the *De Fato*, (*Correspondance*, II, 155). Kickel's interpretation has not been confirmed by the two most
recent American studies of Beza, Jill Raitt, *The Eucharistic Theology of Theodore
Beza: Development of the Reformed Doctrine*, (Chambersburg, Pa., A.A.R. Studies
in Religion, n. 4, 1972) and John Bray, "Theodore Beza's Doctrine of Predestination," unpublished dissertation, Stanford University, 1972. They rightly see
Beza as a better Calvinist and less the rationalist than does Kickel.

Universities of Padua and Bologna and usually associated with Pietro
Pomponazzi and Jacobo Zabarella. It was from this milieu that
Vermigli sprang.

For this reason three scholars in particular have urged a thorough
examination of the role of Peter Martyr Vermigli in the rise of Protestant scholasticism. Robert Kingdon pointed out the Aristotelian
terminology pervading Vermigli's books, his Paduan training, and
his commentary on Aristotle's Nicomachean ethics. He suggested
that Vermigli might be a more important avenue of Reformed contact
with Italian Aristotelianism than Beza.[33] Brian Armstrong urges the
investigation in even stronger terms, pointing out that McLelland's
study downplayed this side of Martyr's theology, while McNair's
biography shows his scholastic training but does not explore its impact on his later theology.[34] John Stanley Bray argues for further research on the influence of Martyr as a source of scholasticism in Beza's
theology and the use Martyr makes of Aristotle.[35]

This book tries to provide the detailed study these scholars request.

It is based on a review of all Martyr's writings, including his correspondence, focusing particularly on his doctrine of man.[36] The arrangement of the coming chapters is topical rather than chronological
since the evolution within Martyr's thought during his years as a
writer was not great enough to urge a chronological arrangement.
But prior to an analysis of Martyr's teaching, his intellectual background and the sources of this thought need to be reviewed.

---

[33] *Bibliothèque d'Humanisme et Renaissance*, XXX, 1968, 386-87. Kingdon's
remarks were part of his review of the fourth volume of the Beza *Correspondance*.
Earlier he had stressed Aristotle's influence on Martyr's political thought, *Geneva and
the Consolidation of the French Protestant Movement, 1564-1572*, (Madison: 1967), 216-17.

[34] Armstrong, 130-31.

[35] Bray, 8, 9, 259.

[36] The particular editions of Vermigli's works that I have used are listed in
the bibliography. Most of Vermigli's correspondence is printed in the *Loci
Communes*. The Parker Society publications of the *Zurich Letters*, *Original Letters*
and *The Works of John Jewel* (see the bibliography) give many letters to and a few
from Martyr not found in the *Loci*. A good number of letters in English archives
were missed by the editor of the *Loci* and can be found in Huelin, Daniel Gerdes,
Scrinium Antiquarum sive Miscellanea Groningana ..., (Groningen: 1753,) and
George C. Gorham, *Gleanings of a Few Scattered Ears During the Reformation in
England and the Times Immediately Succeeding, A.D. 1533 to A.D. 1589*, (London:
1857). The Beza *Correspondance* and the *Calvini Opera* reprint many letters to and
from Martyr. Marvin Anderson has kindly allowed me to use several manuscript
letters he has discovered. Anderson has prepared a checklist of 297 items of
Vermigli correspondence which will be published in the forthcoming Vermigli
bibliography in the *Corpus Reformatorum Italicorum*.

CHAPTER TWO

THE SOURCES OF MARTYR'S THOUGHT

Peter Martyr Vermigli was among the most erudite men of his age.[1] He was not greatly original, but he was able to distill into a unified, personal view the thought and writings of several intellectual traditions that reached back centuries and even millenia. Any adequate study of Martyr's thought must uncover the sources of his ideas and at least try to show in what way Martyr's use of these ideas was distinctive. This chapter highlights what is distinctive in Martyr by contrasting his use of previously existing traditions with John Calvin's use of them. Martyr's theology is no carbon copy of Calvin's, yet their basic theological stance is close enough so that comparison will serve to highlight what is distinctive in each.

There are three kinds of evidence that enable us to reconstruct the sources of Martyr's thought. First, a fair amount is known about Martyr's life and education. This information is readily available in the various biographies of Martyr, starting with that of his friend and confidant Simler. Many of Martyr's friends were themselves very prominent and have been the subject of biographies and monographs. These studies also provide background on the milieu in which Martyr moved. Further evidence of the sources of Martyr's thought is provided by Martyr's library which can be largely reconstructed.[2] The

---

[1] "An Gelehrsamkeit stand er vielleicht höher als Calvin, an Scharfsinn stand er ihm gleich; wenige Theologen des sechzehnten Jahrhunderts waren so vertraut wie er mit den Kirchenvätern und den Scholastikern; Ich glaube, kein Einziger ausser Fagius hat damals die Rabbinen des Mittelalters genauer gekannt." Schmidt, *Leben*, 58. Alexander Schweitzer agrees: ". . . kirchlicher Gelehrsamkeit . . . worin Martyr von keinem andern reformatorischen Manne übertroffen worden sei": quoted in Peter Walser, *Die Prädestination bei Heinrich Bullinger im Zusammenhang mit seiner Gotteslehre*, (Zurich: 1957), 184. ". . . among the reformers he yielded place to no one as a scholar." W. M. Southgate, *John Jewel and the Problem of Doctrinal Authority*, (Cambridge, Mass.: 1962), 20.

[2] Martyr willed his library to his servant Giulio Santerenziano who eventually sold much of it to the Academy at Geneva. Many of these books are still at the Geneva *Bibliothèque publique et universitaire*. Frederic Gardy and Alexandre Ganoczy have attempted to identify those books that once belonged to Martyr. I have relied especially on Ganoczy's investigations. See Frederic Gardy, "Les Livres de Pierre Martyr Vermigli conservés à la Bibliothèque de Genève," *Anzeiger für Schweizerische Geschichte*, N.F., XVII, 1919, 1-6, and Alexandre Ganoczy *La Bibliothèque de l'Académie de Calvin*, (Geneva, 1969), 19-27, 337. I give a systematic reconstruction of Martyr's library in the appendix of the present work.

most important evidence for the sources of Martyr's thought is that provided by his own writings. Even though they contain few personal reminiscences and little autobiographical material, they are rich in references to and citations from Martyr's reading and thereby provide a topography of the sources of his ideas.

According to Simler's biography, Martyr's mother started teaching him Latin at a very early age and gradually introduced him to such classical authors as Terence.[3] As Martyr was a pious and bookish lad, the religious life attracted him, and he determined to enter the Augustinian canons. In his fifteenth year Martyr began his novitiate at the Badia Fiesolana which sits in the hills above Florence about ninety minutes walking time from the center of the city. The hills provide a magnificent view of the city and cool evenings even when Florence swelters. More important in directing Martyr to this particular house was its excellent library and the canons' reputation for piety and learning. Cosimo de' Medici spent 70,000 ducats in refurbishing the monastery and hiring forty-five scribes to transcribe some two hundred volumes for the library. A generation before Martyr's entrance the abbot was a member of the Platonic academy, and here the poet Politian and the philosopher Pico della Mirandola used to repair to reflect and write.[4] Most of Martyr's time would have been spent in prayer and menial tasks, but certainly he found many hours to exploit the treasures of the monastery library.

His talents must have impressed his superiors, for they sent him on to their finest house of studies to complete his priestly training. The monastery of S. Giovanni di Verdara at Padua was Martyr's home from 1518 to 1526. The monastery had its own director of studies and offered a sound grounding in Aristotle. More important still, the training of the young Augustinians was integrated into the great University at Padua. Theology lectures were available in the nearby houses of the Dominicans, Franciscans, and Augustinian Hermits. During Martyr's stay there the University was the finest in Italy, perhaps the finest in the world.[5] Martyr's prior was Alberto da Verona, a scholar "nurtured in the choicest traditions of the humanists." [6] The whole atmosphere of the house encouraged *docta pietas* among

---

[3] Simler, third page. There is no pagination in Simler's *Vita*.
[4] McNair, 70-79.
[5] McNair, 81-88.
[6] McNair, 88.

the young canons regular, and had none of the antiintellectualism that marred the *Imitatio Christi* and certain elements of the *devotio moderna* movement in northern Europe. The monastery possessed an outstanding library. Several professors had bequeathed their private libraries to the monastery so that the selection of books was much wider than might be expected in a monastic library. The noted Averroist Nicoletto Vernia left his library, and Giovanni Calfurnio's bequest brought few works of devotion but seventy-one volumes of Greek classics and eighty of Roman authors. So rich was the library that the great humanist Pietro Bembo frequently met there with his friends for literary discussions. Here it was that Martyr met and became a friend of the future Cardinal. Even deeper friendship developed with two other prominent members of Bembo's circle, the poet Marcantonio Flaminio and the young English nobleman Reginald Pole. Some fifteen years later Pole, Flaminio, and Martyr were all prominent in the movement of Evangelism. Evangelism was an unstable compound; some of the leaders like Martyr espoused Protestantism, others like Pole embraced the Counter-Reformation.[7]

The classical studies pursued by Bembo and his circle were but a condiment to the main fare at Padua. The glory of Padua was its instruction in Aristotle. Most of Martyr's time there was devoted to the study of scholastic philosophy and theology. In later life Martyr had reservations about the value of his theological training, but to his dying day he looked fondly back on his courses in philosophy.[8] Martyr's enthusiasm for his old professors and old school shines through the pages of Simler who here is obviously repeating Martyr's reminiscences: "At that time he wholly dedicated himself to the study of philosophy and spent day and night in reflecting on all the arts. He often used to say that whatever he knew in philosophy and in what are called humane letters he largely acquired during his studies at Padua. Although he used to depreciate his own skill in these disciplines, I and many others always considered it to be great indeed." [9]

---

[7] McNair, 94-100.

[8] *The Works of John Jewel*, edited for the Parker Society by John Ayre, (Cambridge: 1850), IV, xiii.

[9] "Illo igitur tempore totum sese philosophicis studiis addixit, et dies noctesque in omnium artium meditatione versatus est: itaque saepe referre solebat sese quicquid in philosophia et illis literis quas humaniores nominant, sciret, quod ipse quidem parum esse dicebat, ego vero cum aliis multis magnum semper iudicabam,

Simler mentions that three of Martyr's philosophy professors singled him out for special praise. One was the Averroist Giambattista Gonfaloniere. Another was the Milanese Branda Porro, "without any question called the Prince of philosophers of his time." [10] Porro used to affectionately call Martyr his Florentine and frequently used his brilliant pupil as a foil and challenger in the public disputations that were the crowning point of academic life at Padua. [11]

The third and most important of the professors mentioned by Simler was Marcantonio de Passeri, known as Genua: "this outstanding teacher, *quo nemo pertitor Aristotelis interpres*, dominated the School of Philosophy at Padua as Pomponazzi had dominated it before him." [12] Genua started his teaching career the year before Martyr's arrival and was to have many brilliant students, among them Sperone Speroni, Francesco Patrizzi, and Jacobo Zabarella. His only published work, *In Tres Libros Aristotelis de Anima*, appeared posthumously in 1576, so that pinning down his precise philosophical position in his early teaching days when Martyr was his student becomes difficult. [13] Genua's mature philosophy was basically Averroist but with several new twists. The key book for Genua, as for Paduan philosophy generally, was Aristotle's *De Anima*, and the key questions were the unity of the agent intellect and the immortality of the soul. With Averroes Genua insisted that the agent intellect was not a true form animating the human body. Rather, Genua classes the agent intellect as the lowest of the separate intelligences and as common to all men. The agent intellect relates to men as the separate intelligences do to their celestial spheres. Genua breaks somewhat with the Averroist tradition

---

id se magna ex parte acceptum reffere Patavinis studiis." Simler, third page. Throughout this investigation I have modernized sixteenth century Latin punctuation for clarity's sake.

[10] F. Argelati, *Biblioteca Scriptorum Mediolanensium*, II, c. 1115. Quoted by McNair, 108.

[11] ... in publicis congressibus saepenumero Branda Florentinum suum, sic enim Martyrem nominabat, ad disputandum provocaret." Simler, third page.

[12] McNair, 110.

[13] The only modern reprint of Genua's writings is an Italian translation by Tullio Gregory of this commenary on the *De Anima* (ff. 137r, 138r-140v) in *Grande antologia filosofica*, VI, *Protestantismo e riforma cattolica*, ed. M. F. Sciacca, (Milan: 1964), 742-763. The translated passages are an exposition and critique of the arguments of St. Thomas on the unity and immortality of the soul. Many manuscripts of the lectures of Genua and of Juan Montesdoch, another Averroist who taught Martyr, are still extant in many Italian libraries, but they present problems of dating. See P. O. Kristeller, *Iter Italicum*, (London: 1963-67); for Genua manuscripts: I, 189, 284, 289, 291, 294, 341, 348, 352; II, 39, 124, 246, 329, 530, 531. For Montesdoch: I, 168, 289, 367, 380; II, 226, 546.

by preferring several of the older Greek peripatetics, whose writings had recently become available to the Arab *Commentator*. In his view, not only did the Greeks enjoy an advantage over the Arab because Greek was their native language, but they were the source of most of the Arab's ideas which they expressed more clearly and precisely. The Greek commentators that Genua and his disciples preferred were Theophrastes, Themistius, and especially Simplicius. He and his followers soon won the title of *Simpliciani*. To the consternation of old fashioned Averroists such as Marcantonio Zimara, the Simplicians introduced some new philosophical vocabulary based on the Greek commentators and wrote and taught in a Latinity which was heavily indebted to Renaissance humanism. These differences may seem trivial now, but they set the Simplicians violently at odds with the old guard, doubtless to the delight of Martyr and the other students.[14]

As will be shown, Martyr did not follow Genua in upholding the Averroist separate agent intellect, but he does adopt the more classical Latinity, and he does cite the Greek commentators freely. As Martyr's enthusiasm for Aristotle grew, he became less satisfied with the Latin translations of Aristotle which were the basis of his lectures. Even the newer translations made with help of the Greek commentators and the new tools of Renaissance philology seemed inadequate to him. He determined to learn Greek so that he could understand Aristotle directly in his own language.[15] He cast about for a teacher, but surprisingly the chair of Greek studies was vacant from 1524 to 1526.[16] Martyr would not be put off; he undertook the arduous task of teaching himself the language, often sitting up most of the night in the monastic library. Soon his proficiency grew, and he turned the skills acquired over the dense, crabbed pages of the philosopher to the equally demanding but more pleasant masterpieces of Greek poetry and oratory. Still it is worth emphasizing that it was the desire to read Aristotle, not classical literature or the New Testament, that led Martyr to learn Greek.

At Padua Martyr was exposed to a great variety of Aristotelianisms. There was the Simplician Aristotle of Genua. There was the older

[14] Bruno Nardi, *Saggi sull' aristotelismo padovano*, (Florence: 1958), 324, 387-91, 452-53. McNair, 110-12.

[15] ". . . Quia ergo Latini libri non ubique fideliter et perspicue Aristotelis sententiam exprimebant, statuit Graecam linguam addiscere ut Aristotelem aliquando sua lingua loquentem audiret . . ." Simler, third page.

[16] This improbable hiatus is mentioned by Simler and has been verified in detail by McNair, 112-14.

Averroist Aristotle of his professors Juan Montesdoch and Giambattista Gonfaloniere. Most of Martyr's theology professors were
Dominicans and Thomists; from them and his own extensive reading
in St. Thomas he undoubtedly got to know St. Thomas's interpretation of Aristotle. There was still a fourth Aristotle at Padua, the
Alexandrist interpretation. Its greatest spokesman was the most
famous of all the Paduan Aristotelians, Pietro Pomponazzi. Pomponazzi left Padua for Bologna in 1509, nine years before Martyr's arrival,
but his spirit and ideas continued to reverberate in the lecture halls.[17]
Pomponazzi started as an Averroist, but a reading of St. Thomas's
critique of the Arab convinced him that Averroes' position on a
single agent intellect for all men was untenable. This conviction was
deepened by a study of Alexander of Aphrodisias, but Alexander also
led Pomponazzi to a viewpoint quite opposed to St. Thomas: that
the immortality of the soul cannot be proved rationally but must be
accepted as part of the Christian faith. The sincerity of Pomponazzi's
belief in the immortality of the soul is much debated but does not
concern this study. Before Pomponazzi Cajetan and Scotus both asserted that the soul's immortality could not be proved but must be
believed.[18] Their sincerity is unquestionable. Martyr also thought the

---

[17] It was at Padua in the 1530's that Guglielmo Grataroli purchased manuscript
copies of Pomponazzi's *De Incantationibus* and *De Fato*, both long and important
works. After his conversion to Protestantism (under Martyr's indirect influence
according to McNair, 121) and flight to Basel, Grataroli published the first
editions of both these works. He became the dean of the faculty of medicine
at Basel and served as a sort of spy for Calvin on the more liberal Basel Protestants.
He wrote extensively, and his books enjoyed wide circulation. He even secured
a niche in the history of medicine. On his life and ideas, see Frederick Church,
The Italian Reformers, 1534-1564, (New York: 1932), 194-201 and passim; also
Lynn Thorndike, *A History of Magic and Experimental Science*, (New York: 1959),
V, 600-16. Grataroli was a childhood classmate of Martyr's friend Zanchi and
probably fled with him from Italy in 1551: see Church, 195, 199. He sent one
of his books to Martyr with a very warm envoy that suggested that they were in
correspondence: see A. Ganoczy, *Bibliothèque* 169. I examined Grataroli's correspondence preserved in the Basel Universitätsbibliothek. Unfortunately there
was nothing between Martyr and the great admirer of Pomponazzi. I have
subsequently noticed that two letters from Grataroli to Bullinger (December 19,
1553, and January 5, 1554) make it certain that Martyr and Grataroli did correspond. These two letters are printed by Baum, Cunitz, and Reuss, *Ioannis Calvini
Opera quae supersunt omnia*, (Brunswick, 1863-1900) XIV, c. 707; XV, c. 3. All of
Grataroli's correspondence with Bullinger printed in the *Calvini Opera* antedates
Martyr's arrival in Zurich. One can predict with some confidence that when the
projected Bullinger correspondence appears for the years when Martyr was in
Zurich, 1556-62, Grataroli's letters to Bullinger will contain salutations to Martyr.

[18] The literature on Paduan Aristotelianism in general and Pomponazzi in
particular is immense. In addition to Nardi's *Saggi* cited above the following

immortality of the soul could not be proved apodictically but must be taken on faith. Chapter IV will return to this problem in detail.

Martyr's philosophy is a popular Aristotelianism. It cares little for the partisan version of Aristotle championed at Padua and does not center on the abstruse question of the nature of the soul as did Paduan speculation. Martyr's own doctrine of the soul comes closer to that of Pomponazzi and Alexander than to the other schools. Martyr is well acquainted with the writings of Alexander as with all the leading Greek commentators, and he cites their opinions in his works. Again and again his theological and philosophical writings utilize concepts, terms, and methods of exposition and argument borrowed from the Aristotelian tradition.

The adaptation of Aristotelian philosophy to the needs of theology played a role in the development of Protestant scholasticism in the sixteenth and seventeenth centuries quite as fundamental as in the development of medieval Catholic scholasticism in the twelfth and thirteenth centuries. The development was easier, for the earlier scholasticism provided a model for the assimilation of Aristotle to the needs of Christian theology. The Aristotle adopted in Lutheran and Calvinist scholasticism was in large measure the Aristotle of the Paduan professors rather than of the medieval theologians. Martyr pioneered this assimilation.

How important Aristotle and the peripatetic school was for Martyr can be shown in part by a statistical table of Martyr's explicit citations to them scattered through his works. The table that follows deliberately omits all references to Aristotle in Martyr's commentary on Aristotle's Ethics. These are obviously ubiquitous.

The references found in Martyr's commentary on Aristotle's *Ethics* are tabulated separately from those found in his writings, which are all theological. Those found in the *Ethics* commentary reveal Martyr's

are particularly helpful: Bruno Nardi, *Studi su Pietro Pomponazzi*, (Florence: 1965); John Herman Randall, Jr., *The School of Padua and the Emergence of Modern Science*, (Padua: 1961); Randall, *The Career of Philosophy*, I, *From the Middle Ages to the Enlightenment*, (New York: 1970); E. Gilson, "Autour de Pomponazzi; Problématique de l'immortalité de l'âme en Italie au début de XVIe siècle," *Archives d'histoire doctrinale et littéraire du moyen âge*, XXVIII, 1961, 163-279; Gilson, "L'Affaire de l'immortalité de l'âme à Venise au début du XVIe siècle," in *Umanismo europeo e umanismo veneziano*, ed. V. Branca, (Florence: 1963), 31-61; Paul O. Kristeller, *Eight Philosophers of the Italian Renaissance*, (Stanford: 1964); Kristeller, *Renaissance Thought*, II, (New York: 1965); Kristeller, *Le Thomisme et la pensée italienne de la renaissance*, (Paris: 1967); Antonio Poppi, *Introduzione all' aristotelismo padovano*, (Padua, 1970).

References and Citations to Aristotle and Aristotelians:

Name	References in the Ethics	References in other works
Alexander of Aphrodisias	0	4
Ammonius	1	0
Aretinus, Leonardas	1	0
Argyropylus	2	0
Averroes	2	3
Avicenna	0	2
Aristotle	-	98
Eustratius	46	0
Galen	10	5
Pomponazzi	0	1
Simplicius	1	0
Themistius	2	1
Theophrastus	2	1
Trapezuntius	1	0

knowledge of the Aristotelian school, but most of them serve a merely exegetical function there, for instance, all the references to Eustratius. The references and citations found in the theological works are more significant because they witness to the interaction of philosophy and theology. Most of the references are favorable, that is, they adopt a teaching or appeal to the authority of the author referred to. Even the unfavorable references and citations at least indicate that Martyr in developing his theology was conscious of its relation to philosophy.

The importance of Martyr's frequent references to the Aristotelian school becomes clearer when compared to Calvin's practice. In the *Institutes* there are only eight references to the whole Aristotelian school, seven to Aristotle himself and one to Themistius. This is striking even when allowance is made for the fact that the *Institutes* count only 2,000 average modern pages, whereas Martyr's works are several times that long.

There are fifty-six references to and citations from Plato in Martyr's theological works.[19] References to other Platonic authors are strikingly few. Not a single reference to Plotinus and Proclus, only one to

---

[19] Martyr makes an additional forty references to Plato's works in his *In Primum, Secundum et Initium Tertii Libri Ethicorum Aristotelis ad Nicomachum . . .*, (Zurich: 1563). In counting these forty references I did not include one section (138-48) in which Martyr presents and criticizes Plato's theory of the ideas. To have counted the many references in this section would have distorted the larger picture.

Porphyry, and that not to a philosophical work but to his attack on Christianity. Martyr never refers to Giovanni Pico della Mirandola and only once to Marsilio Ficino.[20] There are three references to Cardinal Bessarion, who can be considered a Renaissance Neo-Platonist. Again comparison with Calvin is revealing. The *Institutes* refer to Plato sixteen times, more than twice as often as they refer to Aristotle. Two scholars have recently made determined attempts to read Calvin as a Platonist.[21] In fact Calvin's debt to Plato was relatively minor, but in spite of their exaggerations these two studies serve to highlight an important point: in so far as any philosophical system affects Calvin's theology, it is Platonism rather than Aristotelianism. Later Reformed theology did not follow Calvin's preference for Plato. Reformed theology in the century following Calvins' death builds on Aristotelianism, although Ramism played an important role in certain countries.

All this is not to say that Martyr was hostile to Platonism. Quite the contrary. Very few medieval or Renaissance intellectuals saw Plato and Aristotle as antithetic. They felt little need to choose between them; rather they borrowed liberally from both and tried to combine the insights of both into a higher synthesis. Ficino's and Pico's syntheses gave primacy to Plato. Aquinas preferred Aristotle, as did Genua.[22] So did Martyr. There have always been certain elements in Plato—his moral idealism, his thirst for the beyond and the transcendent, his openness to religion, and especially his belief in personal immortality—that have attracted Christian thinkers down through the ages, just as there has always been an aura of naturalistic scientism in the Aristotelian tradition which has made some Christians chary. Plato did not fail to exercise his charm on Martyr. Martyr is at pains to defend Plato from many of Aristotle's criticisms.[23] He goes

---

[20] *Melachim, id est Regum Libri Duo posteriores cum Commentariis* Petri Matyris Vermilii, (Zurich: 1571), f. 230v. Martyr did have a copy of Porphyry's famous *Isagoge* in his library: Ganoczy, *Bibliothèque*, 266. The *Isagoge* is an introduction to the predicaments and therefore owes more to Aristotle than to Plato. Martyr cites Ficino's commentary on the tenth book of Plato's *Laws*: Peter Martyr Vermigli, *In Librum Iudicum . . . Commentarii*, (Zurich: 1565), f. 141r.

[21] Jean Boisset, *Sagesse et sainteté dans la pensée de Jean Calvin: essai sur l'humanisme du Réformateur Français*, (Paris: 1959); Roy W. Battenhouse, "The Doctrine of Man in Calvin and Renaissance Platonism," *Journal of the History of Ideas*, IX, 1948, 447-71.

[22] Nardi, *Studi*, 380. Even the ancient peripatetics sometimes tended to interpret Aristotle in the light of Plato. Martyr in his only reference to Simplicius very perceptively states: "Simplicius non parum Platoni addictus in multis locis ait . . ." *Ethicorum*, 150.   [23] *Ethicorum*, 74, 144.

well beyond any warrant in Plato's text to attribute to him a very
Christianized idea of God and even belief in the resurrection of the
body.[24] When criticism is necessary, Martyr tends to level it against
the *"Platonici"* rather than against the master himself. Still, Martyr
criticizes several of the Church Fathers and especially Origen for being
too devoted to Plato's teaching.[25] On the critical issues between Plato
and Aristotle, Martyr always opts for Aristotelianism.[26] Chapter IV
will establish this regarding Martyr's theory of knowledge, his metaphysics, and his philosophy of man.

Not all the works of Aristotle and Plato held equal interest for
Martyr. For instance, he seldom refers to the *De Anima*, the work of
Aristotle that most interested the Paduan philosophers. There are
two ways of determing which treatises in Aristotle's corpus interested
Martyr most. The most obvious and important way is the pattern of
citations to Aristotle's works found in Martyr's own writtings. The
second way is an examination of the marginalia in Martyr's personal
copy of the Greek text of Aristotle that is still extant in Geneva.[27] The
pattern of citations and the relative density of marginalia largely reinforce each other. Martyr refers to the *Rhetoric* twenty-two times, to
the *Ethics* twenty-one times, to the *Politics* twelve times. No other
treatise is referred to by title in Martyr's theological works more than
three times. There are, of course, many instances when Martyr refers
to Aristotle's opinion without identifying any particular treatise. The
marginalia in Martyr's Greek Aristotle are heaviest in the *Ethics*. The
heavy marginalia continue through the whole of the Ethics, not just
the first two and a half books covered in Martyr's later commentary on

---

[24] *Ethicorum,* 127; *Melachim,* f. 230v.

[25] *Ethicorum,* 137.

[26] Simler, third page, says of Martyr, "... in suis commentariis testatur
Aristoteleam philosophiam maxime amavit et coluit ob methodum et quod
minus errorum haberet quam reliquae philosophorum sectae." This attitude
was by no means the inevitable result of a Paduan training. A generation earlier
than Martyr, Giles of Viterbo studied at Padua. An Augustinian Eremite, he
was deeply religious and an ardent reformer. Like Martyr, he had a special
interest in Gregory of Rimini and was a deep student of medieval rabbinic lore
and an excellent Hebraist. But in contrast to Martyr, his years at Padua en-
gendered a deep seated hatred of Aristotle. This led him to try to rebuild theology
on a Platonic basis. Like Pico and Reuchlin, he became captivated by the Cabala.
See John O'Malley, *Giles of Viterbo on Church and Reform,* (Leiden: 1968), especially 46, 44, 62, 70.

[27] In view of the publication date (the Erasmus edition, Basel: 1531), Martyr
cannot have had this edition of Aristotle when he was a student, but it was
certainly in his possession while he was still an Augustinian in Italy. See Ganoczy,
Bibliothèque, 22, 253.

the *Ethics*. The marginalia are also very heavy in the third book of the *Politics*. They are heavy in several of the logical works and moderately heavy in the *De Anima*. They are heavy at the beginning of the *Rhetoric* and the *Metaphysics* but quickly fall off. Elsewhere the marginalia are only scattered. Martyr seems to have little interest in Aristotle's biological works; most of his knowledge in this subject comes from Pliny the Elder and Galen. The great speculative works—the *Physics*, *Metaphysics*, and the *De Anima* interested Vermigli but not nearly as much as the treatises that dealt with man in society, the *Ethics*, and *Politics*, and to a lesser extent the *Rhetoric*.

The same general emphasis emerges from an examination of Martyr's references to Plato's writings. Martyr explicitly refers to the *Republic* eighteen times, to the *Laws* thirteen times, to the *Phaedo* and the *Cratylus* seven times, to the *Alcibiades* and the *Timaeus* four times. There are scattered references to many of the other dialogues, but it is interesting to note that there is not a single explicit reference to the most difficult and abstruse of all the dialogues, the *Parmenides*.

Martyr's doctorate from Padua was not in philosophy but in theology. This doubtless absorbed even more of his time at Padua than did philosophy. Teaching theology became Martyr's lifework both as a Catholic and as a Protestant. Most of his theological education came through the lectures given at the Dominician convent at Padua. Simler tells us that Martyr listened to two Dominicans and an Augustinian Eremite. His Dominican teachers were Gaspare Mansueti da Perugia and Alberto Pascaleo da Udine. Fra Gaspare was a Thomist whose strongly medieval cast of mind is evident in the two devotional and the two theological books that he wrote; Fra Alberto was more illustrious and a very poplar professor but he chiefly made his mark as a religious reformer. Both he and Martyr probably played a minor role in the compilation of the great "Aurum Consilium de Emendanda Ecclesia" presented to Paul III by a commission of Cardinals in 1537. Alberto's reward for his services was first the bishopric of Calamona in Crete, then later Chiogga in Italy where he distinguished himself as a reforming bishop. He seems to have left no published works. The two Dominicans were doubtless solid teachers but hardly outstanding theologians.[28]

According to Simler Martyr also attended the lectures of one Augustinian Eremite, but not even McNair's diligence could uncover his

---

[28] McNair, 103-05.

identity.[29] Only once in his writings does Martyr cite the opinion of Giles of Rome, the approved doctor of the Eremite order.[30] McNair suggests that Martyr probably attended the lectures of the two professors who held chairs *ex doctrina Scoti*, Simone Ardeo and Giacomo Bargio, both insignificant figures.[31] My research supports this supposition. Martyr states in his *Defensio* that Stephen Gardiner's theology is Scotist and that he too has spent many unpleasant days in studying Scotism.[32] Scattered through Martyr's works are a dozen citations from or references to Scotus, most of them hostile. Interestingly, there is not a single reference to Scotus in Calvin's *Institutes*, although Scotus is alleged to have exerted an important influence on Calvin.[33]

McNair is undoubtedly correct in stating that Martyr preferred his theology *in via Thomae*.[34] Simler states that while at Padua Martyr's favorite reading among the scholastics was Thomas Aquinas and Gregory of Rimini.[35] In his commentary on Romans Martyr says that the leading scholastic theologians are Thomas, Scotus, and Bonaventure.[36] Martyr cites Bonaventure only three times and rejects the contention that Scotus is the greatest of the scholastic theologians.[37] In contrast, there are more references to Thomas than to any scholastic except Peter Lombard. Aside from the explicit references there are many instances in which Martyr's text has obvious but unacknowledged doctrinal and even verbal borrowings directly from St. Thomas. Some of these will be pointed out in the coming chapters.

The range of Martyr's reading in the scholastics is best illustrated by a table of explicit citations, quotes, and references.

----

[29] McNair, 103.

[30] Martyr cites Giles to support his position, *In Epistolam S. Pauli Apostoli ad Romanos . . .*, (Basel: 1558), 168.

[31] McNair, 105-06.

[32] *Defensio Doctrinae Veteris et Apostolicae de Sacrosancto Eucharistiae Sacramento . . .*, (Zurich: 1559), 116.

[33] François Wendel, *Calvin: the Origins and Development of his Religious Thought*, trans. Philip Mairet, (New York: 1963), 127-29.

[34] McNair, 106.

[35] Simler, third page.

[36] *Romanos*, 175: "praecipui inter scholasticos."

[37] *Defensio*, 381. Martyr never calls St. Thomas the greatest of the scholastics, but phrasing such as the following suggests as much: "Firma itaque sententia esto, quam etiam scholasticos 2 Sent. dist. 8 et inter eos praecipue Thomas, nedum antiqui patres, ratam habuerunt . . ." *Iudicum*, f. 87r.

Martyr's References to Christian Writers, 1000-1500. [38]	
Name	Number of References
Albert the Great	4
Anselm	3
Bartolus	1
Bernard	3
Biel, Gabriel	2
Bonaventure	3
Boniface VIII	1
Capreolus	1
Durandus	1
Gerson, John	1
Giles of Rome	1
Gratian	1
Henry of Ghent	1
Hostiensis (Henry de Segusio)	3
Hugh of St. Victor	1
Leschetus	1
Nicholas of Lyra	3
Occam, William	2
Panormitanus	2
Paul of Burgos	1
Peter Commestor	2
Peter Lombard	31
Peter de Palude	1
Peter Tarantasius	1
Richard de Media Villa	2
Scotus	12
Thomas Aquinas	23
Ulrich of Strasbourg	1
Valla, Lorenzo	4
William of Auvergne	3
Zorobellus	1

[38] The table excludes writers already listed as peripatetics or Platonists. I include only instances in which Martyr explicitly names an author. This and the following tables cover all of Martyr's works except his letters. As I was especially interested in Martyr's references to scholastic theologians, the table includes every single explicit reference Martyr made to them. I would not claim such a high degree of completeness for the other tables in this chapter, particularly that to classical authors. Still all the tables are more than adequate to present a picture of Martyr's readings and bear the weight of useful generalization. Absolute statistical accuracy is almost unattainable since there are borderline cases when it is not easy to decide whether a reference should or should not be counted, or whether several references to the same author in a passage should be counted once or several times. In some instances I have recognized quotations from such poets as Vergil in passages in which Martyr mentions no author by name. I have not counted such instances. In several places Martyr refers to the teaching of the *scholastici* globally on a particular passage in the *Sentences* which Martyr

Five of the authors are lawyers—Bartolus, Gratian, Hostiensis, Panormitanus, and Boniface VIII. Two are among the greatest medieval exegetes: Peter Commestor and Nicholas of Lyra. Martyr's references to Valla are to his annotations on the New Testament which Martyr values very highly.[39] All the other references are to theologians and philosophers. The number of references to Lombard is easily explained. His *Sentences* was the standard medieval introductory text in systematic theology. The lectures that Martyr heard at Padua were almost certainly based on it.[40] Anselm, Bernard, and Hugh of St. Victor belong to the period when scholasticism was only emerging. Anselm's thought was central to Martyr's soteriology.

The weight of Martyr's references falls on the thirteenth century. The fewness of references to nominalist authors is striking; their importance is even less that the statistical table suggests. The only two references to Occam are not real citations at all; in both instances Martyr simply states that the chief scholastic schools are those of Thomas, Scotus, and Occam.[41] One of these passages goes on to

specifies. I have not counted such instances as references to Peter Lombard. Rather arbitrary decisions cannot be avoided, but I do not think that they affect the purpose of the tables—to present a picture of Martyr's intellectual background, his reading, and the sources of his thought.

In a very few instances Martyr gives a cluster of references to several scholastic authors where there are grounds to suspect he has not consulted the authors themselves individually but may be using a second hand summary. One instance is an extended passage his *Defensio . . . ad Riccardi Smythaei . . . duos libellos de Caelibatu et Votis Monasticis . . .*, (Basel: 1559), 601-604 (henceforward I will refer to this work as the *Defensio de Caelibatu* to distinguish it from Martyr's other *Defensio* on the Eucharist). In the above pages Martyr summarizes the teaching of Aquinas, Scotus, Peter de Palude, Bonaventure, Albert the Great, and Cajetan on the relaxation of vows. A passage which is even more likely to contain second hand references to the scholastics occurs in Martyr's *Dialogus de Utraque in Christo Natura* (Zurich: 1561), f. 64v, in which Martyr quotes verbatim the opinion of Albert the Great on an aspect of the communication of idioms between Christ's two natures and then adds, "Possem et aliorum Scholasticorum suffragia colligere, Udalrici, Gabrielis Biel, Riccardi de Media Villa etc." The reference to Ulrich of Strasbourg is certainly to his *Summa de Bono*, V, I, 8, none of which was published until the twentieth century. See Ulrich of Strasbourg, *La "Summa De Bono"* . . . *Introduction et édition critique* par Jean Daquillon, ("Bibliothèque thomiste," Vol. XII; Paris: 1930), 23.

[39] Valla is *"acutissimi iudicii scriptor."* Peter Martyr Vermigli, *In Selectissimam S. Pauli Priorem ad Corinthios . . . Commentarii*, (Zurich: 1551), f. 215v.

[40] In some of the northern Italian universities and convents the *Summa Theologiae* was beginning to replace the *Sentences* as the basis for lectures. This development is traced by P. O. Kristeller, *Thomisme*, 37ff. Kristeller dwells on the strong Thomist tradition at Padua but does not mention it as a pioneer in replacing the *Sentences*.

[41] *Defensio de Caelibatu*, 466; also *Loci*, 1050.

say that the chief interpreters and disciples of Thomism are Capreolus and Cajetan, of Scotism they are Leschetus and Zorobellus, of nominalism they are Biel and Gregory of Rimini.[42] The other reference to Biel says only that he agrees with a quotation Martyr gives from Albert the Great.[43] The sole reference to Gerson bears on a historical point.[44] In a number of instances that will be pointed out in subsequent chapters Martyr brings up the scholastic distinction, especially important for nominalism, between God's *potentia ordinata* and his *potentia absoluta*. But he raises this distinction only to reject considerations resting on the *potentia absoluta*. The fact that nominalism so little affects Martyr is significant. That the roots of Luther's theology go back to nominalism is a commonplace. The roots of Calvin's theology are sometimes traced to Scotism, sometimes to nominalism.[45] Martyr's career shows clearly that a Protestant theology could rest on a Thomistic base.

Martyr's references to the scholastic theologians are often precise and sometimes extensive. Three quarters of his references to Lombard mention a particular book of the *Sentences*; over half mention the precise distinction. In one instance Martyr devotes two-thirds of a folio page to summarizing Lombard's teaching.[46] Martyr refers by name to four of Thomas's works: the *Summa Theologiae*, the *Summa contra Gentiles*, the commentary on the *Sentences*, and the commentary on Galatians. Martyr's library also possessed a copy of the *Questiones Disputatae*. In several instances Martyr quotes Thomas word for word; often his references to the *Summa Theologiae* specify part, question, and

---

[42] Opus illi (sc. Peter Lombard) fuit infinitis interpretibus: antesignandi constituti sunt Thomas, Scotus, et Occamus, qui nil potuerunt dicere tam scholastice, tamquam (ut loquuntur) magistraliter, ut veritatem e tenebris educerent. Expositoribus Thomae fuit opus. Caietanum et Capreolum habuit. Scoto accessit Zorobellus et Leschetus. Occamo Gabriel Biel et Gregorius Ariminensis adiunctus est. *Loci*, 1050.

[43] Peter Martyr Vermigli, *Dialogus*, f. 64v.

[44] *Melachim*, f. 192r.

[45] Although some scholars have traced Calvin's doctrine of divine sovereignty manifesting itself in the decrees of predestination and reprobation to the nominalist doctrine of *potentia absoluta*, this contention is vigorously denied by Calvin's own text: see the *Institutes*, III, 23, 2; also *Brevis Responsio . . . de Aeterna Dei Praedestinatione . . .*; "Passim Calvinus commentum de absoluta Dei potentia, quod in scholis suis ventilant sophistae, acriter repudiat et detestabile esse asserit, quia ab aeterna Dei sapientia et iustitia separari non debet potestas." *Calvini Opera*, IX, c. 259. On the discussion over nominalist and Scotist influence on Calvin, see François Wendel, *Calvin: The Origin and Development of His Religious Thought*, trans. Philip Mairet, (New York, 1963), 127-129.

[46] *Romanos*, 303, summarizes *Sentences* 4, distinctio 48.

article.[47] Some of his references to the Sentence commentary are
equally precise.[48] In one instance Martyr compares Thomas's early
teaching in the *Sentence* commentary with his mature teaching in the
Summa Theologiae and points out precisely how his opinion changed.[49]
Many of Martyr's citations to Thomas are hostile, but many are
friendly.

Besides the references to scholastic theologians by name, there are
many more which simply refer to the *scholastici* in general. A particularly striking example of this is provided by a fourteen page section
in Martyr's Romans commentary which six times refers to the opinion
of the *scholastici*.[50] There must be over a hundred such references
scattered through Martyr's writings.

Martyr's general attitude toward the scholastics differs sharply from
Calvin's: "For there were very wise men among the scholastic theologians, and indeed those not a few."[51] Calvin's references are almost
uniformly hostile and derisive; Martyr cites the opinion of the scholastics nearly as often to agree with it as to oppose it. Martyr's friend
Zanchi carried this a step further; his references to particular scholastic authors, especially St. Thomas, are almost uniformly friendly.
Martyr's reading in medieval theology seems much broader than that
of Calvin. The last edition of the *Institutes* cites Peter Lombard frequently, but aside from two references each to Gratian and Aquinas
and one to Anselm and Gerson, only one other medieval theologian
is mentioned. He is St. Bernard. Calvin refers to him in twenty-one
different passages, more often than to any author save five of the leading Church Fathers.[52] Bernard was a favorite with Luther too.
Strangely Martyr refers to him only three times. In fact the whole
literature of medieval piety and mysticism, in which Bernard was a
key figure, held no attraction for Martyr. In this he contrasts strongly
with Luther.[53] The only distinctly mystical author he cites with any

---

[47] *Dialogus*, ff. 61v, 63r; *Corinthios*, f. 270r.

[48] *Iudicum*, ff. 87r, 145v.

[49] *Defensio de Caelibatu*, 602.

[50] *Romanos*, 179, 181, 186, 187, 191, 193.

[51] "Proinde fuerunt inter scholasticos theologos sapientissimi et quiden non
pauci." *Ethicorum*, 156.

[52] My comments on the sources of Calvin's theology are largely drawn from
the treatments given by Wendel, 123-139, and Boisset, 221ff. Boisset gives a
statistical table of citations in the *Institutes*, 220. In some instances I thought
particularly important (Plato, Aristotle) I have verified the figures I use myself.

[53] Martyr's theological anthropology simply does not have the kind of background that Steven Ozment found in late medieval mysticism for Luther: see

frequency is Dionysius the pseudo-Areopagite, and most of the half dozen references to him are hostile.

Martyr's hostile remarks toward the scholastics stem from two sources. He thinks they delve into too many abstruse questions. More importantly, his Protestant convictions range him against them on many issues. But when Martyr opposes other Protestants he is prompt to summon the scholastics as allies. This is very well brought out by an extended section of his *Dialogue* against the Lutheran Johann Brenz. In the course of six pages he summarizes or quotes the opinions of Lombard, Thomas, Ulrich of Strasbourg, Biel, Richard de Media Villa, Albert the Great, Bonaventure, and Peter Tarantasius.[54]

Martyr's ordination to the priesthood in 1525 and his reception of the doctorate in theology marked the end of one stage in his life and the beginning of another.[55] He was assigned to preaching and to teaching scripture and philosophy in various houses of study belonging to his order. He taught at Padua, Ravenna, Bologna, and Vercelli. The time left over from teaching Martyr devoted to the further study of philosophy and scripture. At Vercelli Martyr also lectured on Homer.[56] The Homer lectures should guard the student of Martyr from any inclination to set up a neat dichotomy between scholasticism and humanism.[57] This study is primarily concerned with the scholastic side of Martyr, but Martyr was as least as much a humanist as a scholastic.[58] The range of humanist literature that Martyr cites and the number of humanist volumes in his library surpass the scholastic. Martyr started to learn Greek to deepen his knowledge of Aristotle

---

his *Homo Spiritualis: A Comparative Study of the Anthropology of Johannes Tauler, Jean Gerson, and Martin Luther (1509-16),* (Leiden: 1969).

[54] *Dialogus,* 62v-65r.

[55] McNair, 117.

[56] Simler, third page.

[57] I use humanism in the sense of an acquired skill in certain studies rather than in the sense of the content of a particular view of man's place in the universe. I entirely subscribe to the following definition of Kristeller's: "Thus Renaissance humanism was not as such a philosophical tendency or system, but rather a cultural and educational program which emphasized and developed an important but limited area of studies. This area had for its center a group of subjects that was concerned essentially neither with the classics nor with philosophy, but might be roughly described as literature ... the *studia humanitatis* includes ... morals," *Renaissance Thought, the Classic, Scholastic, and Humanist Strains,* (New York: 1961), 10.

[58] McNair rightly emphasizes both aspects of Martyr's training: 122, 124, 104-115. In contrast, the dichotomy that Armstrong sets up in his book on Amyraut between scholasticism and humanism leads to an oversimplified explanation of the origins of Protestant scholasticism. See especially 129-39.

but he continued his studies until he could understand exactly the Greek poets and orators without the help of a translation.[59] Martyr's interest in the classics continued all his life, as his library witnesses, and reached to a wide range of authors and subjects. A table of Martyr's explicit references to and quotations from classical literature illustrates this best. The authors previously listed are omitted.

Name	Number of Times	Name	Number of Times
Aemilius Probus	1	Lucan	1
Aphthonius	1	Lucretius	1
Appian	1	Meander	1
Apuleius	1	Ovid	4
Aulus Gellius	5	Pausanias	1
Celsus	1	Philo Alexandrinus	3
Cicero	65	Philostratus	2
Cleanthes	1	Pindar	3
Coelius	1	Plautus	4
Columella	4	Pliny the Elder	14
Curtius	1	Pliny the Younger	1
Diodorus Siculus	1	Plutarch	22
Diogenes Laertius	3	Posidonius	1
Dioscorides	1	Quintillian	6
Dionysius of Halicarnassus	1	Sallust	1
Democritus	1	Seneca	18
Demosthenes	1	Servius Grammaticus	2
Epictetus	3	Sophocles	2
Euripides	3	Statius	1
Gaius Iurisconsultus	1	Strabo	4
Heraclitus	1	Suetonius	2
Hermes Trimegistus	4	Symmachus	1
Herodotus	1	Terence	6
Hesiod	4	Thucydides	2
Hippocritus	1	Tibullus	1
Homer	8	Ulpian	6
Horace	7	Valerius Maximus	1
Josephus	11	Varro	1
Juvenal	1	Vergil	32
Livy	7	Vitruvius	2

Thirty-one of the authors in the list wrote in Latin, twenty-nine wrote in Greek. In a few cases (Heraclitus, Democritus, Posidonius, Menander, Cleanthes, and Varro) Martyr's knowledge of the authors

---

[59] "... eum saepe integras fere noctes in Bibliotheca vigilasse ... ut Graecum aliquem auctorem interpretatur. Hac autem diligentia tantum profecit ut non modo Graecos oratores et philosophos, sed poetas quoque omnes ... absque ullo interprete intelligeret." Simler, third page.

cited was probably second hand and based on quotations from them included in such works as Diogenes Laertius' *Lives of the Philosophers*. All the other instances seem to represent a first hand acquaintance with the works of the authors cited. I do not think Martyr made much use of *florilegia* of classical quotations.

Citations from and reference to Cicero's writings easily lead all the rest in the table. This is entirely to be expected. No pagan author except Aristotle was read and studied as much in the Renaissance as Cicero. Eighty percent of the time when Martyr specifies which work of Cicero he is referring to, the source is among the philosophical treatises. There are seven references to the *De Finibus*, six to the *Tusculan Disputations*, four to the *De Officiis*, three to the *De Natura Deorum* and to the fragments of the *De Republica* available in Martyr's time. Cicero's influence on Martyr was probably not as great as the number of citations from his philosophical works might suggest. Cicero was himself an eclectic, and the interlocutors in his dialogues express the viewpoints of nearly all the philosophical schools of the first century before Christ. His works provide a quarry of arguments and viewpoints, but lacking any sharp philosophical focus themselves, they left no particular impress on Martyr's thought.

The number of references to Stoic writers, eighteen to Seneca and three to Epictetus, is surprisingly high because Martyr frequently exhibits a clear hostility to the Stoic tradition.[60] Martyr was even more hostile to ancient skepticism and Epicureanism. Martyr's four references to Hermes Trismegistus are intriguing in view of the widespread vogue of Hermeticism in the sixteenth century. I find no influence of Hermeticism in Martyr's thought. One passage in Martyr does repeat the Hermetic canard that all the philosophy of the gentiles derives from the Egyptians, but this passage does not refer to thrice greatest Hermes.[61] Those passages in Martyr that do refer to the *Corpus Hermeticum* are hostile.[62] The number of references to Plutarch is surprisingly high, but his vivid biographies were immensely more popular in the sixteenth century. Martyr never refers to the works

---

[60] I feel that Sturm overemphasizes Stoic influence on Martyr: 207, 211, 212, 259, 262-64.

[61] Peter Martyr Vermigli, *In Primum Librum Mosis qui vulgo Genesis dicitur Commentarii . . .*, (Heidelberg: 1606), f. 152r. On the immense vogue of Hermeticism in the sixteenth century, see Frances A. Yates, *Giordano Bruno and the Hermetic Tradition*, (New York: 1964).

[62] *In Duos Libros Samuelis prophetae qui vulgo priores libri Regum appellantur*, (Zurich: 1567), f. 163, 164r; *Melachim*, f. 142v; *Genesis*, f. 3r.

of Xenophon, Polybius, Caesar, or Tacitus. Still other writers notable
for their absence in the table above are Catullus, Propertius, Aeschylus,
Aristophanes, and the Greek poets of the Hellenistic period generally.
A single reference to Demosthenes represents the whole canon of
Attic orators.

Today Greek and Roman writers are read primarily for their literary
excellence. In the sixteenth century they were read primarily for the
information and ideas they could impart. This is true of the list of
authors Martyr cites. Less than a third are pure belles-lettres. There
are eleven poets and five dramatists, but there are also eleven historians. Martyr's two intellectual hobbies seem to have been law and
medicine. Martyr made frequent use of legal arguments in his theological works. His library held a noteworthy collection of legal works,
and his writings reveal a solid knowledge of both ancient and medieval legal commentators. His references to Hippocritus, Celsus, Galen,
Dioscorides, and Pliny give substance to Simler's anecdote that on his
death-bed Martyr insisted on long discussions of his sickness with
the doctors.[63]

Of what use was all this erudition in pagan authors when Martyr
came to write his theological works? A few examples illustrate this.
In his Samuel commentary Martyr has occasion to ask what are demons
and what can they do. Martyr summarizes the views of Aristotle,
Plato, Avicenna, Alexander of Aphrodisias, Hermes Trismegistus,
Apuleius, and Plutarch on this arcane question, all by way of background to the definitive answer provided by scripture.[64] The tenth
chapter of the first book of Kings expatiates on the wisdom and
wealth of Solomon. In commenting on the chapter Martyr refers to
works by Vergil, Strabo, Columella, Pliny the Elder, Cicero (two
different works), Aristotle (two different works), Galen, Ulpian, Lucan,
Tibullus, Celsus, Theophrastus, and Dioscorides, plus three medieval
rabbis. The twenty-seventh verse mentions a sycamore tree—four
Greek writers are called on to explain what a sycamore tree is.[65] This
may seem sheer pedantry, but Martyr's students and readers seem to
have appreciated such erudition.

---

[63] Simler's *Vita*, second last page, in *Loci*.

[64] *Samuelis*, f. 163.

[65] *Melachim*, ff. 78v-84r. Another superb example of how Martyr uses the
resources of his varied background is provided by his short tract *De Dolo* (*Iudicum*,
ff. 55v-57v). He draws on biblical, ancient, and medieval history, Roman law,
pagan poets, rabbinic exegetes, and the Church Fathers.

In May 1530 Martyr became vicar of the Augustinian house in Bologna, a post he held for three years. During these years Martyr began to learn Hebrew. For a generation Hebrew had been recognized as one of the three classical languages whose mastery was the aspiration of every well rounded Renaissance humanist. Many aspired but few achieved. Martyr's task of teaching scripture gave him a personal reason to learn the language. The chair of Hebrew at the University of Bologna was vacant during Martyr's stay there. Nothing daunted, he turned to the flourishing Bolognese Jewish community and fastened on a physician named Isaac. From the caustic comments in Simler, Isaac seems to have been a bad teacher. But Martyr persisted in his Hebrew studies, very likely helped by his Jewish Christian friend Emanuel Tremellius who was with him in both Lucca and Strasbourg. In the end Martyr became one of the finest Hebrew scholars of early Protestantism. His Old Testament commentaries make very extensive use of previous rabbinic commentaries. There are four rabbis that Martyr refers to regularly, over twenty times each: David Kimhi, Abenezra, Levi Ben Gerson, and Rabbi Salomo (today better known as Rashi). There are a citation or two to Rabbi Aquila, Rabbi Samuel, and Moses Maimonides. Martyr does not seem to know Maimonides's great work, the *Guide for the Perplexed*. He also cites two first century Jews writing in Greek, Philo of Alexandria and Josephus. Outside of his Old Testament commentaries Martyr very rarely cites the rabbinic commentaries.[66] Martyr finds the rabbis helpful in solving particular philological and exegetical problems, but they exercise no real influence on his thought, and he has no real respect for them.[67] At root his reading of the Old Testament was Christological and theirs was not. Noteworthy is the fact that Martyr never refers to the Cabalistic literature which fascinated so many of the Christian Hebraists of his time. Neither the mystical nor the magical interested him.

On August 30, 1561, Theodore Beza wrote a letter to John Calvin in which he expressed his desire for Peter Martyr's participation in the forthcoming Colloquy of Poissy, which brought together under the auspices of the French crown leading Catholic and Protestant spokesmen. Beza felt that Martyr had two skills that the Protestant cause needed: his skill in answering scholastic arguments and his mastery of

---

[66] There are only three instances: *Defensio*, 38; *Corinthios*, f. 123r; *Romanos*, 520.
[67] *Iudicum*, f. 70v: "Rabbini Haebraeorum nugas afferunt . . ."

patristic literature.[68] Martyr's use of the Fathers is an immense subject which demands a monograph of its own.[69] Some obvious generalizations can be made. Martyr's references to the Fathers cover all the major figures and most of the minor ones, both Greek and Latin. Among the Greeks Chrysostom is easily his favorite. Indeed, Martyr seems to rate Chrysostom highest of all the Fathers as an exegete. In this he agrees entirely with Calvin.[70] In general Martyr prefers the Cappadocians and the Antiochean school to the Alexandrians. Theodoret is cited with surprising frequency, Cyril of Alexandria, Athanasius, and John Damascene less often than might be expected. In general Martyr prefers the earlier Fathers to the later ones. In contrast to Calvin he seldom cites Gregory the Great. Martyr had high esteem for Ambrose and Jerome and cites them far more often than any others except for Chrysostom and Augustine.

Augustine is easily Martyr's favorite author. References to Augustine outnumber those to any other nonscriptural source several times over.[71] For Martyr Augustine is *"summus theologus."* [72] Still Martyr

---

[68] *Correspondance*, III, 143.

[69] The use of the Fathers by early Protestant theologians has been the subject of several fine studies, especially Peter Fraenkel, *Testimonia Patrum: the Function of the Patristic Argument in the Theology of Philip Melanchthon*, (Geneva: Droz, 1961); Luchesius Smits, *Saint Augustin dans l'œuvre de Jean Calvin*, (Assen: Van Gorcum, 1957-58), 2 vol. Joseph McLelland devotes a useful appendix (267-71) to Martyr's patristic sources, but this deals only with the authority of the Fathers and a few minor technical problems. McLelland does not attempt to measure the range of Martyr's reading in the Fathers nor his use of them.

[70] Wendel, 124.

[71] There are six times as many explicit references in Calvin's *Institutes* to Augustine as to any other non-biblical writer. The proportion of references in Martyr would not be so high, but he refers several times as often to Augustine as to any other non-biblical author. The whole sixteenth century might well be termed the age of *Augustinus redivivus*. Not only is he the master theologian for Luther, Calvin, and Martyr, but also many for Roman Catholics: "S. Augustin est le maître incontesté de tous les théologiens de Louvain au XVIe siècle": R. Guellury, "L'Evolution des méthodes théologiques à Louvain d'Erasme à Jensenius," *Revue d'Histoire ecclésiastique*, XXXVII, 1941, 124. In many ways the humanists sought to revive patristic theology as a substitute for scholasticism; Wimpfeling, Vives, Colet, Budé, Petrarch, Salutati, Guarino da Verona, and Lorenzo Valla were all deeply indebted to Augustine. See Charles Béné, *Erasme et saint Augustin, ou l'influence de saint Augustin sur l'humanisme d'Erasme*, (Geneva: 1969), 429. The thesis of Béné's massive study is ". . . Erasme a choisi Augustin, de préférence à Jérôme et à Origène, mais aussi de préférence à Platon et Cicéron, comme guide pour renouveler la piété, l'exégèse et la prédication chrétienne . . ." p. 13.

[72] *Defensio*, 352; also ". . . maximus optimusque theologus Augustinus." Martyr to Peter Sturm, May 24, 1562; printed in *Operum Theologicorum G. Zanchii...*, (Geneva: 1605), VIII, II, 108.

does not hestitate to disagree with Augustine on particular points.[73] In a few instances a comparison of Martyr's summary of Augustine's teaching with the original text of Augustine to which Martyr refers as his source indicates that Martyr is reading Augustine through scholastic glasses.[74] Martyr's library possessed the magnificent ten volume Froben edition (Basel, 1543) of Augustine's *Omnia Opera*, but Martyr did not draw on all of Augustine's writings to the same extent. Some of his works he cites repeatedly, others seldom or never. Most of Martyr's Augustine citations are to the *De Civitate Dei*, the *De Trinitate*, and especially to the anti-Pelagian tracts. In short, late Augustine. He refers to Augustine's *Confessions* and his scripture commentaries less than might be expected. Martyr hardly ever refers to the early, more neo-Platonic treatises such as the *Soliloquia, De Magistro, De Quantitate Animae, De Immortalitate Animae, De Beata Vita*, and the *De Libero Arbitrio*.[75]

What did Martyr borrow from Augustine? In Martyr's view his sacramental theology and his theology of grace, justification, and predestination were derived (after scripture) from Augustine. Martyr's philosophical view of man owes very little to Augustine, but his view of the fallen human condition owes a great debt to the *Doctor Gratiae*. Martyr would have entirely agreed with the statement of Aquinas: "Augustine speaks of human nature not in so far as it has natural being but as it is ordered to beatitude." [76] Martyr borrowed Augustine's understanding of man's relationship to God and of his path to happiness. In contrast, Martyr's theological method and his manner of exposition owed more to Aristotle and medieval scholasticism than to Augustine. Martyr insisted upon orderly, even rigidly methodical exposition, upon neat technical definitions, upon clarity and precision in theological vocabulary. These are not the hallmarks of Augustine.

---

[73] See *Corinthios*, f. 179v ; *Romanos*, 37, 129.

[74] See *Samuelis*, ff. 222v, 280r; *Iudicum*, f. 92v. M.-D. Chenu notes a similar transformation of Augustine texts at the hands of St. Thomas: *Toward Understanding Saint Thomas*, trans. A. M. King & D. Hughes, (Chicago: 1964), 173.

[75] Ganoczy is mistaken when he says: "Il est permis de penser que sa (Martyr's) préférence pour Platon, surtout au début de sa carrière, fut conditionnée par son attachement à Augustin" (22). At every stage Martyr's preference was for Aristotle rather than Plato. His highest enthusiasm for philosophy largely antedated his enthusiasm for Augustine. Finally, Martyr's preferred reading in Augustine did not include the early and more Platonic works.

[76] "Augustinus loquitur de natura humana non secundum quod consideratur in esse naturali, sed secundum quod ordinatur ad beatitudinem." Quoted by Chenu, 76.

"In Augustine, who had a dislike for abstractions, language was altogether fluid and responsive to the continuities, to the radiating action, and to the fringes of the intelligibleness of things rather than to the fine edges of concepts." [77] Because of this fluid use of language, Augustine's thought cannot be reduced to capsule formulas, and very diverse theologies have claimed his patronage down the centuries.

The beginning of Martyr's interest in and study of Augustine and the Fathers cannot be pinned down to a particular time as can his study of Greek, Hebrew and Aristotle. Martyr's introduction to Augustine undoubtedly coincided with his entrance into the Augustinian Canons Regular. Every religious order directs its younger members to the writings and deeds of its founder, whether real or putative. Augustine and his rule were surely proposed to Martyr as a source of inspiration. The Augustinian house at Padua has been called a "roccaforte dell' agostinismo." [78] As was seen, Aquinas and Gregory of Rimini were Martyr's favorite reading during his theological studies there; both of them were far more faithful to Augustine's theology of grace than were the majority of scholastic theologians. Gregory in particular would have led Martyr back to Augustine's anti-Pelagian tracts. [79]

---

[77] Chenu, 110.

[78] McNair, 94.

[79] That Martyr should read extensively in Aquinas is entirely expected. His theological training was in the *via Thomae*, and Thomas was one of the greatest of the scholastics. Martyr's interest in Gregory is more surprising since Gregory is far less prominent. There were editions of Gregory's *Sentence* commentary at Venice in 1518 and in 1522, which suggests interest in him at Padua. McNair's only comment on Martyr's interest in Gregory is the following footnote (106): "Martyr probably derived his high opinion of Gregorio da Rimini from Gaspare Mansueti da Perugia, for Gregorio wrote a commentary on the *Sentences* of Peter Lombard which was much quoted by Paolo da Soncino, Gaspare's tutor in Perugia. Nardi (*Saggi*, p. 349) describes Gregorio and John of Baconsthorpe as 'più averroisti di Averroe'." First, to see Gregory as an Averroist is to miss the thrust of his theology and its probable impact on Martyr. Second, that the teacher of Martyr's teacher frequently quoted Gregory may explain the occasion of Martyr's looking into Gregory, but does not explain his avid reading of him. The best explanation of why Martyr took to Gregory is the simplest and most obvious: he found him congenial. Gregory was a nominalist in method but a thorough Augustinian in his theology of the fall, justification, and predestination. Gregory energetically opposed the Pelagian bent of much of the theology of his day. If Martyr's own writings are any guide, it was the Augustinian rather than the nominalist side of Gregory that attracted him. McNair repeatedly stresses that it was belief in justification by faith alone that led Martyr to Protestantism. Reflection on the text of Augustine and of Paul led Martyr to his understanding of justification. Martyr's contact with Evangelism and the Valdes circle at Naples and his readings in Protestant literature confirmed his belief in

Martyr's development as a patrist and his interest in Augustine must have gone on apace during the 1530's although precise documentation cannot be supplied. It was reflection on the writings of the Fathers that led him to an implicit denial of purgatory in a famous sermon at Naples in 1540. The sermon aroused the wrath of the Viceroy, and Martyr was forbidden for a time to preach.[80] By the time of his arrival at Lucca in 1541 "his patristic learning was positively formidable, already giving evidence of a lifelong predilection for St. Augustine."[81] He encouraged his subjects at Lucca to study the Fathers and especially Augustine.[82]

The final source of Martyr's thought is the contemporaries that he read, especially other Protestant theologians. Again Martyr's education in this source dates back to his Italian years.[83] What reading of Protestant theology Martyr did in Italy must have been quite limited compared to the materials available to him after his flight to Zurich and then Strasbourg.

The extent of Martyr's reading in contemporary theology and its effect on him are the hardest of all Martyr's sources to assess. Sixteenth century writers spatter their pages with quotations from previous writers. They love to quote scripture or insert a tag from Horace. But this propensity to quote draws upon a set canon. Whenever possible scripture, the Church Fathers, and the writers of antiquity are identified as the source of ideas and quotations. This gives a misleading

---

justification by faith alone. Without simply equating Gregory of Rimini's doctrine of justification with that of Luther and Calvin, I think that Gregory's strong doctrine of grace and his anti-Pelagian stance played an important part in Martyr's transition from a Catholic doctrine of justification by faith and charity to Protestant solafidism. At the Leipzig debate Luther asserted that Gregory of Rimini was the only scholastic who was not a Pelagian—quoted by Heiko Oberman, *The Harvest of Medieval Theology: Gabriel Biel and Late Medieval Theology*, (Cambridge, Mass.: 1963), 144. As did Martyr later, Gregory rejected Thomas's view that works performed in the state of sin are not necessarily sins. *Ibid.*, 142. In failing to pay attention to Martyr's interest in Gregory, McNair has, I feel, overlooked an important ligature in the anatomy of Martyr's apostasy.

There is a telling objection to the role I assign Gregory in Martyr's development: Martyr never quotes him and refers to him only once. I think there is an explanation. Precisely those things Martyr probably took from Gregory he found later in others more fully developed and sealed with higher authority. He found them in Paul, Augustine, and the Protestant theologians. Gregory's doctrine of grace was but a stage in Martyr's development; once well past it, there was little reason to recall it.

[80] McNair, 161-63.
[81] McNair, 230.
[82] See the letter of Zanchi quoted by McNair, 228.
[83] McNair, 149, 230.

impression to the modern reader. Often the real debt of sixteenth century thinkers is less to antiquity and more to medieval and contemporary writers. But these do not belong to the canon of approved authorities, and they are seldom identified.[84] Martyr largely follows this unfortunate practice. In the area of contemporary literature the citations in his published works are not a good guide to his reading or to the sources of his ideas. For instance, to judge from explicit references in his published works, Martyr read only one work of Calvin's; his correspondence makes it clear that he read several others, as will be shown in later chapters.

Martyr's References to Contemporary Authors	
Name	Number of Times
Beza, T.	1
Bude, G.	3
Bucer, M.	2
Bullinger, H.	1
Cajetan, T.	6
Calvin, J.	1
de Castro, A.	1
Cochlaus, J.	1
Colonienses	2
Eck, J.	2
Erasmus, D.	24
Fisher, J.	2
Gardiner, S.	—
Hosius, S.	2
Luther, M.	8
Melanchthon, P.	3
Oecolampadius, J.	3
Pellican, C.	1
Pighius, A.	—
Pole, R.	2
Polydore Vergil	1
Pomponazzi, P.	1
Schwenckfeld, C.	2
Smith, R.	—
Zwingli, H.	9

I have deliberately not counted the number of references to Gardiner, Smith, and Pighius. Martyr wrote very lengthy books to

---

[84] On the tendency of sixteenth century writers not to identify contemporary sources, see the remarks of G. Mattingly, "International Diplomacy and International Law," in the *New Cambridge Modern History*, III, *The Counter Reformation and the Price Revolution, 1558-1610*, ed. R. B. Wernham, (Cambridge: 1968), 168-69.

refute previous works by Gardiner and Smith; his references to their books number in the hundreds, but Smith and Gardiner are obviously not a source of Martyr's ideas. The same considerations apply to Albert Pighius whom Martyr sees as the chief spokesman for the Roman Catholic theology of grace, original sin, and free will. Martyr attacks him by name dozens of times, especially in his commentary on Romans.

It is perhaps curious that the largest group in the list of contemporaries cited by Martyr are Roman Catholic theologians, mostly polemicists: Cajetan, Alphonso de Castro, John Cochlaus, John Eck, John Fisher, Stephen Gardiner, Stanislaus Hosius, Albert Pighius, Reginald Pole and Richard Smith, as well as a collaborative work by a synod at Cologne. With some justice Erasmus could be added to the list. Martyr attacks the *Hyperaspistes* of Erasmus as upholding a Pelagian view of predestination.[85] But for the most part Martyr cites Erasmus' annotations on the New Testament which he values highly.[86]

The two Protestant theologians which Martyr refers to most are Luther and Zwingli, and in four instances he links their names together as the twin upholders of the Gospel against Roman darkness. Martyr praises Zwingli more than Luther, and his linking them together is a device for exalting Zwingli. In contrast, Calvin esteemed Luther much more highly as a theologian than he did Zwingli.[87] Of all Protestant theologians, Martin Bucer probably contributed most toward Martyr's development. Martyr and Bucer were linked together as friends and fellow professors at Strasbourg from 1542 to 1547, the years when Martyr's new Protestant faith was crystallizing into an articulate and developed theology. In his earlier years as a Protestant Martyr admired Melanchthon; this seems to have cooled somewhat later on, for Martyr does not hesitate to disagree with Melanchthon, very gently in print, more forthrightly in a letter to Calvin.[88] Melanchthon's example of the use of Aristotelian concepts in the *Loci Communes* may have encouraged Martyr along the same road, although Martyr goes further than did Melanchthon. Martyr and Calvin became good friends and admired each other, as the correspondence between them in the *Opera Calvini* reveals, but they seem never to have met

---

[85] *Romanos*, 383.

[86] *Defensio*, 12: "Erasmus in recognoscendis authoribus acerrimi vir iudicii."

[87] Wendel, 135-36.

[88] *Iudicum*, f. 195v; *Romanos*, 520; Martyr to Calvin, March 8, 1555: *Calvini Opera*, XV, c. 493.

each other. Although Calvin and Martyr are quite close on almost all doctrinal points, later chapters will argue that this is not because of any massive influence of Calvin on Martyr.

Martyr's reading ranged very wide, but there are some important absences among the works he cites that should be underlined. The most obvious is Martyr's total failure to refer to any vernacular literature or books. His writings never mention Dante, Petrarch, or Boccaccio. Martyr never quotes any neo-Latin poetry. Yet two of Martyr's friends, Marcantonio Flaminio and Theodore Beza, were accomplished neo-Latin poets; moreover, a volume of Latin and Greek verse appeared in England to commemorate the solemn re-burial of his wife.[89] Another friend, Pietro Bembo, was the literary arbiter of Italy and strongly encouraged the vernacular. Martyr's library possessed Bembo's works in three volumes. A large percentage of the works of sixteenth century scholarship found in Martyr's library are commentaries on the ancient classics or aids to the study of antiquity. There are grammars for Latin, Greek, Hebrew, and even a study of Egyptian hieroglyphics, but his library contains nothing on any vernacular language.

The same bookish veneration for antiquity also pervades Martyr's approach to the visual arts. In one passage of his Samuel commentary Martyr wishes to describe the delight that comes from artistic creation. He makes his point by citing a passage in which Seneca describes the artistic skill of Apelles in painting and Praxiteles in sculpture. Martyr was fifteen centuries removed from Seneca, and Seneca five centuries from Apelles and Praxiteles. Had Martyr been raised in Dublin or Danzig, citing Seneca would have been sensible. But he was raised in Florence in the first two decades of the sixteenth century, surrounded by the fruits of the greatest artistic flowering of human history. So he cites Seneca! [90]

Which vernacular languages did Martyr know in addition to his native Italian? In a letter from Oxford to Bucer, Martyr says that he cannot read English.[91] In a letter to Bullinger from Poissy Martyr

---

[89] James Calfhill et al., *De Katherinae . . . Vermilii exhumatione . . . Carmina*, (London: 1561).

[90] *Samuelis*, 104r. Martyr's tendency to see the world through the books of the ancients was shared by many Renaissance intellectuals. Erasmus visited Italy, yet his letters leave no trace of any reaction to Italian art. Martyr's silence may have been partly conditioned by his theological hostility to the religious use of painting and sculpture.

[91] McLelland prints the letter, p. 29.

says that he can understand spoken French but cannot speak it.[92] On Martyr's knowledge of German no such direct evidence is available. It cannot be assumed that because of his many years in Strasbourg and Zurich he learned German. Zanchi and Calvin lived in Strasbourg without learning German. In the sixteenth century a scholar could manage in a foreign city with Latin, plus a few polite phrases in the vernacular. Frenchmen such as Calvin, Farel, and Beza regularly corresponded with one another in Latin rather than French. Still there is some evidence that Martyr learned German. Three theological works in German have been identified as probably belonging to his library.[93] In a letter to Calvin, Martyr summarizes the contents of some page proofs of a German work (probably by J. Westphal) which he managed to get hold of in Strasbourg.[94]

This completes our survey of Martyr's intellectual development and the sources of his teaching. We have emphasized the Italian origins of the intellectual skills later manifested in his copious writings. That Martyr burst upon the northern Protestant divines like some Pallas Athene born fully armed from brow of Zeus appears from a letter of Bucer to Calvin: "A man has arrived from Italy who is quite learned in Latin, Greek, and Hebrew and well skilled in the scriptures; he is about forty-four years old, of serious demeanor and keen intelligence. His name is Peter Martyr."[95] Almost immediately Bucer assigned Martyr the key post of teaching Old Testament at the Strasbourg Academy. The next four chapters examine the use Martyr made of his accumulated erudition in developing a personal theology.

---

[92] Martyr to Bullinger, Oct. 2, 1561: "Quemobrem cum ea lingua nequeam loqui, licet illam intelligam, nihil dixi . . ." *Loci*, 1140. This raises the interesting question of how Martyr communicated with his first wife, Catherine Dammartin of Metz. His second wife was Italian.

[93] Ganoczy, *Bibliothèque*, 200.

[94] Martyr to Calvin, June 14, 1556: *Calvini Opera*, XVI, c. 197.

[95] Bucer to Calvin, Oct. 28, 1542: *Ibid.*, XI, c. 450. "Advenit ex Italia vir quidam grace, hebraice, et latine admodum doctus, et in scripturis feliciter versatus, annos quadraginta quatuor, gravis moribus et iudicio acri, Petro Martyri nomen est."

CHAPTER THREE

REASON, REVELATION, AND MARTYR'S METHODOLOGY

Since New Testament times Christian thinkers and theologians have debated the relationship between reason and revelation and the precise part each is to play in the elaboration of a Christian world view. Some, such as Origen and Thomas Aquinas, have allowed a very substantial role to reason; others, such as Tertullian and Luther, have drastically restricted its role and have emphasized the dichotomy between reason and revelation. Both schools appealed to scripture passages to support their position. Almost all Christian theologians have subordinated reason to revelation, but very few have excluded reason altogether from the theological process.

The popular assumption that scholasticism stood for the massive interjection of philosophy into Christian theology needs qualification. The *via antiqua*, especially its Thomist wing, certainly brought reason and revelation into a close relation and took an optimistic view of man's rational powers. But the *via moderna*, with William of Occam as its chief spokesman, made a more modest assessment of man's rational capacities. Even within the *via antiqua* there were figures such as St. Bonaventure who saw a threat to revelation in the rising tide of Aristotelianism. Peter Martyr's training at the University of Padua was largely in the *via antiqua* tradition.

Martyr never wrote a treatise on the proper relation of philosophy and theology and the role that reason is to play in theology. There is such a treatise in Martyr's published writings, but it is from the hand of Julius Santerenziano, his servant, factotum, and friend who accompanied him on all his travels from Lucca until his death.[1] Santerenziano's treatise takes the form of a preface to Martyr's posthumously published commentary on Aristotle's *Ethics*. The preface attempts to

---

[1] Short biographical accounts of Santerenziano can be found in McNair, *Peter Martyr*, 271-74, and in Paul Boesch, "Julius Terentianus, Factotum des Petrus Martyr Vermilius and Korrector der Offizin Froschauer," *Zwingliana*, VIII, 1948, 587-601. Neither McNair nor Boesch seem to know about the preface to Martyr's *Ethics* commentary, which is very intelligent and easily the most important thing that has come down to us from Santerenziano's hand. That Martyr retained the services of Santerenziano through twenty years of wandering is a further evidence of his gift for winning and holding men's affection and loyalty.

steer a middle course between those Protestants who would totally exclude philosophical considerations and the idolatry of Aristotle reputedly rife among the scholastics. Santerenziano states that the leading divines at Zurich decided to publish Martyr's incomplete commentary on the *Ethics* because it provided an almost perfect model for studying philosophy.[2] The published commentary is the most important evidence of Martyr's interest in philosophy. It puts into print lectures Martyr delivered during his second Strasbourg period, 1553-1556.[3]

As Martyr wrote no systematic treatise on the subject, his teaching on reason and revelation and on theological methodology must be culled from his scattered remarks and from his actual practice. This chapter will examine first his statements, then his practice. The contribution such examination can make to deciding whether and to what degree Martyr can be called a Protestant scholastic is obvious. But it also sheds light on Martyr's view of man. Methodological commitments condition every facet of a theologian or a philosopher's thought, unless he is unusually inconsistent. Martyr's understanding of the role of reason definitely affects his understanding of man.

In Martyr's writings two seemingly contradictory themes can be separated out. There are many passages which are warm encomia of reason and its contribution to theology. There are also passages which inveigh against over-subtlety and the invasion of philosophy into theology. But there is no real contradiction. Martyr's position on the question is a *via media*; therefore he must cover both his flanks. He attacks not only anti-intellectualism which poses as Christian piety and a biblical positivism which accepts nothing not explicit in scripture. But he also rejects excessive rationalism which would reduce the Word of God to an equal or even subordinate level with the dis-

---

[2] "... pene perfectum exemplar interpretandi philosophiam." *Ethicorum*, preface, unpaginated.

[3] *Ibid*. Martyr and Jerome Zanchi alternated in lecturing on Aristotle, Zanchi handling the physical works while Martyr covered the *Ethics*. Martyr's commentary is incomplete because he was called to Zurich before he finished it. At Zurich Conrad Gesner was already covering Aristotle, so Martyr lectured only on the Old Testament. Martyr's printed lectures derive partly from his own lecture notes, partly from those taken down by friends from his lectures. *Ibid*. At one point Santerenziano compares Martyr to Aristotle: "... Aristotelem vero, ut omnes merito admirantur ac laudant, qui philosophiam et eloquentiam simul docuit, ita etiam iure ego hoc nomine Martyrem meum laudare possum, qui non tantum philosophiae cognitionem cum sacrarum litterarum studio coniunxit, verum etiam simul philosophiam et theologiam publice docuit." *Ibid*.

coveries of human reason. In the anti-intellectualist camp, Martyr singles out Anabaptists, Johann Brenz (and by implication conservative Lutherans) and much monastic piety (of which the *Imitatio Christi* is the best example). Martyr levels the charge of excessive rationalism against Origen, Dionysius the pseudo-Areopagite, and the scholastics generally. He attacks the false doctrines of many pagan philosophers and very likely has their modern disciples in mind. Martyr's seeming contradictions largely vanish when his need to protect his *via media* on both flanks is kept in mind. Moreover, a given remark is often conditioned by the specific scripture passage Martyr is commenting on. Thus Martyr's emphasis differs when he is commenting on the Old Testament's praise of Solomon's wisdom and on St. Paul's strictures on the dangers of philosophy.

This chapter first outlines Martyr's eulogies of reason and philosophy, then his cautions about their use, then his statements about the knowledge of God and His law that reason affords. There follows a brief examination of the role of revelation, of the act of faith, and of several features of his methodology which indicates his debt to earlier scholasticism. The chapter closes with a few examples of Martyr's use of philosophical arguments in his theology.

According to Martyr all human knowledge is either revealed or acquired. Revealed knowledge is the province of theology; acquired knowledge belongs to philosophy. He divides philosophy into contemplative or speculative and active or practical. Martyr insists that this distinction does not flow from the distinction of intellect and will. Rather Martyr follows the scholastics in dividing the sciences according to their formal objects.[4]

For Luther reason is the devil's whore. Martyr takes a different stand. He quotes Cicero's magnificent eulogy of philosophy, although making philosophical knowledge clearly subordinate to revelation. The purpose of philosophy is to feed and teach the soul. Dialectics is a gift from God, an inseparable part of wisdom, that is most useful for life. The study of philosophy should bring man great pleasure.[5]

Martyr's commentary on St. Paul's First Epistle to the Corinthians brought him face to face with one of the scripture passages most beloved by Christian anti-intellectuals. In the first chapter (verses 18-31) Paul tells his readers that the Greek seek for wisdom but that he

---

[4] *Ethicorum*, 1, 2.
[5] *Ethicorum*, 4, 10; *Defensio*, 377; *Corinthios*, f. 42r; *Loci*, 488-89.

preaches Christ crucified. Paul points out that God has made the wisdom of the world foolishness and that God will destroy the wisdom of the wise and reject the prudence of the prudent. Martyr's comments on this passage cover pages, and he rejects excessive rationalism and points out that philosophy is not salvific. But what strikes the reader is Martyr's moderation. A short sample must suffice:

> The wisdom of the world is that which is acquired by our natural faculty and light and which avails for directing and protecting and administering the affairs of this world—for instance, medicine, politics, dialectics, rhetoric, and so forth. There is need for these factors in this world, for in the future there will be no room for them. Nor do we teach that the wisdom of this world is to be scorned provided that it keeps within its bounds. For thus it has its usefulness. This only is forbidden it: that it presumes to lead man under its guidance to salvation. This wisdom must be prevented from daring to utter falsehood with its reasons against divine truths. That the wisdom of Paul and the gospel remove or weaken the wisdom of this world is a widely held error that must be destroyed.[6]

Martyr frequently rebukes the Christian anti-intellectualism that cites Paul's condemnation of philosophy. Martyr counters that Paul's condemnations of philosophy apply to false philosophy such as the Stoic doctrine of *apatheia*, academic skepticism, the Epicurean deistic concept of God, the common ownership of goods, the common use of women, and the views that pleasure is the supreme good, that the world is eternal or consists of a mere concurrence of atoms.[7]

Martyr believes that knowledge, even natural knowledge, has an important contribution to make to Christianity. Why else did Paul write his epistles, if not to teach? True philosophy can rise from a knowledge of creatures to a knowledge of God's justice. It is a great joy to know the exact limitations of natural knowledge, for this gives a greater appreciation of revelation. Man should master the data of

---

[6] *Corinthios*, f. 42r: Sapientia saeculi dicitur, quae naturali facultate ac lumine acquiritur, quaeque ad res huius mundi regendas, tuendas, et administrandas valet, ut medica, politica, dialectica, rhetorica, et id genus. His facultatibus opus est in hoc mundo, quae cum illo quoque finientur, nam in futuro saeculo illis minime locus patebit. Neque istam huius mundi sapientiam docemus aspernandam, modo se intra suas fines contineat. Sic enim suas habet utilitates. Id tantum ei non permittitur, ut praesumat hominem suis auspiciis ad salutem perducere. Absterenda etiam est ne divina suis rationibus metiri ausit. Atque id explodendum est, quod multi falso arbitrantur, sapientiam Pauli et evangelii hanc huius mundi sapientiam vel tollere vel debilitare.

[7] *Corinthios*, f. 198r; *Melachim*, f. 99v; *Ethicorum*, 7; *Romanos*, 302.

both revelation and of natural knowledge, for the knowledge of one helps man to guard against possible errors in the other, and the two sources of knowledge can serve as checks on each other. Dialectic is God's matchless gift which helps man to refute error and heresy, and it was so used and treasured by the church Fathers. Martyr eulogizes Aristotle for his peerless work in developing the theory and rules of the syllogism in his *Posterior Analytics*.[8]

Martyr's acceptance of philosophy as an auxiliary of theology led him to reject a mere biblical positivism: that Christian theology should teach only what was explicitly contained in scripture. Martyr allows those conclusions which can be gathered from the scriptures by clear and evident argument. Martyr admits, for instance, that the Anabaptists are right in claiming that there are no explicit endorsements of infant baptism in the Bible, but this does not settle the issue. Jesus himself (Mark 12:26, 27) used an obscure text and a rather drawn out theological argument based on it to refute the Sadducees' arguments against the resurrection of the body; the Christian theologian is entitled to do the same.[9] In Martyr's *Dialogus* the speaker who represents the Lutheran Brenz several times rejects Martyr's arguments as mere philosophy and brands Martyr as a slave to Aristotle. Martyr admits that his arguments are drawn from philosophy and from Aristotle, but they are not therefore invalid or false. As to being Aristotle's slave, Martyr replies that he retains from the philosopher that which is consonant with the teachings of the Church and the Fathers. When Aristotle teaches things contrary to true religion, Martyr insists that he stoutly opposes him.[10] In a number of passages Martyr justifies his borrowings from the philosophers by appealing to the example of St. Paul, who quoted the pagan comedian Menander.[11] He maintains that he does not accept the teachings of Aristotle *authoris causa* but because they are true. He argues that "we embrace the truth, regardless of by whom expressed, as though spoken by the Holy Spirit."[12] Perhaps the best indication of Martyr's

---

[8] *Ethicorum*, 7, 10; *Defensio*, 377; *Romanos*, 535; *Samuelis*, f. 101r.

[9] *Romanos*, 558; *Melachim*, f. 219rv; *Loci*, 545.

[10] *Dialogus*, ff. 3r, 9r, 71r; also see *Defensio*, 630.

[11] *Dialogus*, f. 3r; *Corinthios*, f. 420v.

[12] *Dialogus*, f. 3r: Sed verum a quocunque dictum fuerit, ut a spiritu sancto prolatum amplectimur. Martyr develops this idea, *Corinthios*, f. 420v: "Quoniam a quocunque dicatur, a spiritu sancto est; et quando eam ex libris impiorum accepimus, non aliena rapimus, sed quae sunt nostra ab iniustis possessoribus nobis vindicamus. Revelavit Deus infidelibus nonnunquam permulta vera, idque non raro in eorum condemnationem, quo minus habeant excusationis:

attitude toward Aristotle is the final section of each chapter of his commentary on the *Ethics*. This section compares the teaching of Aristotle with that of scripture. Usually Martyr finds the two in agreement.

According to Martyr the teachings of reason and those of scripture have much in common, but also sharp differences. The purpose of philosophy is that man achieve that happiness which can be reached by merely human powers. But scripture is ordered to faith, and faith to justification, and justification to upright deeds and the recovery of God's image in man. Proofs can be drawn from either causes or effects in both the wisdom of this world and in the wisdom of the Spirit. Both distinguish necessary arguments from the merely probable. Both devise and define a suitable technical vocabulary. But there are also differences. One arises from the light of nature; the other depends on faith and the Holy Spirit. The one takes its principles from the senses, from observation, and from experience; the other adheres to the word of God.[13] In a number of places, Martyr gives a division of the various branches of philosophy. But the findings of human reason are always strictly subordinate to the Word of God.[14] There is never any question of an Averroist double truth in Martyr.

A passage in Martyr's Kings commentary indicates clearly Martyr's debt to St. Thomas in his understanding of the relation of reason and revelation. Martyr asks whether apodictic arguments for the resurrection of the body can be given by natural reason alone. He answers that only probable arguments can be given since the resurrection surpasses every power in nature. Martyr then discusses what constitutes apodictic proofs or arguments. Some arguments resolve the questions they treat into principles which are self evident to natural reason (*principia primo et per se nota in rerum natura*). Such proofs are few in number and are confined to mathematics. Many other arguments do not consist of self evident principles but can be reduced to these principles. Still other arguments rest on necessary principles but these principles are not evident in the subalternate science that uses them but are demonstrated only in a superior and higher science.

---

quandoquidem nullus ex ethnicis invenitur qui tantum factis praestiterit quantum notitia assecutus. Hinc docemur libros ethnicorum non esse prorsus abiciendos, sed vera qua in eis leguntur, studiose audienda, modo tempus impartiendum lectioni sacrarum literarum non huc transferatur."

[13] *Dialogus*, f. 75r; *Ethicorum*, 8; *Corinthios*, f. 45v.

[14] *Ethicorum*, 1; *Melachim*, f. 34v. On the subordination of reason to scripture, see *Ethicorum*, 10, 36.

For examples, musicians borrow their principles from the higher science of mathematics; the arguments used in music are not apodictic for the musician since he does not know mathematics and therefore cannot himself demonstrate the principles of his discipline, but the arguments and principles are apodictic to the man who knows both music and mathematics. The arguments offered for the resurrection are not convincing and apodictic to the natural philosopher because he cannot trace them back to natural causes. They rest on supernatural causes which are known only through revelation. For the faithful the arguments become apodictic because they can trace them back to their foundation in the word of God.[15] In this discussion Martyr never refers to St. Thomas but his teaching is little more than a paraphrase of passages in Aquinas, especially the second and eight articles of the very first question of the *Summa Theologiae*. Martyr repeats not only Thomas's doctrine but also much of his terminology. Thomas also uses the example of the relation of the musician and the mathematician and applies his teaching to the resurrection. A better example of residual Thomism in Martyr's theology would be hard to find.[15]

Along side his encomia of reason and philosophy, Martyr utters words of caution. Mere philosophy cannot remedy human and social evils. Martyr finds shortcomings even in the teachings of the Platonists and peripatetics, the schools he most admired. There is much that Christianity must reject in the teachings of the philosophers, and even their best passages are far inferior to the least valuable passages in scripture. The failings of Aristotle and Plato are due neither to lack of genius, for the two Greeks were abundantly endowed, nor to positive errors, but rather to the inevitable limitations of mere human reason. Their view of man and of ethics is good as far as it goes and is not so much erroneous as incomplete. Without revelation the Greek philosophers simply could not take into account supernatural facts and factors; they could neither grasp the depth of human depravity nor the heights of man's supernatural calling. Because they were without the light of revelation, their teachings can be a source of error. With this in mind Martyr recalls that Tertullian dubbed the philosophers the patriarchs of heretics.[16] Even those truths which are affirmed by the philosophers and believed by the faithful are not held in the

---

[15] *Melachim*, 217rv. Rist, "Modernité," sees Calvin as rejecting sharply this view of theology as a science, 31-32.

[16] *Ethicorum*, 31, 32, 257, 292-94; *Romanos*, 18; *Corinthios*, f. 44r, 141r, 396r; *Dialogus*, f. 25r.

same way. According to Martyr, what is believed cannot be naturally known, at least not with the necessary fulness.[17]

Martyr often criticizes the Roman Catholic scholastic theologians, both medieval and contemporary. His criticism takes two main forms. The scholastics are enslaved to the papal anti-Christ, and their teachings are too subtle and argumentative. Martyr becomes very bitter about the Catholic scholastics' acceptance of papal decrees, especially those regarding the Eucharist. He writes of a conscious conspiracy against the truth, of a blind, pertinacious, and insane worship of the decretals. He castigates the Roman Catholic universities, especially Paris, Louvain, Salamanca, Bologna, and Padua; these have herds of theology professors, but there is scarcely one sincere theologian among them. Their style is dark and contentious, thorny and rustic.[18] He criticizes the scholastics for raising curious questions, for exampel about the future life and about angels, which they discuss with excessive subtlety and very little scriptural foundation. They invent a pretentious jargon full of quiddities and formalities so as to impress others with their erudition.[19] Indeed, after denouncing the gladiatorial shows of ancient Rome, Martyr goes on to say that theological controversies are "easily the worse of gladiatorial fighting. I do not object to moderate colloquies on religion; but I reject loud quarrels about abstruse and arcane questions."[20]

Martyr's cautions about the use of philosophy and his rejection of scholastic subtlety and contentiousness should not be taken too seriously. Perry Miller observes that: "though Puritan literature abounds with condemnations of scholasticism, almost no limits can

---

[17] *Melachim*, f. 218rv: Atque haec de naturalibus rationibus quae, ut dictum est, probabiles sunt, non apodeichticae, sint satis. Et quod hac de re affirmatum est, de caeteris quoque articulis fidei sentiendum est. Etenim quae ab aliquo creduntur, ab eodem naturaliter sciri non possunt. At dixerit quispiam: Nos credimus unum Deum, quem tamen esse naturali rationi concluditur. Ad hoc respondemus philosophos quidem physica investigatione ad unum summum principium pervenisse, quod Graeci θεός et latini Deum dixerunt, sed ille non est is quem fides Christiana profitetur. Non enim simpliciter ac nude credimus unum Deum, sed illum qui creavit coelum et terram, quique habet filium et spiritum sanctam. Has utique appendices philosophi suis rationibus minime apprehenderunt. Unde verissime constat, quod Apostolus ad Hebraeos docuit, fidem argumentum esse rerum non apparentium.

[18] *Loci*, 1060, 1064; *Defensio*, 113.

[19] *Romanos*, 330; *Corinthios*, f. 64v, 364r.

[20] *Samuelis*, f. 188r: Hoc longe omnium deterrimum est genus gladiaturae. Colloquia quidem de religione moderata non improbo: rixas autem et clamores de rebus abstrusis et reconditis reprehendo.

be set to its actual influence."[21] The fact is that Martyr considered Aristotle a valuable ally against the Catholics.[22] Scholastic terminology, metaphysics, and subtlety of argument were simply too valuable as weapons for the Reformed theologian to omit them from his panoply. Martyr repeatedly denounces his Catholic opponent Gardiner for his failings precisely as a scholastic metaphysician and logician. Gardiner errs not because he is a scholastic, but because he is a bad scholastic.[23] Historians have generally concurred with Martyr in denouncing the medieval scholastics for arguing abstruse questions with excessive subtlety. Yet there were two theological questions closest to Martyr's heart: predestination and the Eucharist. Both were abstruse. The scriptural data about both was meager. Still Martyr argued them both at great length with extreme subtlety. Martyr, of course, justifies his procedure by insisting on their importance.[24]

Modern historians have praised Martyr's appeals for charity in theological dispute and have seen them as signs of moderation in an age when invective and billingsgate were the rule.[25] In his *Dialogue* against the Lutheran Brenz, Martyr's manners are impeccable, but against his Roman Catholic adversaries Martyr is guilty of *ad hominem* attacks.[26]

---

[21] Perry Miller, *The New England Mind: The Seventeenth Century*, (Cambridge, Mass.: 1963), 104.

[22] *Ethicorum*, 265.

[23] Sed quis hic risum teneat cum vident istum (i.e.: Gardiner) ita incogitanter dicere species visibles in hoc Sacramento esse pro forma, corpus autem et sanguinem Christi esse pro materia? Ego semper audivi materiam a forma longe dignitate superari . . . Noli, Inconstanti (Gardiner had written under the pseudonym of Constantius, which Martyr mockingly twists), si me audis, inter philosophos aut etiam inter Scholasticos ista dicere, ne te gradibus illis tuis, quos tu forte inter eos aliquando accepisti, spolient . . . O Sorbonistas fungos et stipites, qui istam tam exquisitam et subtilem philosophiam numquam didiceritis. Transmittite in Angliam et a novo isto Magistro sententiarum discite ea quae neque ex Lombardo vestro neque ex aliis omnibus doctoribus discere hactenus potuistis. *Defensio*, 350.

[24] Non tamen omnes prorsus questiones ut inutiles damnandae sunt. Itaque probare non possum quosdam prudentes quidem vero in aliis rebus et attentos, sed hac in re una certe minus consideratos, quae hodie passim agitatur de Eucharistia, intempestivam esse putant et inutilem. *Romanos*, 614.

[25] W. M. Southgate praises Martyr's moderation, p. 20; McLelland entitles his long biographical section on Martyr as "Portrait of an Ecumenical Reformer." *Visible Words*, 1-68. Also Young, I, 488.

[26] Martyr's three chief Roman Catholic targets were Richard Smith, Stephen Gardiner, and Albert Pighius. Smith had been ousted from his chair at Oxford to make room for Martyr and used to attend many of Martyr's lectures. In their later controversy over celibacy Smith incorrectly stated that Martyr had been a

Now that Martyr's eulogies and cautions about reason have been seen, a further question arises: what kind of knowledge about God and his law can human reason afford? Martyr turns to the question several times and his answer always contains two elements: human reason can know God, but this rational knowledge is insufficient and must be supplemented by scripture. St. Paul's statement on the matter (Romans: 1: 20-25) determined Martyr's thinking much more than any philosophical proofs for God's existence that Martyr had come across in his readings. Such proofs seem to have little interested him. Martyr's most thorough treatment of man's natural knowledge of God occurs in his commentary on the above Pauline passage to the Romans. Martyr thought that atheism was psychologically impossible: some men might pretend that God did not exist and try to convince themselves of this, but they could not really succeed because their consciences would inevitably rebel against atheism.[27] Martyr believed that several of the Greek philosophers had worked out successful proofs for God's existence and for some of his basic attributes.[28] He credited Plato with a very Christian concept of God: that God was

---

Carthusian when in Italy. In fact, Martyr was a former Augustinian canon. Smith's mistake seems a guileless and understandable slip. Martyr reacts: "Quantus quantus est totus ex mendaciis conflatus videri possit." *Defensio de Coelibatu*, 4. Stephen Gardiner, bishop of Winchester and a powerful figure in ecclesiastical politics under Henry VIII and Mary (he enjoyed the hospitality of the Tower under Edward VI), published a controversial work on the Eucharist notable for its patristic learning. Martyr had reason to be grateful to Gardiner, who secured funds for Martyr's journey back to Strasbourg after the accession of Mary put his life in some danger. Martyr's mocking tone toward Gardiner is clear from footnote twenty-three immediately above. Martyr attempted to undermine Gardiner's patristic arsenal by relating some hearsay he had picked up in Rome about Gardiner years before. Gardiner was in Rome to argue Henry VIII's divorce. Curial canonists rumoured that Gardiner was fabricating legal citations to bolster the King's great matter. Martyr dredges up this rumor and suggests that Gardiner's patristic quotations are equally bogus. This no doubt eased the drudgery of verifying and refuting Gardiner's citations, but it was bad manners and bad method in scholarly debate, doubly so as Gardiner was several years in his grave when Martyr first published his *Defensio*. Curiously Martyr also had personal contact with his third major Roman Catholic adversary, Pighius. In 1533 the Dutchman stayed at Martyr's monastery when he visited Bologna as part of Charles V's entourage. Pighius was safely dead sixteen years when long sections of Martyr's commentary on the Epistle to the Romans (first published 1558) excoriated Pighius's views on free will, predestination, and original sin. McNair, *Peter Martyr*, 126, mentions Pighius's sojourn at Bologna.

[27] *Romanos*, 30. Atheism ran counter to the prevailing mentality of the sixteenth century. See Lucien Febvre, *Le Problème de l'incroyance au XVIᵉ siècle*, (Paris: Albin Michel, 1942), 361-501.

[28] *Romanos*, 29.

one and ineffable, infinite and ubiquitous, that God created all things out of his mere goodness.[29]

But the knowledge of God drawn from reason alone is not only insufficient and not salvific but in fact of itself leads only to damnation. Martyr writes:

> We posit a twofold knowledge of God. One is general and perceived naturally but is so vague and weak that it avails only to make men inexcusable. It offers some light but not enough to change the heart. The second knowledge of God is had through faith and depends on the Word of God and divine revelation. This is found only in those who have been reborn through Christ and is so efficacious that it changes our souls and makes us partakers in the divine nature.[30]

Needless to say, for Martyr not even the knowledge of God through faith is perfect or exhaustive. God's creaturely effects only mirror the creator imperfectly.[31]

Martyr never attempts any detailed rational proof of God's existence. His most explicit passage on man's natural knowledge of God is a bit ambivalent, for while part of it seems to echo St. Thomas's five ways, it also develops the view that God has implanted in man certain foreshadowings or an inchoate knowledge of himself, and that these foreshadowings develop into a sort of knowledge of God under rational reflection on nature.[32]

---

[29] *Ethicorum*, 137.

[30] *Corinthios*, f. 23v. ". . . Dei cognitionem duplicem statuamus: unam quidem communem et naturaliter perceptam, quae adeo tenuis et infirma est, ut solum valeat ad reddendos homines inexcusabiles. Aliquid sane lucis affert, sed non tantum ut cor immutet. Altera est quae per fidem habetur et ex verbo Dei atque divina revelatione pendet. Et haec, quae est solum in renatis per Christum, adeo est efficax, ut animos transmutet nosque naturae divinae consortes efficiat." Martyr makes the same point in *Romanos*, 30.

[31] *Iudicum*, f. 82r. Sturm, 103-107.

[32] On St. Pauls' words "Deus enim illis manifestavit" Martyr comments: "Hinc colligitur omne verum a Deo esse. Non enim ex nobis nascitur. Sed quomodo sit a Deo duplex est sententia. Dicunt nonnulli, hoc ideo esse quod Deus ea condiderit per quae possumus haec vera praecipere: alii vero, quibus magis assentior, quod Deus inserverit animis nostris . . . anticipationes et informationes, per quas impellimur ad opinandum praeclara et eximia de natura Dei. Atque hae notitiae de Deo nobis naturaliter insitae observatione rerum creaturarum in dies magis ac magis confirmantur et expoliuntur . . . Haec autem signa, quae ab initio Deum nobis declararunt, sunt creaturae: Quas dum perpendunt physici quoad naturae proprietates et qualitates admirabiles, deducuntur ad notitiam Dei. Noverunt enim seriem causarum earumque coniuctionem cum suis effectis; et cum facile intelligerent nequaquam statui oportere infinitum progressum concludebant ad aliquod primum pertigendum: et ita concludebant esse Deum." *Romanos*, 20.

Martyr's treatment of man's knowledge of morality and of God's will and law for man parallels his treatment of man's knowledge of God. Reason provides man with an understanding of God's moral law, but very imperfectly. This imperfect knowledge is not accompanied by the means to carry it out, with the result that man's natural knowledge of the moral law leads only to his increased culpability before God.[33] The one solid source of moral knowledge is God's Word in scripture. Martyr drives home this point with a rare burst of rhetorical fireworks at Strasbourg during an exhortation to the study of theology:

> Wherefore it belongs to God alone to set up and define by his Word, as by the certain measure of all rectitude and justice, what is the mean of the virtues. Whatever he teaches, whatever he praises, whatever he approves, is sincere virtue and solid justice. The man who thinks he can learn this elsewhere is seeking water from a stone and wool from a donkey; he is hunting the winds with a net, building on sand, and drawing water with a sieve.[34]

Even here Aristotelianism creeps in: morality is understood as the cultivation of virtue, and virtue as the mean between two extremes.

There is still another dimension to Martyr's understanding of man's rational knowledge of God and of his law. Not only is this knowledge restricted by the inherent limitations of man's knowing faculties, but it is positively depraved by original sin. The unregenerate human intellect not only does not grasp the truth about God but

---

[33] *Romanos*, 30, 156; *Corinthios*, f. 141v; *Loci*, 1058.

[34] *Loci*, 1059-60: Quamobrem solius est Dei Verbo suo, tamquam certa mensura omnis rectitudinis et iustitiae, de vero virtutum medio constituere et definire. Quicquid is praecipit, quicquid is laudat, quicquid approbat, syncera est virtus et solida iustitia: quam aliunde quisquis arbitratur se posse disceri, is e pumice aquam petit, ab asino lanam, reti venatur ventos, in arena aedificat, cribo aquam haurit . . ." The general impression that Martyr's statements on morality give is that God forbids certain actions because they are intrinsically wrong. This was the Thomist view. But in at least one passage Martyr seems to swing over and hold that actions are wrong because God forbids them. This brings him closer to Luther and the nominalists. The passage in question regards Jacob's lie that he was Esau. Martyr claims that Jacob told the lie under divine impulse. He expands: "Si humana ratione ista aguntur, omnia sunt plena dolis. At si divina moderatione, iam hic nullum est peccatum: si quidem actiones haud ex suo genere sunt aestimandae, sed respicienda est Dei voluntas, nam si id ipse iubeat ut fiat, iam ratio peccati evanescit, quae maxime in hoc sita est ut adversetur divinae legi et voluntati. Interficere filium sua natura est parricidium, expoliare Aegyptum furtum censetur, interficere sine publica authoritate et legitimo iudicio homicidium; tamen in Abrahamo primum laudatur, secundum iussit Deus filiis Israel, tertium in Phinees commendat." *Genesis*, f. 102v.

finds the truth positively repugnant, just as some sick men find whole-
some food distasteful. Vermigli never tires of repeating Paul's statement (1 Cor. 2:14): "A man who is unspiritual (*animalis homo*) refuses
what belongs to the Spirit of God; it is folly to him; he cannot grasp
it, because it needs to be judged in the light of the Spirit." [35] Martyr
defines *animalis homo* as the man who knows and acts with the powers
of the lower and the higher parts of his soul. He trusts his own reason
and sees no need for faith, for grace, and for the help of the Holy
Spirit. He accepts nothing but rational demonstrations and depends
upon nothing but his own natural light and prudence. Still, for
Martyr the intellect remains a powerful tool in the theological process,
despite the wounds of original sin. Only the unregenerate feel the full
impact of original sin. In regenerate theologians grace has done its
healing work on the intellect's wounds, and they work under the
light of scripture and the Spirit. [36]

Martyr attributes to scripture the paramount role in teaching man
about God and his law. Like all mainstream sixteenth century Protestants, he teaches a strong doctrine of *sola scriptura* and tries earnestly
to make scripture the source and norm of all his theology. Contrary
to the Roman Catholics, he rejects extra-scriptural tradition and
ecclesiastical authority as doctrinal norms. His writings are sprinkled
with attacks on the Anabaptists, and he has no use for appeals to the
inner light or inner Spirit against the biblical text. He stands no less
resolutely against evangelical rationalism. He supported the burning
of Servetus whom he regarded as the devil's own son. He was involved
with anti-Trinitarian tendencies among his fellow Italian exiles
(especially Blandrata, Stancaro, Socinus, and Ochino) and tried to
moderate them by personal contact in Zurich and check the spread of
their ideas in Poland by letter. [37]

Marvin Anderson has treated Martyr's scriptural principle in a
recent article, so the treatment here can be brief. [38] According to
Martyr, man must believe everything that is in scripture and only

---

[35] I use the *New English Bible* for scripture quotations except in a few instances
in which I have felt it necessary to translate Martyr's Latin myself in order to
retain his stress.

[36] *Corinthios*, f. 49rv; *Romanos*, 125, 585.

[37] McLelland, *Visible Words*, 48-50, 54, 55.

[38] Marvin Anderson, "Word and Spirit," 195-97. He also touches on the same
subject in "Pietro Martyre Vermigli on the Scope and Clarity of Scripture,"
forthcoming in *Theologische Zeitschrift*.

what is in scripture. Nothing can be the object of faith that is not in scripture. The authority of scripture is independent of the Church. Human reason alone is not enough to understand the Bible, for the help of the Spirit is also essential.[39] Perhaps Martyr's finest statement of the scriptural principle is in his letter to the Polish evangelicals, embattled by Catholic power on the one hand and radical subversion on the other:

> The dignity and luster of no creature should blind our eyes—not kings, not the Fathers, not the Bishops, not the Roman Pontiffs, not the Councils, nor finally the learned men of our age, though they are many indeed and can compare fully with the ancients. This is the prerogative of holy scripture alone, that it be the master of our faith, that it be the certain rule that prescribes what we must believe. No other creature should be believed save in so far as it agrees with it.[40]

The previous chapter traced Vermigli's patristic learning. But what value did he attribute to the writings of the Church Fathers in theological investigation and argument? Martyr allows the Fathers no dogmatic authority whatever. The Fathers were mere men, and all men are fallible. Only the scriptures contain the infallible Word of God.[41] To the Roman Catholic argument that the Fathers are a necessary supplement to scripture because the Bible is often obscure and needs clarification from writings of the Fathers, Martyr replies that the reverse is the case. The Fathers themselves are often obscure and contradictory. The Bible is self-clarifying since the clear passages provide the light needed to elucidate the obscure ones. Martyr does admit that his study of the Fathers has often led him to deeper insights into the meaning of scripture than he might have obtained otherwise. Martyr felt that the Protestant theologian needed to master the Fathers because the papists constantly appeal to their authority and twist their meaning into support for the Roman position. This impresses the ignorant and must be met by patristic counter-argument showing that the Fathers of the early Church generally support

---

[39] *Romanos*, 126; *Defensio*, 1, 2.

[40] *Loci*, 1110: Nullius creaturae dignitas aut fulgor oculos nobis perstringat, non reges, non patres, non episcopi, non Romani antistites, non concilia, non denique viri docti nostrae aetatis, qui sane permulti sunt et cum veteribus optimo iure conferri queunt. Unius sanctae scripturae sit haec praerogativa ut nostrae fidei dominetur, illa, ceu regula certissima, quid nobis credendum praescribat, nulli praetera creaturae nisi quantum cum ea facit credatur.

[41] *Defensio*, 68; *Romanos*, 541.

Protestantism in its quarrel with the Roman Church. Martyr's writings are filled with examples of just this counter-argument. He admits that there are issues on which the weight of patristic testimony (for instance the patristic hyper-esteem for virginity) favors Rome. In such cases Martyr simply falls back on the Bible, which is alone decisive. The patristic line of defense is valuable, but only an outwork. Martyr has no hesitation in disagreeing with individual Fathers. He recognizes the preponderant Platonic influence over them, sometimes with unfortunate results for their theology.[42]

Scripture alone provides the dogmatic content of faith. Reason aids man in elaborating the content of revelation into a coherent theology and in defending it. But man makes the teachings of scripture his own only by the act of faith. Faith is central to Martyr's theological noetic no less than to his doctrine of justification. Faith means freely accepting what another person says because one trusts that person. In every act of faith, human or divine, there are always two elements: the person who is trusted and the content which is believed. The New Testament and Luther clearly emphasized the fiducial, personalist aspect of faith. Medieval scholasticism emphasized the content of faith, the intellectual aspect. Protestant scholasticism tended to follow the medievals and as it neared the eighteenth century came close to reducing faith to an assent to a series of propositions. Especially when speaking of faith in conjunction with justification, Martyr is alive to the personalist, fiducial aspect, but this treatment of the act of faith has a strong intellectual tinge that requires investigation. For Martyr the intellect and not the will holds primacy in the act of faith, although his description is far from rationalistic

> We do not teach that faith depends upon a command of the will. Whence, indeed, is the will moved to command that the articles of faith should be accepted as good and worthy of faith unless this is first commanded through the intellect? We admit that those things which we believe are obscure and far from clear to human reason. But they become evident to the intellect by the light of divine revelation and the brightness of the Holy Spirit. Therefore they are recognized and admitted by a judgment of reason with the highest certitude. When they are so known and received, the result is that the will delights and so eagerly embraces them that it orders the soul's other faculties to those actions which the mind believes consistent with

---

[42] *Loci*, 1060; *Genesis*, f. 25v; *Romanos*, 541; *Defensio de Coelibatu*, 462ff. Also see McLelland, *Visible Words*, 267-71.

that truth. And in this wise charity arises from faith and hope follows from them both.[43]

The content of faith is everything contained in scripture, but Martyr does not see the *everything in scripture* as an undifferentiated farrago of propositions. Faith looks first to a single master truth (*una veritas praecipua et eximia in quam aliae omnes diriguntur*). This master truth is that "Christ the Son of God suffered for us so that through him we might receive the forgiveness of our sins."[44] Just as the dignity of man's faculties depends on the dignity of their objects, so the various assents contained in the act of faith vary in dignity. All else in Scripture is believed for the sake of faith in Christ's death which reconciles men to God. It is faith in this truth that pleases God most. As a major premise in establishing the higher dignity of his master truth, Martyr quotes the scholastic axiom: *"propter quod unumquodque tale, illud ipsum erit magis tale."*[45]

So far this chapter has discussed Martyr's statements about reason, revelation, and methodology. But what is Martyr's own practice? Do his theological works exhibit scholastic characteristics? The com-

---

[43] *Romanos*, 128: "Nos vero non ita fieri docemus ut fides a praecepto voluntatis pendeat. Unde enim illa moveretur ut res credendas recipi iuberet tamquam bonas et dignas fide, nisi id prius per intellectum percepisset? Obscura quidem et parum evidentia humanae rationi fatemur esse ea quae credimus. Sed ea intellectui conspicua fiunt lumine divinae revelationis et fulgore Spiritus Sancti. Quare a iudicio rationis apprehenduntur atque admittuntur summa certitudine; quibus ita cognitis atque receptis ut consequens est voluntas sese oblectat et ea tam vehementer complectitur ut caeteris animi facultatibus opera praecipiat ei veritati, cui mens credidit consentanea." Martyr gives several different definitions of faith, but their differences are not important. "Est ergo fides assensus et quidem firmus verbis Dei, non ex ratione sed ab authoritate dicentis, vi Spiritus sancti afflatus," *Loci*, 485. "Est itaque fides firmus certusque animi assensus verbis Dei, a Spiritu divino afflatus ad salutem credentium," *Loci*, 511. Martyr discusses the act of faith also in *Genesis*, f. 56r. Martyr's treatment of faith is less rationalistic than that of Melanchthon and Ursinus: see Althaus, *Prinzipien*, 83. Sturm describes Martyr's treatment of faith, 103-107, 264.

[44] *Romanos*, 565: "Christum filium Dei pro nobis passum esse ut per eum acciperemus condonationem peccatorum." Elsewhere he puts it even more briefly: "placatum fore nobis Deum propter Christum," *Loci*, 486. This master truth was, of course, so basic that it was not controverted in the sixteenth century. Hence it does not set Martyr apart from his contemporaries. Much of Martyr's literary activity dealt with the Eucharist, but as Martyr's constant theme is that too much emphasis has been placed on the Eucharist, it is not the center of his theology as a whole. The most distinctive note in Martyr's theology is the central importance given to predestination. Predestination is more central for Martyr than for Calvin.

[45] *Romanos*, 565.

monplace are true. Actions do speak louder than words. The medium is the message. Very likely Martyr's practice in elaborating his theology proved more influential than his scattered statements on the nature of theology.

At the outset of the Reformation Luther urged that lectures on the text of scripture replace the *Sentences* of Lombard, the innumerable commentaries on it, and the summas of the later scholastics. Protestant theological academies accepted this suggestion. The bulk of Peter Martyr's published writings are his lectures on scripture. At Oxford he lectured on Paul's two most important epistles, Romans and First Corinthians. His audience at Oxford was still largely Catholic in sympathy, and Martyr chose these two epistles as his subject matter because they brought up most of the major questions at issue between the old and new faiths. At Strasbourg and Zurich Martyr's chair was in the Old Testament, and his hearers were mainly students for the Protestant ministry. Throughout his career Martyr seems to have enjoyed great latitude in choosing the books of the Bible upon which to lecture. His choice when on the Continent almost always lay with the historical books of the Old Testament. The single exception among his extant writings was the Lamentations of Jeremiah, finally published sixty-seven years after Martyr's death.[46]

In preparing his lectures Martyr drew upon his own immense erudition. Still, he seems to have deliberately narrowed his sources when he came to write his commentaries. In every instance his commentaries take as their immediate guide a philologically competent but doctrinally neutral previous commentator. Apparently Martyr wanted to look afresh at the large scale doctrinal content of the book he was glossing but also found useful having at his elbow a commentary which would shed light chiefly on grammatical and philological difficulties. For instance, in the introduction to his commentary on the Epistle to the Romans, Martyr says explicitly that he has read the commentaries of Calvin and Bullinger on that Epistle and implies familiarity with the commentaries of Bucer and Melanchthon as well. But his commentary does not refer to these illustrious predecessors. There are repeated references to one work of contemporary scholar-

---

[46] Peter Martyr, *In Lamentationes . . . Commentarium*, (Zurich: J. J. Bodmerus, 1629). These lectures were given during Martyr's first Strasbourg period, 1542-1547, but the text was lost until J. R. Stukius discovered it in 1629 and published it as appropriate to the desolation of the Thirty Years War. See his preface to Martyr's commentary.

ship: Erasmus' *Annotations*. It is equally obvious that in preparing his commentary on First Corinthians Martyr had the *Annotations* on his desk. Obviously Martyr does not depend upon Erasmus for his general theology of grace, free will, predestination, or original sin. What he borrows from Erasmus is the precise meaning of a word or of a turn of phrase. Various rabbinical commentators play a similar role in the preparation of Martyr's Old Testament lectures. For long stretches Martyr refers to certain rabbis nearly every other page, almost always for the precise import of the Hebrew. Martyr's Hebrew guides vary from book to book, the most important being Rabbis Salomo, Ebenezra, and David Kimhi. Thus in the first thirty-five pages of Martyr's Genesis commentary he refers at least thirteen times to Rabbi Salomo and eight times to Ebenezra.[47] This pattern becomes more striking when one observes the almost total lack of references to contemporary or medieval commentaries. Even references to patristic comment on the passage under discussion are scant. Martyr follows a similar pattern in his commentary on Aristotle's *Ethics*. Every few pages of his commentary on the first book of the *Ethics*, Martyr cites Eustratius, the eleventh century Archbishop of Nicaea whose commentaries were noted for concentrating on the meaning of individual words and expressions and ignoring larger issues raised by the text.[48]

Martyr's commentaries set as their first aim to give a clear interpretation of the literal meaning of the text. In the preface to his Corinthians commentary, addressed to Edward VI, Martyr states that he has three ends in view: First, that the Apostle's meaning be clearly understood and expressed. Second that there be no statement containing superstition. Third, that nothing conformable to God's Word be reprehended out of love for scholarly quarreling.[49] Martyr laments that his style lacks the eloquence that theology deserves but consoles

---

[47] Salomo: ff. 4r, 12r, 16r, 16v, 17r, 18r, 19v, 22v, 25r, 27r, 29r, 31v, 34r. Ebenezra: 3v, 9v, 20v, 27r, 28r, 29r, 31v, 32v.

[48] Martyr probably used the Aldine edition (Venice, 1536) of Eustratius' commentary on the first and sixth books of the *Ethics*. Alexandre Ganoczy, *Bibliothèque*, (265, 271) found two copies of this edition in the library of the Geneva academy, which had acquired Martyr's library. He does not identify either copy of Eustratius as having been Martyr's, but that seems likely. For Eustratius, see the article on him by Martini, *Paulys Real-Encyclopädie der classischen Altertumswissenschaft*, ed. Georg Wissowa, (Stuttgart: 1909), VI, cc. 1490, 91.

[49] *Corinthios*, f. 3r. The British Museum has a copy of Martyr's *Tractatio de Sacramento Eucharistiae* with marginalia in the hand of the young king. See *British Museum General Catalogue of Printed Books*, (London, 1964), Vol. 247, c. 829.

himself that he achieves clarity, teaches truth, and fosters piety with his writings.[50] Martyr's prefaces are usually dedicated to prominent individuals and cultivate a more elevated and flowery style than do his commentaries proper, although Martyr's every page owes an obvious debt to Renaissance Latinity in the richness of its vocabulary and complexity of its syntax. Martyr's commentaries are chiefly straight forward line by line or pericope by pericope explanations of the text.

Martyr always tries to interpret the Bible literally. Vague passages are elucidated with the help of clear ones elsewhere in scripture. Martyr confirms his teaching and interpretation with citations from the Fathers. Martyr's occasional allegorical interpretations are always brief and rather chaste and usually borrowed from the Fathers. In them he seems to be consulting the future preaching needs of his listeners rather than a personal penchant.[51]

The most striking feature of Martyr's commentaries remains. This is the *loci* or scholia, digressions in the form of systematic tracts which pepper Martyr's commentaries. They are usually set off from the body of the commentary by titles in bold type, for instance *De Pre-destinatione, De Fortitudine*. Sometimes the title takes the form of a question: *An Deus Sit Author Peccati?* Martyr seems to have borrowed this technique from Bucer but carried it further. The *loci* make up a large portion of his text. Sometimes editions of his commentaries have a special index to these scholia or *loci*. They are certainly the most interesting and theologically important part of his writings. Martyr's posthumously compiled and published *Loci Communes* is scarcely more than a catena of these scholia. The scholia vary greatly in length. Many are less than a page, but those on predestination and on justification from the Romans commentary could stand as small books. The scholia are relatively few in number in Martyr's New Testament commentaries where Paul's text touched frequently on subjects of intense current interest and of vital doctrinal importance. The scholia in the New Testament commentaries clearly represent a desire for systematic development that was impossible in Martyr's

---

[50] *Defensio de Coelibatu*, 253.

[51] Some instances of Martyr's use of allegorical interpretation can be found in these places: *Genesis*, ff. 15v, 33r, 70v, 78r, 103r; *Melachim*, 214v, 233v; *Iudicum*, f. 90rv. The men of the sixteenth century loved allegory as dearly as did their medieval forefathers, even if they preferred their Bible straight.

usual line by line exegesis. This desire for systematic exposition is also present in the scholia of Martyr's Old Testament commentaries but it seems subordinate to a desire to give the lectures greater relevance to the ministerial students before him. The exploits of the Hebrew kings and judges which comprise the bulk of Martyr's Strasbourg and Zurich lectures could have aroused only academic interest among the students and must have seemed remote from the concerns of sixteenth-century Christians. Therefore Martyr repeatedly widens the discussion by inserting scholia on questions of theological or practical import. For instance, the first hundred pages of the commentary on 1 Kings has scholia on asylum, on exile, on church ornamentation, on Christian marriage with non-believers, and on whether man can love God with his whole heart in this life. The longest of these is nineteen folio pages, the shortest two; most are about six pages. The frequency of the scholia increases in Martyr's later works.

The internal organization and structure in Martyr's scholia varies, but two patterns seem especially noteworthy. Very many of Martyr's shorter scholia start with an etymological discussion of the subject, giving the Latin, Greek, and Hebrew roots with special attention to biblical usage and examples. Then Martyr usually gives a philosophical definition of the subject which contains the four Aristotelian causes. Martyr then breaks down the definition and discusses each of the four causes.[52]

Martyr puts great stress on definitions and distinctions. He praises Aristotle for his diligence and method in making definitions and

---

[52] Good examples of Martyr's pattern of definition followed by a discussion of the four causes are Martyr's treatment of temptation (*Genesis*, f. 85r), heresy (*Iudicum*, ff. 38v-39r), and fortitude (*Samuelis*, f. 231v). The scholion on fortitude is discussed more fully in chapter four. Martyr even uses the schema of the four causes when he admits that it cannot be neatly applied. For instance, Martyr assigns formal and final causes for predestination but then argues that there cannot be a material cause (because God is simple) nor an efficient cause (because there can be no cause of the divine will act outside of and prior to the divine will itself): *Genesis*, f. 94v. The theory of the four causes is particularly important in Martyr's sacramental writings. He explicitly appeals to his scholastic predecessors when assigning the four causes. The material cause in the sacraments is the material object used, water, bread, wine. The formal cause is the words of the rite. The final cause is to stir man's hearts to grasp God's promise by faith. The efficient cause is God. See *Romanos*, 106-07. It is doubtful if the schema of the four causes, which was originally intended to apply to objects, really helps to understand the sacraments, which are actions. Certainly Martyr did not find scripture assigning the four causes of the sacraments. See Chenu, 116, on the importance of definitions in medieval scholastic methodology.

distinctions since this practice greatly aids clarity. Martyr claims that it is harder to give a good definition than to explain it once it has been given. Careful distinctions are also necessary because what is confused or involved cannot be clearly understood until it is accurately broken down into its parts.[53] Martyr's care about clear definitions and distinctions and the careful order followed in his lectures contributed greatly to his popularity as a teacher. Josiah Simler, Martyr's friend and first biographer, tells us that these features so endeared him to his students at Strasbourg that they preferred him to Bucer.[54]

More important than the pattern of development by the four causes is the structure of Martyr's longer scholia, which are often similar to the scholastic *quaestio disputata*.[55] These scholia are often posed in the form of a question. For instance, in his commentary on 1 Corinthians Martyr asks whether there are works of supererogation. After stating the question he gives six reasons for the existence of supererogatory works, then fourteen short reasons against them.

---

[53] *Ethicorum*, 187-95. Martyr's stress on distinctions naturally suggests that Peter Ramus may have influenced him. I find no trace of Ramism in Martyr's writings. Martyr rightly attributes his emphasis on logical distinctions to Aristotle, the *bête noire* of Ramism. Peter Ramus did not make Peter Martyr a Ramist. But Martyr may have helped make Ramus a martyr. Ramus became a Protestant martyr in the St. Bartholomew's Day Massacre. Ramus's internal conversion to Protestantism seems to have resulted from listening to the Protestant spokesmen at the Colloquy of Poissy. Martyr was one of the leading spokesmen. Ramus's external conversion came while at Heidelberg, then a hotbed of Vermiglianism (see chapter seven). The crucial figure was Emmanuel Tremellius, under whose direction Ramus devoted himself to the study of theology. Martyr converted Tremellius to Protestantism at Lucca, and they were faculty colleagues later at Strasbourg. For the conversion of Ramus, see Charles Waddington, *Ramus: Sa Vie, ses écrits, et ses opinions*, (Paris: 1855), 134, 199.

[54] Simler writes of Martyr as lecturer: "Martyr autem omnia quae tractanda erant cum apte in certas partes dividebat, tum neque ullius earum in quantumvis prolixa tractatione obliviscebatur, neque novam aliquam in media tractatione inserebat, neque ordinem quem initio proposuerat invertebat, sed eum quem semel proposuisset partium numerum et ordinem constanter ad finem usque persequebatur." Simler's funeral oration-biography is unpaginated at the beginning of the *Loci*. This passage and Simler's comparison of Martyr and Bucer are on the sixth page. Martyr lacked one gift of a great teacher: wit and a sense of humor. His lectures are unrelentingly serious. He lacks Luther's earthy bonhomie and any eye for colorful detail or telling phrase.

[55] M.-D. Chenu, O. P., *Toward Understanding Saint Thomas*, trans. A. M. Henry and D. Hughes, (Chicago: 1964), discusses the nature of the scholastic *quaestio* and how an article was built up. According to Chenu the basic literary genres of thirteenth century scholasticism were the commentary first and the *questio* second. See p. 99. Martyr of course combined these two forms. Chenu also points out that "the building up of a definition is one of the traits of the scholastic method" (p. 166). The importance of definitions for Martyr was just shown.

Martyr then gives a short discussion of the whole problem and then concludes by answering the six arguments supporting works of supererogation. The whole scholion occupies ten quarto pages.[56] A bit later in the same commentary he takes up the legitimacy of administering communion under one species. He gives nineteen arguments for and eight against the practice and concludes by answering the nineteen arguments supporting communion under one species.[57]

Earlier this chapter mentioned Martyr's praise of Aristotle for developing the rules of logic and of the syllogism. Martyr's writings seldom contain fully developed formal syllogisms, any more than do the writings of the medieval scholastics. There are two exceptions to this. Martyr's commentary on the *Ethics* almost regularly recasts the philosopher's text into strict, fully developed syllogisms. This is a pedagogical device, and a very successful one, for Martyr's recast Aristotle is notably clearer than the original. Martyr's polemical *Defensio* against Stephen Gardiner on the Eucharist also makes extensive use of the formal syllogism, sometimes with explicit reference to the kind of figure or form of the syllogism.[58]

Martyr agreed with Luther that the text of the Bible should replace Lombard's *Sentences* and the Summas as the prime source from which theology should be taught. Yet his introduction of the scholia, the massive interjection of systematic theological tracts into the exegesis of the biblical text, was basically subversive of Luther's program for theological education. The scholia in Martyr's Old Testament commentaries are only loosely connected with the text, and the motive for their introduction was almost certainly to give contemporary relevance and theological depth. Apparently the bare text and its explanation did not suffice as a theological education. More significant was the introduction of long and complicated tracts such as those on predestination and justification into Romans lectures. Here the barren-

---

[56] *Corinthios*, ff. 225r-229v.

[57] *Corinthios*, ff. 263r-271v.

[58] A few examples from the *Defensio* illustrate Martyr's use of the syllogism: Obiectum CIX: Si panis mutatur, et sit corpus Christi, certe generatur. At non generatur. Ergo non mutatur in corpus Christi (p. 355). Obiectum CXII: Si corpus Christi crucifixum non sit factum ex pane, et corpus Christi crucifixum idem fuit cum eo quod sumebatur in coena, sequitur corpus Christi quod sumebatur in coena non fuisse factum ex pane (p. 359). Each of the *obiecta* includes several pages of development and argument. The formal syllogism actually plays far less a role in Martyr than in many Protestant scholastics. In most of Jerome Zanchi's writings each subsection starts with a formal syllogism which the whole subsection then explains and defends.

ness of the scripture text was not a motive. The tracts followed directly upon Martyr's thorough exegesis of Paul's longest and most profound reflections on two basic doctrines that lay close to the heart of the Protestant attack on Roman theology. These scholia were an implicit confession that the theological process must go beyond an exposition of the Bible text. Martyr has taken the important step of introducing systematic, highly speculative, and rather scholastic theology right into the citadel of biblical exegesis. Was this a Trojan Horse? The second step Martyr did not take: the gathering of these scholia, tracts, or *loci* into a single systematic handbook, a summa. His friends did this after his death in the *Loci Communes*. The third step was, of course, replacing the Bible with the *Loci Communes* as the basic handbook of theology. A comparative reading of Martyr's *Loci* with the last edition of Melanchthon's *Loci Communes* indicates that Martyr's was markedly the more scholastic work. Melanchthon's *Loci Communes* was an important source of Lutheran neo-scholasticism; Martyr's *Loci* played a similar role in Reformed circles.

In Christology Calvin, Martyr, and the whole Reformed tradition tended to stress the distinction of the two natures in Christ, and its affinities were strongly with the Antiochian school of the fourth and fifth centuries. To be sure, the Reformed stopped far short of the Nestorian separation of the two natures, a charge the Lutherans hurled at them. Werner Elert, Friedrich Loofs, and Hermann Bauke have seen the philosophical axiom *finitum non capax infiniti* behind much of Calvin's thought. Not only is the axiom the key to Calvin's Christology and the stress on the distinction of the two natures, but also according to these historians of theology, it lies behind Calvin's emphasis on the transcendence and majesty of God and the distance between God and His creatures. Among others, G. C. Berkouwer and David Willis have rejected this interpretation. Berkouwer has pointed out that the axiom never once occurs in Calvin's writings.[59] But the axiom does occur in Martyr where it is used as a premise to show that human nature cannot receive infinite power, wisdom, goodness and justice, and is directly applied to Christology and the quarrel of the Reformed with the Lutherans. No less than Calvin, Martyr

---

[59] The problem of the *finitum non capax infiniti* in Calvin is discussed, with full references to the scholarly debate, by E. David Willis, *Calvin's Catholic Christology*, (Leiden: 1966), 4-8, 74-76.

emphasizes God's transcedence.[60] Given that Martyr's thought has a more philosophical orientation than that of Calvin, the axiom *finitum non capax infiniti* may well have had widespread repercussions in Martyr's thought even in areas where it is not specifically invoked.

Perhaps the best illustration of the interaction of philosophy and theology is a passage in Martyr's Samuel commentary dealing with Christology:

> I will reduce to a few points the way he (Christ) made satisfaction to the Father. Some have thought that the death of Christ and his obedience, in so far as it belongs to the human nature, have finite dignity and therefore did not satisfy the Father except in so far as He chose to accept them. They do not want to concede that the satisfaction was full if it is considered in itself. They add also that God could have acted in various other ways, but that He chose to accept this way. There is another explanation that I think far better: the obedience of Christ and his death should not be considered merely as regards the human nature because, as is said, actions belong to the supposites, the persons, and individuals (who perform them). Although Christ had two natures, he is only one person. His actions are therefore those of the Son of God: as his human nature must not be considered separately, we can say that the divine nature operates through the human. Thus His actions truly merit the remission of sin and are condign and full (satisfaction). Some will object that these actions were owed (to God) since Christ was a creature and owed all his works (to God). Rather, he was God and of the same substance with the Father. He had the fullness of grace, not a quantity measured out. He therefore satisfied not only for man's guilt but also took away punishment. If the faithful are punished, it is for some other reason, as we shall hear. Therefore we should seek no other satisfaction since this one is given freely.[61]

In this passage Martyr brings together his doctrine of the Trinity of Christology (on the nature of Christ) and his soteriology (on the saving work of Christ). From the philosophical principle that actions pertain to the supposit rather than to a thing's nature and from the fact that it is the divine person who acts, he deduces the infinite merits of Christ's theandric acts. At the end of the paragraph he deduces a further conclusion: the Protestant doctrine of *sola gratia*. The

---

[60] Verum quod tu annectis, filium hominis, id est, naturam humanam evectam esse ad infinitam potentiam, sapientiam, bonitatem et iustitiam, non facile dabo: quia *quod finitum ac terminatum est, infinita non capit.* Sufficit quippe hominem illum assumptum, bona quae commemorasti ultra omnes creatures quae vel cogitari vel nominari possunt esse consequutum. *Dialogus*, f. 19v.

[61] *Samuelis*, f. 332r.

view that he rejects—that Christ's death satisfied for sin only because the Father accepted it as satisfaction—is the view of Scotus and many late medieval scholastics. The view he asserts on the infinity of Christ's merits goes back to Anselm's *Cur Deus Homo?* It is also the teaching of St. Thomas.[62] For Martyr the teachings of faith are true because they derived from God's Word, but the various truths are logically interrelated and re-enforcing. They are not just a collection of isolated or juxtaposed propositions. Philosophical principles have a proper place in the theological process which lays bare the inter-connections between the truths of faith.

Martyr often adopts the tools of scholasticism to refute its con-clusions. He severely criticizes the medieval scholastics for breaking penance up into contrition, confession, and satisfaction. He then analyses this division to show that it leads necessarily to various contradictions.[63] Against the scholastic doctrine that charity is the form of faith, Vermigli argues that one quality cannot be the form of another quality of the same kind. One accident cannot inhere as a form in another, especially not two qualities. According to Martyr, by saying that charity is the form of faith, the scholastics intend to assert that charity perfects faith as form perfects matter.[64] Martyr thinks that a better analogy of the relation of charity to faith is the relation of wisdom to the intellectual virtues or of prudence to the moral virtues. Yet wisdom is never considered the form of the intel-lectual virtues nor prudence the form of the moral virtues.[65] Against the Lutheran doctrine of ubiquity, Martyr analyses the notions of local motion and being-in-place. During this scholastic analysis, he appeals to the authority of Aristotle, Aquinas, Averroes, Alexander of Aphrodisias, and Themistius.[66]

This chapter has shown that Martyr explicitly advocates considerable room for human reason in the theological process, that he borrows several methods of argument and exposition from the Aristotelian and scholastic tradition, and that he actually uses the terminology, doctrines, and conclusions of scholastic philosophy as a source for elaborating and defending his own theology. All these developments

---

[62] *S.T.* III, 1, 2; III, 48, 3 and 6.
[63] *Samuelis*, ff. 328v, 332v.
[64] Chapter IV discusses Martyr's use of hylomorphism.
[65] *Corinthios*, f. 355v.
[66] *Dialogus*, f. 23v-24r.

represent a distinct departure, at least in degree, from the practice of Luther and Calvin. These developments have important consequences for Martyr's view of man, both philosophical and theological, as will be seen in Chapters IV, V, and VI. Chapters VII and VIII will show their importance for the evolution of Reformed Theology.

CHAPTER FOUR

MARTYR'S PHILOSOPHICAL VIEW OF MAN

Peter Martyr Vermigli never wrote a philosophical tract on human nature. In fact he wrote only one philosophical work, an incomplete commentary on Aristotle's *Ethics* that was published posthumously.[1] Most of Martyr's philosophy of man is not found in the *Ethics* commentary but is scattered throughout his theological writings. Unlike John Calvin,[2] Martyr's theological works do not contain any unified tractate on man. His theological works are either Scripture commentaries or controversial work on celibacy and the Eucharist, and in them his comments on man are not developed systematically but rather as scholia and *obiter dicta* or as illustrations, examples and analogies. Still Martyr's philosophical comments on man are cumulatively extensive and present a rather sharply defined and consistent picture.

There should be no methodological difficulty about extracting Martyr's philosophical comments from his theological works and arranging them systematically. Historians of medieval philosophy have long done this to theological works of the medieval scholastics; the method should prove equally legitimate when applied to the Protestant scholastics of the sixteenth and seventeenth century. This chapter will take philosophy of man to mean that understanding of human nature and man's faculties which the scholastic tradition thought was attainable by human reason. This was virtually synonymous with Aristotle's doctrine of man as elaborated by later commentators.

Martyr's philosophy of man is quite pedestrian in content and barely repays the effort needed to extract it from his lengthy *opera* and arrange it. More significant than the content is the brute fact that Martyr, a major Reformed theologian, had an elaborate philosophy of man; more significant still is the fact that the elements of this philosophy are found intermeshed with his theology. Because Martyr's theological use of his philosophy of man is often more important

---

[1] *Ethicorum*. Martyr's commentary stops halfway through Aristotle's third book.

[2] *Institutes*, I, 15.

than its particular tenets, it is often crucial to indicate the theological context of his philosophical examples, analogies, and *obiter dicta*.

Man in an Aristotelian World

For Martyr a basic given is the fact that God created the universe—man as well as all the material things that surround him and affect his life. God's bringing the world into creation does not imply any change in God.[3] Because God created both the universe and man, he he has total dominion over man; indeed, God's dominion is so absolute over man that he would be perfectly within his rights to demand human sacrifice.[4] God not only created the world, he also conserves it: "The duration of things depends on the pure will of God."[5] God governs all events by his providence, even seemingly fortuitous events and human actions. Men cannot see the *ratio* of secondary causes in events that seem fortuitous, but God sees and directs them. Strictly speaking, there is no luck in Martyr's world. Divine Providence and dominion are major themes in Martyr theology.[6]

But even beyond divine creation, conservation, and providence, Martyr teaches that divine concurrence is metaphysically necessary for every action, especially the actions of man. Martyr develops this doctrine in a thoroughly scholastic context. God is pure act, and therefore his action is needed to incite and move all things to act.[7]

---

[3] *Genesis*, ff. 2rv, 23r. Martyr sharply rebukes the philosophers who claim that the world has always existed, but his case for creation in time rests on the testimony of Scripture rather than philosophical evidence, a position which is further evidence of his Thomistic training. Also *Romanos*, 302; *Ethicorum*, 64.

[4] *Melachim*, f. 206v.

[5] *Romanos*, 302: ". . . rerum duratio a mera Dei voluntate pendeat. . . ."

[6] *Samuelis*, f. 57v. "Quare homo eximendus non est a providentia Dei. Multo autem minus excludenda sunt ea quae videntur agi fortuito. Etsi enim nos secundarum causarum rationem non videamus, Deus tamen eam videt. Imo philosophi docent omnem causam, quam appellant per accidens, revocandum esse ad causam per se. Nam quod est per accidens non potest esse causa. Itaque Aristoteles in libello de bona fortuna, cum quaesisset cur alii essent fortunati, alii non essent, respondit: id propter impetum quendam et impulsum fieri, cuius tamen is qui impellitur rationem non possit reddere." In his *Genesis*, ff. 109v-110r, Martyr rejects St. Ambrose's definition of providence because it includes only the notion of divine foreknowing without sufficiently bringing in the divine will. He also attacks Averroes for claiming that if divine providence descended to each particular action of all men, the divine intellect would be cheapened. Martyr counters that God sees all things in himself so that there is no question of God depending upon creatures or cheapening himself. Compare Aquinas, *S.T.*, I, 14, 5 and 6.

[7] *Samuelis*, f. 20r.

> First it can hardly be denied that God concurs in the production of every physical action. For he is the prime mover in the production of all things and the author without whose divine power nothing can exist . . . Whatever happens is produced not only by inferior and secondary causes, but also flows from God the first efficient cause.[8]

The philosophical doctrine behind this is obviously Aristotle's theory of act and potency and of the prime mover, the same presuppositions that underlie the most famous passage of all scholastic thought, Aquinas's first three of the five ways of proving God's existence.[9] The question arises: does not divine concurrence rob creatures of their autonomy, does not secondary causality become a charade, would not an occasionalism such as that of Malebranche have the merits of greater consistency and sincerity? Martyr rejects any such notions. God acts in creatures, but he acts in each according to its own nature. In stones God acts so that they do not sense and will anything, in animals so that they exercise their senses and appetites, in men God "so acts that they use the powers of their rational soul with which they are endowed."[10] The question of divine concurrence becomes of crucial importance with reference to morally good or evil actions. Does not concurrence make God the cause of sin? Moreover, like many medieval scholastics Martyr develops his theory of actual grace in terms of what kind of concurrence God gives to a man faced with a moral decision. The doctrine of concurrence thus ramifies directly from God as first cause and pure act into the theology of grace, of sanctification, and of predestination.[11]

---

[8] *Samuelis*, f. 19v. Primum haud negare potest Deum ad omnem physicam actionem producendam concurrere. Nam est primus omnium rerum producendarum movens et author sine cuius numine et vi nihil potest existere . . . Quicquid enim fit, non modo ab inferioribus et secundis producitur causis, verum etiam a Deo prima efficiente causa dimanat.

[9] *S.T.* I, 2, 3.

[10] *Romanos*, p. 210; *Samuelis*, f. 20r.

[11] The *locus classicus* for this problem in Martyr is *Samuelis*, f. 280rv: "Cum ergo motus animi sint res quaedam, hoc pacto a Deo pendare non est dubium. Agit quiden Deus ut causa summa, cooperantur creaturae. Unde Anshelmus scripsit in libro de Casu diaboli, ipsum male velle diaboli, quatenus velle est, a Deo pendere: res autem ipsa prava non est nisi quatenus ipse male vult. Quod vero ille actus quaepiam res sit, ex eo patet quod est in genere vel praedicamento actionis: ut ergo quidpiam est, a Deo est et creatura est. Imo dixit Augustinus in lib. 9 de Trinitate cap. 10 animi accidentia praestantiora esse quam corporum propter nobilitatem subiecti. Unde forma vel species ut in animo, nobilior est quam ut in corpore invenitur exterius. Ipsa item anima qua anima est, utut prava fuerit, adhuc est nobilior quovis corpore. Cum itaque actus animi quibus postea vitio nostro inhaeret privatio, quatenus res sunt, sine Deo non productorem

Martyr locates man in an Aristotelian universe. He accepts with Aristotle the doctrine of the four basic elements (earth, air, fire, and water) and the doctrine of natural motion. Celestial bodies move in a circle, sublunar objects in a straight line. Species are stable and discrete. All individual material things are subject to generation and corruption as well as to accidental changes. This orderly world is geo-

---

non substantialium tantum, sed accidentialium, universalium, et motuum voluntatis etiam malorum. Vis quippe Dei est infinita: quare nihil potest produci cuiusmodi sit quod non subiicitur eius actioni. Nam si eam quidpiam subterfugeret, tunc non esset infinita, non omnia impleret. Ne voluntas nostra posset in actum erumpere nisi una agente voluntate illa summa." It is worth noting that the passage Martyr cites and paraphrases from Augustine takes on Aristotelian coloring in the course of the paraphrase.

Martyr continues on the next page: "Est igitur Deus causa omnium rerum: agitationem primae causae res inferiores iuxta earum naturam recipiunt. Unde si vitium contrahitur, secundarum causarum natura contrahitur. Simili rem illustrabo. In animantibus vim habeamus quae Locomotiva dicitur movetque animalia vel ad ambulandum vel ad currendum. Ea vero ut recipiunt motum a Locomotiva moventur. At si tibia fuerit vitiata, luxata aut crura, ille motus cursus claudicationem coniunctam habet; sed illa claudicatio, ut motus est, a facultate animi motiva est; ut vitiosa et clauda, pendet a vito tibiae quae fracta fuit. Sic est de motu illo Dei perenni quo agitat creaturas ... motusque Dei quandoque transit per animum depravatum; unde actionis vitium non a Deo sed a proxima causa contrahitur. Quid vero Deus ibi agat, et quomodo regat illam deformitatem, expositum est supra. Nunc de actu ex voluntate nostra erumpente agimus. Unde recte dicitur privationem rectitudinis non sequi opus voluntatis nostrae et motum eius quatenus est in genere naturae, sed ut est in genere motus. Augustinus de civitate Dei libro septimo, cap. 30 dicit: Deum sic administrare creaturas ut illas proprios motus exercere et coagere sinat. Non enim solus agit Deus, sed pravi, ut supra dixi, et diabolus suam malitiam in agendo adhibent. Sed cum dicimus actum ipsum qui postea vitio nostro malus est, a causa suprema, id est Deo, et nobis, id est voluntate nostra, produci: quomodo id accipiemus? An quod Deus totum faciat, et nos totum? An quod ille partem et nos partem? Atque hic productionem contrahimus ad ipsum actum voluntatis nostrae. Respondetur: si ratio toti (sic: totius?) referatur ad causam, uno modo est dicendum si referatur ad effectum, aliter si totum referamus ad causam, ita ut intelligamus voluntatem nostram totam causam actionis esse, ut per se absque Deo possit producere, verum non est. Quia nisi Deus innuerit, non posset actionem edere. Ita Deus etsi absoluta potentia sua per seipsum opus facere posset, tamen ut est cursus rerum, non vult solus agere sed vult creaturam coagentem habere. (n.b.: the distinction between *potentia absoluta* and *ordinata*, so important for nominalism, but very rare in Martyr's writings). Hoc pacto nec voluntas nec Deus dicuntur tota causa. At si ad effectum ipsum referatur, Deus et voluntas causa sunt plena. Nam Deus et voluntas totum effectum faciunt, licet coniungantur in actione. Exemplo rem ostendam. Ad actionem producendam, voluntatem habemus et intelligentiam: et voluntas totum effectum facit et intelligentia est causa totius effectus. Sed una est propinqua, altera est remotior. Ita est de voluntate et Deo: ipsa totum facit et Deus totum facit, sed una causa est prima, altera secundaria." (n.b.: the real distinction Martyr's last example makes between intellect and will).

centric, and Martyr accepts the Aristotelian notion of intelligences governing the spheres, but like most Christian theologians he makes these intelligences angels. Angels are doubtless higher and more noble than man in the order of nature, but Martyr considers it rash to extend this judgement to the order of grace. In any event, man is to rule as lord of creation over the birds of the air, the fishes of the sea, and the beasts of the earth. But this theme of man as lord of creation is not very important for Martyr. Neither are two other favorite renaissance themes, man as microcosm and man as a central link in the great chain of being.[12]

In commenting on the first verse of Genesis, Martyr warns against reading into the Bible the philosophical principles of being.[13] But his theological works are in fact shot through with the Aristotelian principles of being. These principles are an essential part of Martyr's philosophical doctrine of man. The most basic of the Aristotelian antinomies is that of act and potency. We have already seen how the doctrine of God as pure act leads to concurrence. The philosophical doctrine of act and potency applies, of course, to man as well, but Martyr does not much exploit it except as defining the relation between the principles of being, substance/accidents and matter/form.[14] Man is made up of substance and accidents which are related as potency to act. Created substance cannot exist without accidents and accidents obviously cannot exist without inhering in a substance as in a subject. Martyr is peculiarly anxious to insist that man has the same substance (that he is the same individual and remains in the same species) even after the resurrection and its gift of risen qualities.[15]

---

[12] *Corinthios*, ff. 424v-25r; *Ethicorum*, 33; *Defensio*, 111; *Samuelis*, f. 163. In this last passage Martyr does not wholly accept Aristotelian doctrine since he rejects Alexander of Aphrodisias' interpretation of miracles and Aristotle's statement that the intelligences cannot interrupt their work. The scriptures clearly teach Martyr that Joshua stopped the sun.

[13] *Genesis*, f. 2r. This is precisely what Zanchi later did: *Opera Theologica*, III, 217.

[14] The first act of a living creature is to be, which it has from the union of body and soul. The second act is its operations. "Ad quod respondeo vita accipi bifariam, nam interdum vivere nihil aliud significat nisi esse, quod universa quae animam sortiuntur ex ipsius coniunctione cum corpore statim habeant. Philosophi hoc appellarunt actum primum. Deinde vivere idem est quod operari et id philosophi secundum actum dixerunt: atque ista posteriori significatione modo accipiendum est recte vivere." *Ethicorum*, 76. Martyr applies extensively the Aristotelian notions of act and potency to refute Roman Catholic eucharistic doctrine. See *Defensio*, 267-68. Martyr does not make the distinction between existence and essence is so important for modern Thomism. Martyr's disciple Jerome Zanchi does express it, indeed, better than almost anyone in the sixteenth century: *Opera Theologica*, II, 65, 66.

[15] *Dialogus*, ff. 21v-22r; *Defensio*, 39, 40, 137, 154, 351; the passage on the

Although the metaphysical notion of person was developed largely in response to Trinitarian and Christological controversies, it is properly a philosophical concept. Martyr accepts the traditional definition: a person is an individual substance of a rational nature. The notion of person is important for Martyr's Trinitarian and Christological doctrine, but is not an important category in his philosophical and theological anthropology.[16]

In all material creation, including man, substance is divided into matter and form. The soul is the form of the body for Martyr. Matter is in potency to receive various forms. Martyr does not call matter a pure potency but speaks of it as *per se rudis, inculta, confusa*. Matter is terminated and perfected by form. So great is the exigence of matter for form that Martyr sees a sort of intimation of the resurrection of the dead in the peripatetic doctrine of matter and form as applied to the human body and soul. He sees little strength in the objection against the resurrection in the argument that man's body is reduced to prime matter by the separation from the soul.[17]

The Aristotelian concept of accidents plays an important part in Martyr's philosophy and theology. God's immutability and impassibility can be deduced from his simplicity, that is from the fact that God, being simple, has no accidents. Man is a composite being, therefore he can undergo accidental change while remaining substantially

---

resurrection reads: "Non mirum tibi videatur nos dicere: corpus quod in morte deponemus et recipiendum in resurrectione quoad substantiam idem esse, sed habere diversitatem per qualitates; quandoquidem in natura vides idem usu venire. . . . In hoc Pauli argumento, caro quoad genus accipienda est, cui variae differentiae adiungi possunt, licet eius generalis natura non mutetur quoad naturam sive substantiam. Et cavendum est ne putemus corpus a nobis recipiendum specie differre ab eo quae posuimus. Nam differentiae quae generi adduntur, quando adaptantur inferioribus, magnam diversitatem inducant, siquidem species diversas efficiunt: verum si ad genus eas retuleris, quodammodo sunt eius accidentia, neque diversitatem eius naturae faciunt." *Corinthios*, ff. 424v, 425r. This is a clear example of Martyr's use of the philosophical doctrine of substance and accidents to dispose of an objection against a revealed truth.

[16] *Dialogus*, f. 16v; *Defensio*, 388; Subsistentia enim, aut hypostasis, neque ad definitionem hominis neque ad eius essentiam pertinet.

[17] *Defensio*, f. 21v; *Ethicorum*, 47, 72, 253; *Melachim*, f. 216r; *Corinthios*, f. 422r. Martyr is unmoved by the standard objection that a man raised totally as a cannibal from childhood would not have any matter of his own at the resurrection of the dead. He points out that even in this life we are constantly taking in new matter by eating and excreting old matter. "Caeterum si tota materia simul auferretur, unitas illa nequaquam servaretur. Verum quia per partes abscedit materia et nova quae hauritur ex cibo ac potu adiungitur prae-existentibus, ideo retinetur unitas, praesertim cum eadum forma duret et conservet." *Melachim*, f. 231r.

the same individual throughout life.[18] The accidents that inhere in the human substance are many and varied. As a means to organize and discuss them, Martyr uses the Aristotelian categories or predicaments. Substance is the first predicament; there are nine predicaments for the nine kinds of accidents. "Nothing can be found in the world which does not pertain to the predicaments."[19] Martyr finds that everybody can easily understand some of the predicaments or categories, for instance, substance and quality; but others are exceedingly subtle, for instance, relation.[20] No single passage in Martyr's writings enumerates all the categories, but most are discussed in one place or another. He can be rather fussy about precisely under which predicament a given accident fits.[21]

MAN'S BODY

Martyr does not devote much attention to the human body. The body is an outstanding example of God's workmanship; it is a marvel, a wonderful monument to God's wisdom that surpasses man's ability to explain. He rejects the opinion that men are determined for life by the quality of their material and by their early upbringing; men can lessen their inborn propensity for evil and become outstanding for moral virtues and external deportment. The head is the organ or seat of man's senses and motor faculties, but reason and the supernatural

---

[18] *Dialogus*, f. 21v: "Humanitas autem fit res composita et variis accidentibus obnoxia, quae et substantiam rei non mutant et praeter subiecti (ut dialectici loquuntur) corruptionem adesse possunt et abesse." Martyr's chief theological exploitation of accidents is in his eucharistic tracts, for instance *Defensio*, 128, 386, 641; *Dialogus*, ff. 22r, 111v.

[19] *Romanos*, 231: ". . . nihil inveniri potest in rerum natura quod ad illa praedicamenta non pertineat. . . ." In this passage Vermigli goes on to draw an analogy between the ten predicaments and the ten commandments. Just as all reality can be reduced to one of the predicaments, so every kind of wickedness is reducible to one of the commandments; and just as all the predicaments relate to substance, so every sin reduces to desire (*cupiditas*). And just as substance has form and matter as its basic principles, so every human consent to sin derives from the depravity of our nature. The reader will recall Luther's statement about the pernicious influence of the predicaments on theology that was quoted in the first chapter.

[20] *Ethicorum*, 153-54. These pages also discuss the transcendentals (*ens, bonum, verum*, and *unum*) and how they are co-extensive yet distinct.

[21] *Defensio*, 128. Vermigli's knowledge of the predicaments depended not only on his reading of Aristotle and the medieval scholastics but almost surely on the third century Neoplatonist Porphyry whose *Isagoge*, a famous introduction to the predicaments, was in Martyr's library. See Alexandre Ganoczy, *Bibliothèque*, 266.

life pervade the whole body. From Aristotle he draws the idea that warmth provides life. This warmth depends upon the humours which old age and overwork break down and thereby hasten death. Still the theory of the four humours plays only a minor role in Martyr's thinking, even though he refers to the humoral physio-psychology and is well acquainted with the works of Galen, the great expositor of the humoral theory. In commenting on the statement of Genesis that Adam and Eve were naked but did not blush, Martyr insists that there was nothing shameful in either the human body or the soul as instituted by God. Martyr admits that bodily pleasures must be checked and mortified, but this is *per accidens*—due to sin. Martyr refuses to concede to Plato and Porphyry that the body is a hindrance to the soul; indeed the senses are a help, as Aristotle teaches.[22]

Martyr insists that our knowledge comes to us from external objects through our senses.[23] He enumerates the five senses and describes their functions and emphasizes that for all their diversity, they do not constitute five distinct sensing persons but a single man who uses all five.[24] For all their power the external senses do not reach to the substances of things but only to accidents and properties; it is the reason that attains an understanding of substances by relying on knowledge of accidents provided by the senses.[25] The senses are generally reliable, but they can fail us in many ways; charlatans can deceive us by dexterity and sleight of hand, atmospheric conditions can trick us, and in certain sicknesses everything tastes bitter. Sometimes too the devil intervenes in our sense faculties.[26]

DIVISIONS WITHIN THE SOUL

Now that we have outlined Martyr's statement on the body and the external sense faculties, we stand on the threshold of the more philo-

---

[22] *Ethicorum*, 65, 281; *Samuelis*, f. 167v; *Corinthios*, f. 284r; *Melachim*, ff. 1v, 146r, 231r; *Genesis*, ff. 12r, 135v, 136v; *Romanos*, 185.

[23] *Ethicorum*, 399: Nec requiritur ut sit principium primum motus in nobis: nostra quippe notitia ex obiecto provenit quamvis ille motus quo sensus ab obiecto afficitur est alterius ordinis.

[24] *Dialogus*, f. 42rv. Martyr insists on the unity of the person who uses his five distinct senses and sees in this an analogy of the unity of Christ as a person whose divine omnipresence does not entail the ubiquity of his human body, thereby excluding a corporeal presence in the eucharist. Martyr argues the point analogically from the fact that the soul has acts distinct from those of the body, yet there remains but one human person.

[25] *Defensio*, 107; *Iudicum*, f. 143r.

[26] *Samuelis*, f. 167v. But the devil cannot intervene in the intellect. *Samuelis*, f. 165v.

sophical part of his complex faculty psychology. Before taking up the
remaining faculties individually, an overview or outline of the divisions that Martyr posits within the soul will provide a useful guide.
Because Martyr sees the body as Aristotelian prime matter and the
soul as a substantial form, none of man's functions originate, strictly
speaking, from the body, but all relate in some way to the body. All
result from the form, from the nature. But levels are distinguishable
within man's functions based upon their relative dependence upon
man's spiritual faculties of intellect and will. There are three levels,
the vegetative, the sentient, and the rational. The vegetative level is
common to all living things: plants, brute animals, and man. This
vegetative level within man totally lacks reason. The stomach is deaf
—digestion goes on whether we want it or not.[27] Above the vegetative
there is the sentient level which man largely shares with the brutes;
to this level belong the external and internal senses and the sense
appetites. The sentient level differs in man from that in the brutes in
that the human sentient powers work under the control of reason, at
least in the continent man. Martyr uses the analogy of the moon and
the sun to explain the relation of the sentient powers to reason: they
depend on the reason for guidance just as the moon borrows its light
from the sun. The sentient powers in beasts are also guided by reason,
but by the external reason of nature and instinct which God has built
into the world. Finally there is the rational level, proper to man alone,
which includes the spiritual faculties of intellect and will.[28] Martyr
sometimes varies his terminology; instead of speaking of the vegetative, sentient, and intelligent (or rational) levels of the soul, he often
speaks of the rational or superior part of the soul and the irrational or
inferior or gross (*crassior*) part of the soul. This inferior level then sub-
divides into a sentient and a nutrient or vegetative level, as we have
seen. The superior/inferior terminology Martyr borrows from Plato's
Republic but adapts it to his own Aristotelian system.[29] Martyr holds
that these distinctions are not merely mental precisions made by human
ratiocination but correspond to really distinct powers within man's

---

[27] *Ethicorum*, 279, 284, 287, 281. In the last passage Martyr becomes very
precise, arguing that *nutrire* and *augere* are really distinct powers within the *vis
vegetandi*. Martyr also points out that the various divisions of the soul are not
quantitative but based on the various powers: "Divisio haec subiecti est in
accidentia; quando istae animi partes nil aliud quam vires eius dici debent neque
anima corpus est quae instar eius discerpi queat." *Ethicorum*, 279.

[28] *Ethicorum*, 335, 280, 282, 287.

[29] *Ethicorum*, 284; *Corinthios*, f. 49r; *Romanos*, 152.

make-up. Following Aristotle he goes to considerable pains to prove this, his arguments mainly revolving around the opposition, even the struggle, that all men experience between the sense appetites and the dictates of reason. Nevertheless Martyr stoutly maintains the unicity of the human soul against those who advocate a multiplicity of forms within man corresponding to the vegetative, sentient, and rational levels. Martyr admits the difficulty of proving the unicity of the human form and never attempts a demonstration.[30]

Martyr has little to say about the soul itself as distinct from its faculties and operations. He accepts the standard definition of the soul: "it is the act of a physical organic body having life in potency."[31] The "in potency" refers to the fact that the body has no life in itself but only from the soul. The empirical signs of the soul's presence in the body are movement and the operation of the senses, for these are the chief effects of the soul according to Aristotle and the ancient philosophers. All man's actions find their font and origins in the soul.[32] The soul is a spirit. From its spirituality Martyr argues that Christ's body in the Eucharist can be present to the soul only spiritually, thereby ruling out any Eucharistic real presence.[33] Though it is

---

[30] *Ethicorum*, 284-86. Martyr's best statement on the unity and multiplicity of the human soul is the following: "Quia omnium actionum quae ab homine utcunque fiunt, et initium et fundamentum et (sic: est?) vita et ea ut evidens est in homine habetur multiplex, ideo videre oportet, iuxta quam vitam homo discernatur a caeteris viventibus. Et ea erit cuius opus homini proprie adscribetur. Primo loco vita se offert nutriens et augens corpus: at illum communem habemus cum plantis; nam et illae suis radicibus trahunt alimentum a terra ex quo alantur et crescant. Seponetur itaque hoc vitae genus: nam cum non sit homini proprium sed commune multorum, non valet esse initium proprii operis hominis qua homo est. Secundum gradum habet ea vita qua sentimus et progredimur, incendendo quo visum fuerit. Sed haec quoque communis habetur nobiscum cum brutis, nam equi, boves et caetera quae rationis sunt expertia sentiunt et moventur. Proinde removenda est etiam haec vita, quod ab ea non possit oriri proprium hominis opus. Quemobrem restat ea sola vita quae agit cum ratione: ea discernitur homo a reliquis omnibus. Idcirco poterit inde nasci proprium nostrum opus. Habet sane homo comprehensas has vitas in seipso; ast illarum una tantum est ipsi propria. Nec tamen propterea dicimus illum habere tres animos: unus est satis. Nam haec est eius natura, ut quo praestantior fuerit, vires comprehendat ignobiliorum." *Ethicorum*, 186-87. Calvin also insists on the unicity of the soul; *Institutes*, I, 15, 6.

[31] *Romanos*, 539: "Quam autem (philosophi) definiunt animam, aiunt eam actum corporis physici organici potentia habentis vitam." Martyr also calls the soul the form of the body: *Melachim*, f. 215r; *Dialogus*, f. 118rv; *Genesis*, f. 9v.

[32] *Genesis*, f. 9v; *Corinthios*, f. 428v.

[33] *Romanos*, 174; *Defensio*, 633.

a spirit, the soul can be in only one place at a time, yet so that the whole soul is totally in every part of the body.[34]

THE INTERNAL SENSES

In addition to the five external senses, Martyr posits three internal senses within the sentient level of the soul. Like the external senses the internal senses have a localized seat in the body, although Martyr is not specific in assigning these seats. Man shares these three internal senses with the brute animals. In brutes the internal senses and the sense appetites are the highest faculties of the soul. In man the internal senses perform the same operations as in the brutes but also process information received from the external senses for the service of the intellect and will which constitute the highest part of the human soul. As we have seen, the internal senses and sense appetites are directed in their operations by the intellect and will.

Martyr's major comments on the internal senses occur in rather bizarre connections: in his explanation of how Jacob managed to breed mottled black and white sheep (Gen. 30: 38-40) and how the witch of Endor was able to produce an apparition of the dead Samuel for Saul (1 Sam. 28: 12-15). Both explanations involve a discussion of the internal senses. Martyr enumerates three senses: the *sensus communis*, the *phantasia*, and the *memoria*. Images arise from external objects which first reach man's external senses and then are received in the common sense; from the common sense these images are transferred to the phantasy and lastly to the memory where they are retained much as imprints are retained in wax. These images can be recalled from the memory to the phantasy and sometimes even to the senses. So vivid is the reproduction produced by this imprinted image that the sick or even the sleeping sometimes are convinced that they have seen or touched the actual object again. Martyr believed that God, angels, and devils can all intervene in the workings of the internal senses and thereby produce images in the mind of the conscious subject which counterfeit reality perfectly. He explained Saul's vision of Samuel as an example of such an intervention by the devil. Martyr was fascinated by sleep and dreams and explained how dreams can be a mixture of these pre-existing images in the internal sense faculties. He confirmed his explanation by pointing out that the deaf do not "hear" in their dreams nor do the blind "see" colors.[35]

---

[34] *Defensio*, 571. *Dialogus*, ff. 117r, 118rv.
[35] *Samuelis*, f. 167v. The key part of the passage reads: "Potest etiam alia via

The problem of Jacob's mottled sheep led Martyr to compare two alternative explanations, one based on the power of the phantasy, the other on Augustine's *rationes seminales*. It will be recalled that Jacob (Gen. 30) set up black and white sticks in front of the watering place where the sheep generally coupled. Presumably this had such a great affect on their phantasy that they produced mottled offspring. Martyr admits some probability to this explanation. What mothers see with delectation during conception affects the still tender seeds within their wombs. He relates a story borrowed from Quintillian: an ugly man and his ugly wife produced a beautiful child. The husband accused the wife of adultery and seemed to have won his case until the presence in their bedroom of the portrait of a strikingly handsome youth was pointed out. Martyr also attributes the power of the chameleon to change color to its phantasy. Other animals cannot change color because their bodies are less subtle. Martyr even chides Avicenna and Pomponazzi (Martyr's sole explicit mention of Pomponazzi) about the power they attribute to the phantasy, although he immediately adds that this should not limit our trust in their true statements. But despite the power that Martyr attributes to the phantasy, he finally opts for Augustine's solution to the problem of Jacob's sheep which is based on the theory of the *rationes seminales*, latent powers planted in certain creatures which are to produce their fore-ordained effects when so willed by the Creator. Martyr here suggests that the *rationes seminales* are responsible for so-called spontaneous generation.[36]

This is Martyr's only use of the theory of the *rationes seminales*. This

---

illudi sensibus. Quam ut intelligamus, sciendum est ab illis rebus quae sentiuntur oriri imagines et ad sensus pervenire, postea recipi ad sensum communem, deinde ad phantasiam, postremo ad memoriam atque ibi asservari; imprimi autem illas et exculpi in singulis istis partibus tanquam in cera. Cum ergo istae imagines a memoria revocantur ad phantasiam aut ad sensus, referunt secum eadem sigilla atque ita fortiter feriunt et afficiunt ut ea iam sentire et praesentia esse videantur. Potest vis tanta esse phantasiae, ut Aristoteles docet de somno et vigilia, ut quae longe absint ea quispiam se certissime putet videre et tangere. Ista accidunt vigilantibus interdum ut arreptis et phreneticis, interdum etiam dormientibus. Quod ergo naturali ratione fit, id potest etiam fieri a diabolo. Is enim potest imagines rerum a memoria revocare ad phantasiam aut ad sensum atque ita hominum oculos ludificari. Idque non tantum daemones possunt, verum etiam angeli boni. Verisimile enim est illos insculpisse in phantasiis prophetarum ea quae Deus voluit revelare." Martyr's last statement seems dependent on Aquinas, *S.T.* II II, 172, 2; 173, 2. Martyr's best discussion of sleep and dreams is his *In Librum Iudicum . . . Commentarii*, (Zurich: 1565), ff. 90v. ff.

[36] *Genesis*, f. 118v.

bit of Augustinianism seems hardly more than an expedient to lighten a *crux interpretum*. Except for a few unimportant comments,[37] the passages described above from the commentaries on Genesis and Samuel are the only times Martyr discusses the internal senses, although the theory of the internal senses dovetails organically into his whole Aristotelian rational psychology. Martyr neither gives reasons for positing internal senses, nor argues their number and distinctive functions, nor assigns an organic seat. Obviously then he is only taking over and using a traditional teaching and relying on his readers' familiarity with it. Avicenna, who did much develop the theory of the internal senses, assigned five of them. St. Thomas had four; Melanchthon followed Galen in positing three, but as Melanchthon remarked, the precise number mattered little.[38] Martyr owned a copy of Melanchthon's *Opera* and was familiar with Galen, but his terminology differs slightly. Martyr also owned a copy of Juan Luis Vives's *De Anima et Vita Libri Tres* which assigns three internal senses, but again Martyr's terminology varies a bit from that of Vives. Vives like Martyr suggests that the angels and devils can work in the phantasy.[39] But even this is probably less a case of direct borrowing than of two authors expressing a well diffused traditional view that goes back at least as far as St. Thomas.[40]

---

[37] *In Lamentationes Sanctissimi Ieremiae Prophetae* D. Petri Martyris Vermilii . . . *Commentarium*, (Zurich: J. Bodmerus, 1639), 22-23. *Iudicum*, ff. 92rv.

[38] St. Thomas summarizes his own and Avicenna's doctrine of the internal senses, *S.T.* I, 78, 4. Melanchthon gives his views in his *De Anima, Opera Quae Supersunt Omnia*, ed. Carolus Bretschneider, (Halle: 1846), XIII, 120-21.

[39] On Martyr's ownership of copies of the treatises on the soul of Melanchthon and Vives, see Ganoczy, *Bibliothèque*, pp. 190, 287. Hoping that the marginalia might prove helpful, I checked Martyr's personal copy of Vives (Basel: R. Winter, 1538). They proved too few to be of value . Vives's doctrine of internal senses and diabolical intervention in the phantasy are found on pp. 32-33. Vives often praises Aristotle's psychology (pp. 87, 88, 93, 115, 127, 135, 145) but his definition of the soul owes more to St. Augustine: "Dicamus ergo humanam mentem spiritum esse per quem corpus, cui est connexus, vivit, aptus cognitioni Dei propter amorem atque huic coniunctioni cum eo ad beatitudinem" (104). Vives attributes greater freedom to the will (98-104) and takes a more pronounced stand in favor of immortality of the soul (124-44) than does Martyr. Like Martyr he distinguishes vegetative, sentient, and rational levels within the soul but insists on the unicity of the human form (47, 105). I doubt if Vives had much influence on Martyr.

[40] Martyr's suggestion that the devil can intervene in the phantasy is also taught by St. Thomas, *S.T.* I, 111, 3. As both Martyr and Thomas make reference to Aristotle's *De Somno*, I suspect that Martyr is borrowing without acknowledging his source. The one author I have seen whose terminology on the internal senses agrees perfectly with Martyr's is Jerome Zanchi, *Opera Theologica, III,*

The Sense Appetites

Martyr's soul is symmetrical. In the superior part of the soul are both the knowing and appetitive powers, the intellect and the will. So too in the inferior part of the soul there are knowing powers, the external and internal senses, and appetitive powers, the *vis cupiens* and the *vis irascens*.[41] Martyr writes about these sense appetites far more often than about the internal senses, probably because of their ethical and theological implications. Martyr devotes a whole page to proving that the *vis cupiens* and the *vis irascens* are really distinct powers. His whole argument is based on the Aristotelian and scholastic doctrine that there are as many distinct faculties as there are distinct formal objects.[42]

The sense appetite is a sense-level reaction to the information about some external object which derives from the senses. On the basis of this knowledge the sense appetite urges man either to seek the object as a good or flee it as an evil; but this urge, based exclusively on sense knowledge, is often wrong. The intellect understands objects within a wider perspective than their mere sensible attractiveness or repulsiveness. Thus within human nature, considered solely philosophically, tensions can and do arise. This natural tension between sensible and intellectual good is not to be confused, Martyr insists, with the still more profound tension between the carnal and the spiritual man that will be explored in conjunction with Martyr's doctrine of original sin and concupiscence.[43] But in spite of the tensions, the sense appetites are under the control of the reason and the will; consequently the actions taken by a man, even under extreme pressure from his sense appetites, are still free, that is, voluntary and spontaneous; man is morally responsible for them. According to Martyr, sense passions can never overpower the will and impair responsibility.[44] Martyr carries

---

cc. 521-24. Zanchi has an elaborate treatment, whereas Vermigli gives only a few sentences.

[41] *Ethicorum*, 428. Appetitus omnis est tripartitus: aut est nobilioris partis animi et cum ratione coniungitur diciturque voluntas, aut partis crassioris tumque diducitur in vim cupientem et irascentem. Also see *Ethicorum*, 35, 421.

[42] *Ethicorum*, 336. Martyr concludes: "Vis itaque irascens tutatrix est et pugnax, cupienti parti adversatur: illa enim labores et dolores refugit, haec ... perfert, ac ea invita subit." Martyr then adds a homely comparison to prove the distinction of the two powers: a man who is angry at a woman does not desire her, and he who desires her is not angry at her. Calvin holds the distinction between irascible and concupiscible faculties: *Institutes*, I, 15, 6.

[43] *Romanos*, 240; *Genesis*, f. 35r; *Corinthios*, 434v; *Samuelis*, f. 255r.

[44] *Ethicorum* 35, 187, 188. The best expression of Martyr's teaching on human responsibility in spite of the impact of the emotions is the following: "Ratio est huiusmodi. Quia humanae sunt affectiones irrationables quas habemus;

his doctrine of responsibility very far; he describes what certain theologians called the first movements of desire: a natural, pre-reflect-ive inclination for the sensible good. Since this propensity is often contrary to God's law, man can sin even by this non-reflective inclination.[45]

Martyr finds Aristotle's doctrine of the sense appetites in close harmony with Scripture. Because the appetites are not wrong or injurious to man but a real good, Martyr attacks bitterly the Stoic doctrine that man must root out his sense appetites. Jesus, who had an integral human nature, also had the sense appetites and their con-comitant emotions, and he used them in a human way without attempt-ing to root them out or suppress them. Hence there is nothing wrong when spiritual men weep and rejoice, provided that they do this under the control of reason enlightened by the Gospel. Men are flesh and and blood, not tree trunks. A bitter hostility to Stoicism pervades Martyr's writings which contrasts with the attitude of many of the church fathers, Erasmus, and Calvin who found much in Stoicism that could be incorporated into a Christian synthesis.[46]

THE VIRTUES

Vermigli's understanding of the sense appetites links up with his teaching on the passions or emotions (*affectus*) and on the virtues. "An

---

humanaeque sunt actiones quae ab ira vel cupiditate nascuntur, sunt etiam voluntariae atque spontaneae. Quod enim humanum est, est voluntarium. Nemo autem dixerit cupiditates et iras non esse in animis hominum affectiones, quemad-modum ratio in illis eisdem est; unde si actiones humanae sunt quae a ratione eliciuntur quia ratio pars est animi nostri, sic illae humanae fuerint quae ab ira vel cupiditate derivantur. Nam vis irascens et cupiens in animis hominum sunt. Potest fieri ut per occupationem tali occuratur obiectione. Actiones quae ab ira et cupiditate sunt, a parte irrationali proficiscuntur. Verum est, inquit (Aristoteles). Sed tamen istae vires humani animi sunt. Ergo actus inde prodeuntes humani erunt. Et istae facultates, etsi per essentiam rationem non habent, illius tamen sunt participes et ab ea regi possunt: quod non accidit in brutis. Deinde spontanea sunt principia istae affectiones et actiones quia possunt a voluntate coerceri. Neque de illis est ut de vi nutriente atque alente quae vel nobis nolentibus agit. Ideo concluditur absurdum esse statuere haec invita seu coacta." *Ethicorum*, 421.

[45] *Corinthios*, f. 245v: Est autem duorum generum cupiditas. Una statim sese exerit, vel nobis imprudentibus, quando se offerunt voluptates quae divina lege interdicuntur. Ibi animus primo impetu sese oblectat, quamquam non assen-tiatur eas consectari. Atque hoc genus tintillationis recentiores theologi appel-larunt primos motus, in quibus peccatum esse pernegant. Sed res longe aliter habet: quia si diligeremus Deum toto corde, tota anima et omnibus viribus, quicquid occurrert quod eius voluntati adversaretur, nobis horrori esset. . . .

[46] *Samuelis*, f. 255v, 256r; *Ethicorum*, 129. Martyr's whole treatment of the

emotion is a certain power or ability by which we either seek or flee objects that have been proposed to us."[47] In some cases a man's emotional response to an object or course of action antedates his knowledge of it, other times it follows upon or accompanies knowledge. The chief emotions are pleasure and pain. Martyr enumerates four simple emotions: joy, hope, sadness, and fear, but besides these there are the complex emotions such as wrath which combine elements of pain and pleasure. Plato makes the liver the seat of the emotions but Aristotle and Scripture generally assign the heart. The emotions fit under the predicament of quality but are stronger than habits; indeed, they are often stronger than the will itself. Because the emotions are a wild horse and the will is a timid child who must ride the steed, man needs the virtues to rein in his emotions and strengthen his weak will and reason, which must moderate and direct the emotions in attaining good and avoiding evil. Martyr insists that the emotions affect not only the lower part of the soul, but also the will and intellect. At this point Martyr's philosophical psychology links closely with his theology of original sin. Martyr never tires of repeating that the entire man, including intellect and will, is corrupted by original sin. Using the double criteria of faith and emotional control, Martyr makes a four fold division of all men: (1) those who lack both faith and the moral virtues which keep the emotions from running riot; (2) those who lack faith but who possess moderation and can control their passions; (3) Christian believers who are led by passion into sin, although their sin is not imputed; (4) Christians who due to God's gift are free from vicious passions and direct their emotions to the good.[48]

To control his passions or emotions, man needs the virtues. Without the help of the virtues man cannot perform moral actions with due speed, ease, and joy. Martyr repeatedly rejects the Platonic doctrine that the soul is born with all the virtues but is so dragged down by its union with the body that it forgets and neglects its innate virtues and only recovers their use by correct interrogation and teaching.[49] He does concede to the Platonists that the principle of the virtues is from nature. He attacks two Stoic doctrines relating to the virtues:

---

sense appetites agrees closely with that of St. Thomas. See *S.T.*, I, Q. 81, articles 2, 3.

[47] *Ethicorum*, 328. Affectus vis quaedam est seu facultas qua proposita nobis obiecta vel persequimur vel fugimus.

[48] *Defensio de Caelibatu*, 357; *Ethicorum*, 328-35; *Samuelis*, f. 255r.

[49] *Romanos*, 125; *Ethicorum*, 50, 68, 301.

that men are born with a natural propensity for virtue but are corrupted by bad example and that virtue is its own reward.[50] He agrees
with Aristotle that the virtues must be cultivated by repeated good acts
and by good teaching. Often divine grace is needed. Against Valla,
Martyr sides with Aristotle in teaching that virtue is a mean between
two extremes; he even insists against medieval scholastics that the
theological virtues are a mean between extremes. Martyr classes the
virtues as a special kind of habit. He follows Aristotle in distinguishing
the virtues according to their subjects, that is, according to which
part of the soul they perfect and in which they inhere. The vegetative
part of the soul is incapable of virtue. The intellectual virtues such as
wisdom and prudence are accidents of the intellect, while the moral
virtues belong to the lower part of the soul which obeys reason; for
instance, clemency is an accident of the irascible appetite and temperance of the concupiscible appetite. The natural virtue of hope
pertains to the irascible appetite, but the supernatural virtue of hope
inheres in the superior part of the soul. Martyr tries to attain an analogous understanding of this supernatural virtue by going through a
standard scholastic analysis of the natural virtue of hope.[51]

The scholium on fortitude from Martyr's commentary on Samuel
illustrates the scholastic character of his doctrine of the virtues. He
defines fortitude as a habit of the soul by which, in accord with right

---

[50] *Ethicorum*, 64, 125-29, 335.

[51] *Ethicorum*, 275, 291, 301, 385, 393; two brief quotations illustrate the metaphysics behind Martyr's theory of the virtues: "Sed quare virtutes verae non
facile transeant in vitia ex eo liquet quoniam sunt habitus, et hi (ut definiuntur
ab Aristotele in categoriis) difficile amoventur. *Ethicorum*, 254. Sed tamen haud
contra naturam (virtutes) vendicantur: quia se habent ad animam nostram ut
formam erga materiam. Est materia propensa per se ad eam accipiendam sed
efficiente causa indiget. Sic animus noster parandus est consuetudine ac doctrina
quibus excultus virtutes assequitur." *Ethicorum*, 301. Martyr comments on hope
as follows: "Neque praetermittendum est bonum illud, quod spes respicit,
arduum esse atque difficile. Etenim naturaliter in animantibus affectio spei penes
partem animi crassiorem, quam irascentem vocant, consistit; qua erigitur animans
ut bonum sibi propositum persequatur, licet aliquid videatur obstare. Incitatur
enim huiusmodi affectione ad superandum quicquid impediat. Lupo esurienti
occurrit taurus; ille appetendi facultate cupit eam praedam. Sed cum videat
gravem difficultatem imminere sibi pugnae atque certaminis, ab irascente animi
vi incitatur per spem, audetque se mittere in discrimen et dimicare. Atque ita
postremo, remoto omni obstaculo, praeda potitur. Sic Deus in animi nostri parte
nobiliori constituit spem, qua efficitur ut cum offertur nobis bonum summae
foelicitatis, quod et arduum est et longe a nobis positum, ne detereamur sed
audaciam habeamus et accessum ad Deum per fidem ut Paulus ait, cap. 2 ad
Ephesios." *Romanos*, 140. For Martyr's discussion of prudence, see *Corinthios*,
f. 141r.

reason for just and upright ends, man holds to the mean between fear and rashness. Martyr then discusses the four Aristotelian causes that are contained in his definition. He divides the material cause into two aspects; the subject (namely, that part of the soul in which fear and rashness operate) and the object (the danger faced). The formal cause is the holding to the mean. The final cause is the just and the upright and the will of God. The efficient cause according to Martyr, who here cites Aristotle's *Ethics*, is the law and the establishment of the state.[52]

THE INTELLECT AND WILL

Vermigli has many names for the knowing faculty in the superior part of the soul: *mens, ratio, intellectus, intelligentia, facultas intelligens, vis intelligendi, vis cognoscendi, vis ratiocinandi*. He also speaks of *cogitatio* and *ratiocinatio* but these seem to refer to the process rather than the faculty itself. The reason or intellect is the most outstanding part of the soul, the most desirable and powerful force in man; it seems something divine. The mind is to the soul what the eye is to the body and as the eye is good for the body, so the mind for the soul. Martyr then sides with St. Thomas and against Scotus on the pre-eminence of the intellect over the will. It might be argued that the intellect is even more pre-eminent for Martyr than for St. Thomas since the Thomistic doctrine of salvation centers on charity, a virtue of the will, whereas Martyr makes the mind man's highest faculty precisely because justification comes from faith, a virtue of the intellect.[53]

The intellect is an accident of the soul which belongs to the predicament of quality.[54] There are two kinds of accidents, the separable and the inseparable, and the intellect is clearly an inseparable accident, for obviously a man without an intellect is as much a contradiction as a four-sided triangle.[55]

Aristotle and his Greek, Arab, and Christian disciples all posit two intellects in man, the possible or potential intellect (the faculty which knows rationally) and the agent or active intellect (the non-knowing

---

[52] *Samuelis*, f. 232r. Martyr does not give the virtues nearly so central a place in his thinking as does St. Thomas who organizes his whole ethic in the *Summa* around his tract on the virtues. In this Aquinas had few predecessors and few followers. Most theologians, Martyr among them, organize their morality around the ten commandments. This is certainly more scriptural, but Thomas's Aristotelian method has the advantage of giving morality a positive orientation as contrasted to a series of "Thou-shalt-nots".

[53] *Genesis*, ff. 119r, 35v; *Ethicorum*, 169, 291.

[54] *Defensio*, 39, 260.

[55] *Defensio*, 39, 43, 260.

faculty which provides the possible intellect with the intelligible species or images with which and in which the possible intellect knows). Martyr talks about the possible intellect hundreds of times, although he uses the technical term only once.[56] Aristotle's brief and obscure comments on the agent intellect have generated more controversy than any short non-biblical passages in the history of western thought. As the agent intellect itself does not know, introspection cannot discover it. Rather it is a postulate of the whole Aristotelian psychological system: something is needed to provide the possible intellect with its intelligible species or universal concepts. The sense faculties, as they deal with concrete singulars, can at best initiate the process. The solutions suggested to this problem in the long history of Aristotelianism were numerous, abstruse, and bitterly contested.[57]

Martyr never uses the technical term *agent intellect*, but his use of *possible intellect* implies its correlative. His failure to use the term is not significant since so many of his comments on the parts of the soul are found in *obiter dicta*. But there is no doubt that Martyr agreed with Aquinas and several modern commentators on Aristotle in making the agent intellect an intrinsic component of the human mind. He understands quite well the need for intelligible species in the possible intellect. There is no evidence that he held an Augustinian theory of divine illumination. He rejects outright the Platonic theory of the ideas and states clearly that man has within himself the faculty of knowing and the light by which he understands known objects.[58]

How then does the intellect know? Martyr follows Aristotle in his

---

[56] *Defensio,* 630.

[57] David Knowles outlines the medieval controversy, *The Evolution of Medieval Thought*, (New York: 1962), 211. Antonino Poppi's essay, "La Discussione sulla 'species intelligibilis' nella scuola padovana del cinquecento," in his *Saggi sul pensiero inedito di Pietro Pomponazzi*, (Padua: 1970), 139-94, traces the argument at Padua.

[58] "Et istis Plato de repub. 6 adiecit, ideam secum afferre duplicem utilitatem, quarum una est, ut res per ipsum veritatem habeant, altera vero, per quam intelligentes vim habent cognoscendi. Scio quidem haec ab eo dicta, sed non probata: sentiunt alioquin Peripatetici res ipsas qua sunt veras esse. Atque nos absque opera ideae in animis nostris naturae beneficio vim facultatemque cognoscendi habere, necnon *lumen* quo cognita discernamus. Et iuvari homines in inquirendo praecedenti notitia quaesitorum fatebimus, sed species et formas eius generis in animis nostris constituimus, non quae constent et cohaereant per sese aut in mente divina resideant. Nam utrisque his, etiamsi fuerint in nostris actionibus, non iuvamur." *Ethicorum,* 171. The *lumen*, which I have italicized in the passage, probably means the agent intellect. Aquinas, following Aristotle, uses *lumen* as a synonym and simile for the agent intellect: *S.T.*, I, 79, 4. For Aristotle's use, *De Anima*, III, vl.

explanation. The external senses perceive extramental reality and from it receive images (*species, formae, imagines, simulacra*). These images are transferred from the external senses to the internal senses and from the internal senses to intellect. Within the intellect the concept exists as a universal. Martyr uses the analogy of a mirror to illustrate how the forms or images existing in the mind make extramental objects really (*re ipsa*) present in the mind even though man does not have their gross physical substance in his mind. Martyr says this power is called the possible intellect by philosophers because it is *able* to become all things by means of having the intelligible species of all things.[59] But Martyr nowhere gives a thorough philosophical analysis of intentional existence.

For Martyr the intellect is not only the crown of man's faculties to be investigated philosophically, but also of central importance for man's

---

[59] *Ethicorum*, 170; *Samuelis*, f. 165v; *Iudicum*. f. 92v; the most important passage for understanding Martyr's teaching on the intellect is the following from *Defensio*, 630; Martyr is arguing to establish that: "Fides vera tantae est efficaciae ut res praesentes constituat; non quidem realiter, sed spiritualiter; eas enim per fidem ita complectimur ac si essent ante oculos. . . . Speculum enim refert non ea quae in ipso sint praesentia, sed ea potius quae longius absint; Quae tamen ita refert et proponit ob oculos ac si essent re vera coram et in speculo praesentia. Ita ego dico usu venire etiam in fide: eius videlicet vi et efficacia ea, quae longe absint quod ad rem ipsam attinet, fieri quodammodo praesentia. Non potuit ergo Inconstantius (Martyr's ironic name for Stephen Gardiner who published the work Martyr is attacking under the pseudonym of Constantius) commodiori simili meam sententiam confirmare. Et quoniam ipse viam nobis munivit ut exempla et similia petamus a rebus familiaribus, non video cur non mihi quoque liceat idem facere. Vis in nobis intelligendi, quam philosophi appellant possibilem, ut Aristoteles ait, potest fieri omnia. Ornatur enim infinitis rerum simulachris, quae vulgo appellant species aut imagines. Ea vero simulachra, cum a rebus ipsis effluxerint et primum quidem per sensus exteriores, deinde etiam per interiores ad intelligentiam nostram penetrarint, ibi omnium rerum formas quodammodo praesentes efficiunt. Atque ita fit ut res longissime distantes et iam saepe praeteritas in nobis ipsis atque in animo nostro praesentes habere possimus, vel potius re ipsa habeamus, etsi crassa illarum hypostasis et substantia in animo nostro non existat. At ista, inquies, sunt philosophica. Maxime! Non tamen propterea falsa sunt." A close study of this passage is most rewarding for an understanding of Martyr's theological method. Besides stating the existence of the possible intellect and the internal sense, attributing the doctrines to Aristotle, and implying a standard interpretation, Martyr explicitly asserts their valid use in theological argument and in fact uses them to uphold Reformed teaching against the Catholic doctrine of real presence. Martyr's use of the threefold analogy of the mirror, the possible intellect, and faith is highly characteristic of scholasticism which constantly seeks analogies between common physical phenomena, philosophical explanation, and theological conclusions. The analogy is, of course, based on the fact that mirror, intellect, and faith all render present to us that which is physically absent.

supernatural salvation and religious development. It is precisely because man is a rational creature that he can sin; because man has a
rational nature God cannot make it impossible for man to sin, at least
in the natural order. Martyr agrees that God can confirm a man in grace
so that he cannot sin, but this obviously involves the supernatural
order.[60] Because of the religious importance of the intellect, Martyr
reverses the primacy that the Greeks gave to the speculative over the
practical intellect. The distinction between the speculative and practical intellect is not between two different faculties but between two
sets of objects with which the same mind deals. According to Martyr
the objects of the speculative intellect break down into three groups:
metaphysics, physics, and mathematics. Metaphysics treats of God
and the intelligences, that is, things separated from matter. Physics
deals with objects that adhere in matter and cannot be defined without
matter. Mathematics deals with things that cannot exist without matter
but can be defined without it. The speculative is ordered to contemplation, the practical intellect to action. The Aristotelian sources of
these distinctions hardly need emphasis. But Martyr points out that
man can contemplate God without loving him and hence can be alienated from him. Contemplation of God must not be merely speculative
but must be ordered to enjoying him in heaven; it must look to action;
therefore Martyr disagrees with both Plato and Aristotle and awards
pre-eminence to the practical intellect.[61]

This introduces Martyr's treatment of human conscience. Unlike
many later Protestant theologians especially Americans, who make
conscience a special faculty, Martyr follows the scholastic tradition in
defining concience as the action of the practical intellect by which our
actions are either defended or reproached. Martyr sees conscience as
working syllogistically: synderesis (man's innate knowledge of moral
first principles) provides the major of the moral syllogism: adultery
is wrong. Conscience then adds the minor: what you are about to do
is adultery, and draws the conclusion in reproaching us. Whoever acts
against his conscience sins.[62]

Martyr recognizes the difficulty of knowing what is right and wrong.
Scripture provides a sure guide in this dark land, and Martyr constantly
appeals to it, but Martyr sometimes recognizes a natural law and
the need for acting in accord with right reason. He attacks those

---

[60] *Genesis*, ff. 119r, 14r.
[61] *Ethicorum*, 3.
[62] *Corinthios*, f. 202v.

philosophers who seem to preach a moral nihilism and castigates the skeptics for holding that nothing is right of itself but only because law and custom have sanctioned it. He also attacks the Epicureans for trying to root out man's natural repugnance to certain kinds of action: this repugnance is not a mindless taboo but the voice of conscience which echoes the voice of God. Martyr's frequent use of rational argument to buttress and explicate the teaching of Scripture on moral questions implies a considerable natural law ethic, though very subordinate to the Word of God.[63]

The distinction between man's two spiritual faculties was not as sharp in Aristotle as in the medieval scholastics,[64] whom Martyr follows in distinguishing the intellect and will as two clearly distinct faculties.[65] The will relates to the intellect as matter to form and pertains to the predicament of quality. The intellect has the task of directing the will, for only when the intellect has provided knowledge of the end to be sought and the means to attain it, can the will go into action by commanding and administering man's other powers.[66] The act of the will is the intention, which Martyr defines as the will tending to an end by specific means. Martyr rejects the teaching of many scholastic theologians that a habitually good intention makes an action morally good; on the contrary, only an actually good intention makes an action good; hence actions performed with only a habitually good intention are really sins.[67] Vermigli's comments on the will itself

---

[63] *Corinthios*, f. 202v; *Ethicorum*, 48; *Genesis*, f. 10v; *Romanos*, 27; *Iudicum*, f. 103r.

[64] Frederick Copleston, S. J., *A History of Philosophy*, Vol I, Part II, (Garden City, N.Y.: 1962), 81.

[65] *Ethicorum*, 430; *Samuelis*, ff. 56v, 280v.

[66] *Samuelis*, f. 56v; *Iudicum*, f. 103r.

[67] *Samuelis*, ff. 56v, 324v. Martyr writes regarding intention: "Quoad significationem vocis, intentio significat motum animi quo per aliquod medium in finem tenditur, ut si quis per largitiones vel per obsequia studeat ad aliquos honores pervenire. Rerum quippe natura ita se habet ut multa inter sese ita sint connexa, ut per unum ad aliud fiat gradus. Pharmacis enim et potionibus itur ad sanitatem; per studia, lectiones, et praeceptores ad sapientiam. Quamobrem voluntatis actus est intentio, nam illius est movere ac incitare animum. Cum autem voluntas non prius percipiat quae cupit quam ipsi notitia eius praeluceat, non movet neque impellit animum ante notitiam quae in facultate intelligente viget. Ea et finem et illa quae eo conducunt habet prospecta et voluntati subministrat. Proinde intentio ad finem incitat, velut ad terminum, per ea quae in ipsum dirigatur. Sit eius definitio: Voluntas tendens in finem per aliqua media. Voluntas, quae genus eius ponitur, actus est facultatis volentis. Differentia ex obiecto deducitur, nimirum ex fine ac iis quae in eum ordinantur." *Iudicum*, f. 103r. As the survey of the faculties posited by Martyr has been completed, some comparison with Calvin's treatment of the same matter seems appropriate.

are very brief. There was only one aspect of the will that really interested him: its freedom, which he examines again and again. Some of the objections that he considers against freedom are philosophical, others theological, especially those arising from the doctrine of original sin. While it would be proper to consider the philosophical objections to the freedom of the will here, it seems better to handle the whole question of freedom together in chapter five.

The Origin of the Soul

Now that Martyr's treatment of the human faculties has been examined, two further questions arise. When and how does the human soul come into existence? These questions had vexed philosophers and theologians since Plato, and Martyr drew upon their probings to formulate his own position.

There were two main opinions regarding the time when the human soul comes into existence. Origen held that all souls were created at the beginning of the world, but behind Origen's teaching lay the Platonic doctrine of metempsychosis which taught that souls undergo a series of incarnations as punishments for sins committed in a previous existence. Martyr countered the Platonic view that the soul is really the human person (which underlay Origen's position) with his own Aristotelian doctrine of the soul: "Since the soul is the act and form of the body, the production of both should, it seems, be linked together."[68] It is absurd to think the soul remained idle through the long centuries before its union with the body, but neither could it have acted since it lacked the body which is the instrument and organ of its actions. Martyr rejects Origen's scriptural argument that God ceased to work after the sixth day and therefore does not continue to create souls;

Calvin (Institutes: I, 15, 6) posits five external senses and two internal senses (the common sense and the phantasy, but no separate memory). Like Martyr he enumerates three appetitive faculties, the concupiscible, the irascible, and the will. Calvin seems to divide the mind into two faculties, the reason which makes universal judgements and the understanding which contemplates the objects considered by reason. This last distinction is rather strange. Calvin is quite undogmatic about the distinction between the faculties and is rather contemptuous of subtle philosophic argument. His presentation is pragmatic: a simple, clear psychological doctrine that he can use in presenting his theology to the ordinary Christian. There is a summary of Calvin's philosophical doctrine by Carla Gallicet Calvetti, "La filosofia di Giovanni Calvino," in the *Grande antologia filosofica, II Pensiero della renascenza e della riforma*, Vol. VIII, M. F. Sciacca, general editor, (Milan: 1964).

[68] *Genesis*, f. 9v: ". . . cum anima sit actus et forma corporis, utriusque productio videtur iungenda."

strictly speaking God continues to work even now. Besides, Genesis tells us that God breathed forth the soul into the body only when he had made a body for Adam, which is a poetic way of saying that he created it.[69]

Martyr has more difficulty in explaining how the soul comes into existence. He rejects outright the notion that the soul is an emanation of the divine substance, for the divine substance is immutable, whereas man is most inconstant. Nor is the human soul of the same kind or of the same origin as the soul of brute animals. There remain the two orthodox opinions: transducianism and immediate creation. Martyr reviews these two options and makes a somewhat hesitant choice for immediate creation. The problem of the origin of the soul centers on the production of the superior part of the soul. There is no difficulty about the lower part: the vegetative and sentient levels of the soul are obviously procreated by the parents' seed.[70] Martyr relates how Augustine had explored these two options and showed considerable favor for transducianism, the view that a part of the soul of the parents was somehow transferred over to form the soul of their children. The other view held that the soul is created by God from nothing. Vermigli finds no decisive scriptural argument for deciding between these two views. His choice for immediate creation rests on the philosophical argument against transducianism: the soul, which is spiritual and simple, cannot be shared or divided as transducianism presupposes.[71]

THE BODY-SOUL RELATION

One extreme view of the body-soul relationship is the Manichean. The body, being matter, is evil. The soul, being spirit, is good. The Manichees made evil a substance in its own right, not just a corruption or defect in what was otherwise something good. Martyr of course totally rejects this view.[72]

Sometimes Martyr uses imagery with a Platonic ring to describe the relation of the soul to the body; for instance, the soul is in the body as a sword in its scabbard.[73] Martyr rarely uses such terminology since his understanding of the relationship is governed by the Aristotelian doctrine that the soul is the form and act of the body and the body

---

[69] *Genesis*, f. 9v; Vermigli also attacks Origenism elsewhere: *Romanos*, 348; *Iudicum*, f. 141r.

[70] *Romanos*, 152.

[71] *Romanos*, 152-53; *Corinthios*, f. 428v; *Genesis*, ff. 9v, 11v, 35r.

[72] *Romanos*, 241.

[73] *Genesis*, f. 25v.

is matter and potency.[74] In contrast, the Platonic soul was a complete substance so that union with the body always seemed something unfortunate and non-essential, more a hindrance than a help for the soul; indeed, the body was often seen as a punishment. Martyr cites and rejects the favorite adage of the ancient Stoics and Platonists that played on the similarity of the Greek words for body and tomb. He recapitulates and then rejects their basic argument against the body. This viewpoint led these philosophers to forbid sadness and mourning over the death of a loved one; to them death seemed an escape from the tomb and prison of the body. This attitude even led some to suicide. Martyr rejects it as bad philosophy; worse still, it conflicts with scripture and Christian doctrine which teach that death is an evil brought about by sin and divinely imposed as a punishment for sin. By a God-given instinct all living things seek to avoid death. As proof that death is an evil, Martyr cites side by side Aristotle's comments on death and Christ's agony in the garden over the prospect of death.[75]

Contrary to this false philosophy, the body is good for the soul. Sense perception, far from detracting from true knowledge, is its origin. It is sin, not the senses, that blocks knowledge of God, the highest object of our intellect.[76] One must not equate the body with sin since sin exists in the soul as well as in the body just as sanctity exists in the body as well as in the soul.[77] Nor can the body be counted a hindrance to virtue. On the contrary, most virtues relate to the lower part of the soul which is closely connected to matter. Without the body there would be little chance to acquire or exercise the virtues.[78] Martyr refuses to admit that the care of the body greatly draws the pious man from the things of God; but he does admit that by its very nature the body is rebellious to the dictates of the soul and a source of temptation and sin for the soul.[79] To illustrate how the body and soul are jointly responsible for sin Martyr relates the rabbinic story of a blind man and a lame man; the lame man mounts the blind man's shoulders and together they plunder an orchard. When caught they are rightly punished together, so it is also with the body and the soul.

---

[74] *Genesis*, f. 9v; *Dialogus*, f. 118rv; *Melachim*, f. 215r; *Romanos*, 539.
[75] *Genesis*, ff. 135v-36r.
[76] *Genesis* ff. 135 v-36r; *Romanos*, 300; *Iudicum*, f. 75r.
[77] *Romanos*, 249; *Defensio*, 291.
[78] *Genesis*, f. 136r.
[79] *Genesis*, f. 15v; *Romanos*, 175.

The soul indeed grasps, knows, and understands but of itself cannot venture forth by external actions. Though the body is stupid and does not understand, it is still an apt instrument for external actions when impelled and moved by the soul. Since this is the case, reason and justice demand that after death they be joined, whether to receive punishments or rewards.[80]

Without the body the soul is not perfect, for man without his body is not integral, but only a half man. The intimacy of the soul and the body in Martyr's thought is brought out by his answer to the question whether an angel using or conjoined to a human body can be called a man. Martyr says no. Human flesh is that which is informed and brought to birth by a rational soul. An angel using a body does not have an body in this sense since its union with the body is not permanent and it does not constitute one person or hypostasis with the body it has adopted.[81]

The union of the body and soul sets up an intimate sympathy between them so that the condition of the one affects that of the other. The soul is sorrowful when the body is afflicted. Even the physical temperature of the body can affect the soul, though only indirectly since the physical cannot act directly on the spiritual. Men with an abundence of yellow or black bile tend to be temperamental or morose. The sick body resists the soul's direction or at least is not so apt as its instrument. The soul in many of its actions is dependent on the body for powers which are joined to a bodily organ. Without these organs the soul cannot act, and any imperfections in the organs will affect the soul's ability to function.[82]

Still not all the soul's functions are shared with the body, nor all those of the body shared with the soul.[83] This conclusion had important ramifications for Martyr's polemic against the Lutheran doctrine of ubiquity. The Lutherans saw an analogy between the relation of the body and soul and the relation of divinity and humanity in

---

[80] *Melachim*, f. 215r: Animus quidem cognoscit, intelligit, et sapit; verum externa per se non potest obire opera. Corpus vero per se stupidum est nec sapit; quod tamen ab animo cum impellitur et movetur idoneum instrumentum est actionum externarum. Quod cum ita sit, ratio postulat et iustitia ut post mortem coniungantur denuo ad perferendas poenas vel praemia.

[81] *Dialogus*, f. 118v; *Corinthios*, f. 417v; *Iudicum*, f. 143r.

[82] *Dialogus*, f. 119r; *Romanos*, 185; *Genesis*, f. 35r.

[83] *Dialogus*, f. 41v: Quis non videat in commemoratis exemplis quasdam proprietates ita corporis esse ut non ad animum attineant, et vicissim alios animi sic esse ut corpori non queant communicari? Nec tamen ob id animi et corporis hypostatica unio solvitur. Also see *Dialogus*, f. 42v.

Christ. Just as the body and soul constitute one person, so Christ's divine and human natures constitute one person. This much Martyr concedes. But as the soul has functions in which the body does not share, so Christ's divine nature has attributes, especially ubiquity, which cannot be extended to the humanity by invoking the communication of idioms. Martyr's development of this argument teaches much about his understanding of the body/soul relationship and provides another fine example of his use of philosophical doctrine to support his theology:

> Aristotle indeed seems to consider the whole rational soul one subject but divided into powers and faculties. Therefore he makes the soul whole and one, or (as the physicists say in the schools) potestative: something that has many and varied powers. But the soul does not have all these powers in every member and is not whole in each part because it cannot hear, see, smell, and exercise all its actions and works in every member of the body. Therefore the whole soul with all its actions and powers is not in each and every part of the body. For it is an organic form and it has its powers connected with certain organs and members, nor can it pour its powers over into other parts of the body. Hence we say that with respect to its nature and essence (which we express by its definition) the whole soul is in the whole body and in all its parts: seeing that it is the act or form and animates the body. But with respect to its powers, the whole soul is in the whole body because it has all its faculties and powers and actions disposed through the body and arranged in marvelous order. But the whole soul is not in each part; rather the whole soul is in the whole body and partly in the parts.[84]

DEATH

Death is an analogous concept for Martyr. On the lowest level is natural death, the separation of the body and soul. But besides the

---

[11] *Dialogus*, f. 118rv: Aristoteles vero totam rationalem animam videtur opinari subiecto unam esse, sed viribus ac potestatibus dividuam. Proinde facit illam quiddam totum et unum, seu (ut physici loguuntur in scholis) potestativum, quod multiplices et varias habeat potestates, quas omnes cum in omnibus membris non habeat, non est tota in qualibet parte, quia non in omni corporis membro potest audire, videre, olfacere, ac omnes actiones et opera exercere. Unde non est tota cum omnibus suis actionibus et viribus in qualibet corporis parte. Forma enim est organica et vires suas habet certis organis et membris alligatas, nec eas potest ad alias partes corporis transfundere. Quocirca dicimus animam quoad naturam et essentiam suam, quae per definitionem exprimitur, esse totam in toto corpore ac in omnibus eius partibus: siquidem est eius actus vel forma et ipsum constituit animatum. Quo autem ad vires eius, est tota in toto, quia omnes facultates et vires et actiones habet per corpus dispositas et ordine pulcherrimo digestas. Non tamen est tota in omnibus partibus, sed tota in toto et pars in partibus.

death of the body there is also the death of the soul through sin which separates it from God. The death of the soul is twofold, curable and obstinate; the latter leads to damnation.[85] Both the death of the body and the death of the soul destroy life, natural and supernatural life respectively. Both are caused by sin. Herein lies the problem of death that most concerned Martyr. Why do men die? Experience and reason indicate that men, no less than beasts, die from natural causes—sickness, accident, murder, old age. Death is an ineluctable part of the human condition. But the Bible teaches that sin causes death, particularly Adam's sin. Martyr warns Christians against thinking that death, as it in fact exists in the world, flows from natural causes. He admits that men have a natural necessity to die, but any full understanding of death must look to Adam. Adam was created with a mortal nature, that is, with the possibility of dying; but he also had the possibility of not dying had he obeyed God. This possibility of not dying was not part of his human nature but a superadded gift of God. Adam's sin removed for him and for his posterity the gift of being able not to die. Once Adam sinned, the natural dynamism toward death built into human nature went into effect. Hence death as it exists *de facto* results from sin. The penalty for eating the forbidden fruit was to die the death. This immediately took place regarding the life of grace. That sin did not also immediately result in the death of Adam's body was due entirely to God's loving kindness. Martyr concludes from this that no mortal man can promise himself an hour of life.[86] So confident is Vermigli of this conception of death that he uses it as a premise from which to argue against the Pelagians to the existence of original sin in infants: sin is the cause of death, but infants die, therefore they have sin. As infants cannot commit actual sins, they must have inherited sin. Were infants without sin, they would not die.[87]

Martyr assigns the Christian a rather paradoxical attitude in the face of death; death is a sign of divine wrath and therefore inspires sorrow and terror,[88] but the prospect of death should also afford inspiration and solace since death brings rescue from temptation and puts an end to offenses against God. Hence the Christian should ponder and speak of death as pilgrims and sailors do of their arrival in home port.[89]

---

[85] *Genesis*, f. 11r; *Corinthios*, f. 408r.
[86] *Genesis*, f. 11r; *Romanos*, 154.
[87] *Romanos*, 151.
[88] *Romanos*, 154.
[89] *Genesis*, f. 136r.

THE IMMORTALITY OF THE SOUL

As was seen in the second chapter, the most hotly debated question during Martyr's student days at Padua was the immortality of the human soul. A generation earlier Marsilio Ficino, the leading exponent of Florentine Neo-Platonism, made the soul's immortality the cardinal doctrine of his system. Ficino's assertion that the soul was immortal was hardly something new, even if some of his arguments and the centrality he gave to this doctrine struck a new note. In the generation after Ficino, leadership in Italian philosophical speculation passed from Florence to Pavia, Bologna, Venice and especially to Padua. The enthusiastic recovery of ancient letters and thought characterized the whole Italian Renaissance; in Ficinan Florence this centered on studying and making available the works of Plato and the ancient Neo-Platonic or Plotinian school; but during the next generation interest shifted to the ancient pagan commentators on Aristotle, especially Alexander of Aphrodisias and Simplicius. Since these pagan peripatetics sometimes proposed ideas potentially inimical to Christian dogma, tensions were bound to arise, and these were augmented by circumstances surrounding the teaching of philosophy in the Italian universities. Unlike Paris and many northern universities where theology dominated, the Italian universities were traditionally strong in medicine and law and seldom had strong theology faculties integrated into the university structure, although many religious orders provided houses of study associated with the universities where their younger members could complete their theological education. Most of the teachers and students of philosophy were laymen. It is not surprising that in this atmosphere there developed what historians of philosophy have called secular Aristotelianism, or sometimes less accurately, Paduan Averroism. The study of philosophy developed relatively free of theological considerations. A further factor favored this development. During the fourteenth and fifteenth centuries the rising nominalist school tended to polarize theology and philosophy and markedly restricted the contributions that philosophy could make to theology, especially in the area of the preambles of faith, which included the immortality of the soul. In this situation the study of Alexander and Simplicius and their denial that the immortality of the soul can be demonstrated was bound to have profound repercussions and give rise to a many-faceted controversy on the soul. There is no room here to rehearse the roles in this controversy played by Cajetan, Pomponazzi, Genua, Nifo, Contarini, and even the Fifth Lateran Council. Eminent historians of philosophy such as Nardi, Randall, Gilson, and Kristeller have explored it in depth.[90] This controversy touched Peter Martyr Vermigli and provides important background for his statements on the immortality of the soul.

Martyr's teaching on the soul's immortality is complex. The human soul is immortal by its very nature, not merely by a special act of God, although God must of course preserve the separated soul in existence just as he must conserve and concur with all created reality. Contrary to what might be expected from a Christian theologian, Martyr does not direct his discussion of the immortality of the soul against the Italian philosophers who denied that reason could prove that the soul is naturally immortal. Martyr largely agrees with Pomponazzi, Genua, and the rest of the "Paduan" school. Reason can provide only probable arguments, mere intimations of immortality. Martyr directs his attack rather against those radical Protestants who taught a doctrine of psychopannychism or soul-sleep. These radicals held that the soul entered a period of suspended animation, an unconcious sleep, in the interval from the death of the body until its resurrection.

Martyr argues that Aristotle did not believe in the immortality of the soul. This is important because for many in Martyr's thought-world the voice of Aristotle was almost tantamount to the voice of reason itself, and many earlier scholastics attributed to Aristotle either belief in immortality, or at least ambiguity or neutrality on the question. Martyr realizes that his is a controversial opinion and at-tempts to cover his flank from attack by the rigidly orthodox by pointing out that two of the early Fathers of the Church, Tertullian and Gregory Nazianzen, also thought that Aristotle denied the soul's immortality. Obviously Martyr did not have to go back to Tertullian and Gregory for an assessment of Aristotle's position. He immediately adds that Alexander of Aphrodisias taught that the soul was mortal and that Averroes held only one intellect for all men.[91] Martyr does not cite the authority of Pomponazzi or of his old professors Montes-doch and Genua, but his position differed from theirs only in detail.[92]

---

[90] On Paduan Aristotelianism, see the studies cited in chapter II, note 18.

[91] *Dialogus*, ff. 38v, 40r; *Corinthios*, f. 367r; *Melachim*, ff. 217v, 231v. *Ethicorum*, 238.

[92] Martyr cites philosophical support in *Melachim*, f. 217v: "Ad hanc rationem, primum dicerent ethnici pro re certa et evidenti sumi quae naturae lumini obscura est, animum scilicet post mortem remanere ac immortalem esse; nobiles quippe philosophos non paucos longe diversum opinatos, quin et ipsi Aristoteli ascri-

He is perfectly aware that Plato and many other philosophers gave proofs for the soul's immortality but Martyr seems little impressed by their arguments.[93] He summarizes and rejects the view of those peripatetics who sought to show the immortality of the soul metaphysically by arguing that the human soul is essentially different from the form of brute animals, plants, and rocks because it does not depend upon matter and is really free from matter.[94] Martyr is equally unimpressed by arguments drawn from the simplicity of the separated soul.[95]

He saw greater suasive value in the moral arguments for immortality.[96] On one important point he clearly disagrees with Pomponazzi, although without mentioning him by name. Pomponazzi tried to exclude moral arguments for immortality by adopting the Stoic doctrine that virtue is its own reward and vice its own punishment. Hence there is no need of an after life to reward the virtuous and punish the wicked. Martyr considers this position absurd. It is sheer nonsense to argue as did the Stoics that the testimony of an upright conscience renders a man happy even should he be broiled alive in the red-hot bronze bull of Phalaris, the Sicilian tyrant. Martyr goes further: the upright man is actually less happy in this life than is the rake.[97]

---

pitur a doctissimis viris, Tertulliano inquam, et Gregorio Nazianzeno, animam hominis mortalem esse censuerit. Et Alexander Aphrodiseus, peripateticus non obscurus, hoc sensit. Et Averroes in schola peripatetica docuit unum dumtaxat esse humanum intellectum, qui singulis hominibus per phantasmata copulentur. Proinde hoc principium quod asseritur, animam post mortem perseverare incorruptam, cum dubium sit, nec pendeat a per se notis ac perspectis in rerum natura argumentum quod super eo extruitur, nutat et pro firmo haberi non potest." It is interesting to compare Martyr's appeal to the Fathers with a passage from a Pomponazzi manuscript, recently discovered, which according to Nardi summarizes that philosopher's position "in senso perfettamenta alessandrista." Pomponazzi writes: ". . . quare concludendum est animam esse mortalem . . . et quod haec sit opinio Aristotelis confirmant Gregorius Nazianzenus et Gregorius Nyssenus, quod scilicet anima intellectiva sit mortalis." See Bruno Nardi, *Studi su Pietro Pomponazzi*, (Florence: 1965), 94.

[93] *Melachim*, 232r: Ascendit quidem spiritus hominum sursum et spiritus iumentorum deorsum, sed quis hoc novit? Quis firmis et naturalibus rationibus probabit? Non negatur a Salomone ista contingere sed scientiam et notitiam earum rerum, ait, aut omnino aut vix inter homines extare, quoad naturalia principia. Et cum inquit, Quis novit? ut Hieronymus interpretatur difficultatem ostendit, non quod sit penitus impossibile. Etenim ad notitiam immortalitatis animorum utcunque pervenerunt Socrates, Plato, et Pythagoras necnon aliqui alii philosophi, quibus autem rationibus non disputo.

[94] *Ethicorum*, 148.

[95] *Romanos*, 307.

[96] *Samuelis*, f. 332v.

[97] *Corinthios*, ff. 406v, 407r. ". . . si torqueatur vel descendat in Phalarides

Martyr never elaborates this rejection of Stoicism into an argument for immortality and denies that there are any apodictic rational arguments. In confronting the Protestant radicals who denied immortality he bases his whole case on scriptural evidence.[98] His biblical case limps rather badly because he tended to see the Bible as a monolith rather than the gradually built up record of an evolving religious consciousness. Twentieth century biblical scholarship largely agrees that the ancient Jews had little explicit notion of a personal afterlife until very late in the Old Testament period. Immortality of the soul was a typically Greek philosophical notion quite foreign to the thought of ancient Semitic peoples. Only the latest stratum of the Old Testament asserts even the resurrection of the body, a view more congenial to Semites.[99] As did Calvin, Martyr took upon himself a Herculean task in trying to uphold the immortality of the soul with a handful of vague New Testament texts (e. g. Luke, 23:43) against the defenders

---

taurem, et dicat ut hoc est suave, quemadmodum jactat suum sapientem dicturum, inconstantissime proculdubio loquetur . . ." *Ethicorum*, 129.

[98] Martyr was perhaps closer to the advocates of soul-sleep than he realized. George Williams has recently argued that psychopannychism owed more to the Italian secular Aristotelians than to the Bible, but he does not document this interesting hypothesis. "The three religious groups espousing psychopannychism in the Reformation Era were the Spiritual Libertines, the Anabaptists, and the Socinians. All these groups seem to have been directly or indirectly influenced by the speculations emanating from the two schools of interpretaters of Aristotle in the Northern Italian Universities of Padua, Bologna, and Ferrara: the Averroists and the Alexandrines." See Williams' "Camillo Renato," in John A. Tedeschi, editor, *Italian Reformation Studies in Honor of Laelius Socinus*, (Florence: 1965), 106. Williams also discusses psychopannychism in his *Radical Reformation*, (Philadelphia: 1962), 20-24, 104-06, 580-92. Martyr and radicals such as Camilio Renato would have agreed that it is impossible to prove the immortality of the soul by reason. If the real roots of psychopannychism were philosophical, then Martyr's scriptural refutation of their position would have been largely futile.

Martyr and Calvin differed in their teaching on the immortality of the soul. Calvin's first theological tract was directed against psychopannychism. In it he dismisses the philosophers with unconcealed contempt: to examine their conflicting opinions is a waste of time: *Calvini Opera*, "*Quae Conditio et Vita Animarum post Hanc Vitam*," V, c. 177. In this tract Calvin devotes himself exclusively to exploiting and defending those meager scripture texts which assert immortality and to refuting those that seem to deny it. The last edition of the *Institutes*, however, takes a different approach and claims that reason easily knows that the soul is immortal. Calvin briefly suggests several philosophical arguments: I, 5, 5; I, 15, 2. George Williams sees Calvin's position as strongly influenced by the Platonic elements in his thought: *The Radical Reformation*, 582.

[99] For instance, Daniel 12:2. For a summary statement on the development of belief in an afterlife in the Bible, see John L. McKenzie, *Dictionary of the Bible*, (Milwaukee: 1965), 731.

of soulsleep who had a plentiful supply of denials of immortality garnered from the early strata of the Old Testament.[100]

The psychopannychists were not Martyr's only adversaries on the question of immortality; he attacks metempsychosis on both scriptural and philosophical grounds. Philosophy denies that a substantial form (and the soul is a substantial form) can exchange the matter which is its subject for different matter. Martyr's great opponent on metempsychosis is Origen, for he curiously never levels this charge against Plato.[101] He also attacks those who hold that the soul dies with the body and is recreated by God at the resurrection; these first cousins of the psychopannychists err because of a false interpretation of a passage in St. Paul; Martyr tries to set the record straight in his own exegesis of the passage.[102]

The general character of Martyr's philosophy of man is clear enough: the popular Aristotelianism that was the common patrimony of most of the secondary and higher education of Western Europe, a patrimony derived largely from medieval scholasticism, but recently renewed and purified by fresh contact with its Greek roots through the philological tools provided by renaissance humanism. There is nothing original in Martyr's philosophy of man; he is only an intelligent disciple and proponent of the regnant system of his day. Showing little interest in developing a personal position on disputed or arcane points, he simply takes over the main lines of the system and employs them for his own theological ends. There is no evidence to show that Martyr's conversion from Roman Catholicism caused a parallel reassessment of his Aristotelianism. Aside from the rational indemonstrability of the soul's immortality and the enumeration of the internal senses, almost all of Martyr's teaching in this chapter have direct parallels in Thomas Aquinas.[103]

---

[100] *Corinthios*, ff. 366v-369v.

[101] *Genesis*, f. 144v.

[102] *Corinthios*, f. 406rv.

[103] It is noteworthy the T. F. Torrance's *Calvin's Doctrine of Man*, (London: 1949), has no chapter at all on a philosophy of man in Calvin's voluminous writings.

CHAPTER FIVE

MARTYR'S THEOLOGY OF SIN AND FALLEN MAN

This chapter examines successively Peter Martyr Vermigli's thought on the nature and divisions of sin, on original sin, on the necessity of sin, and whether God causes sin. Since Vermigli never wrote a tract explicitly on either theological methodology or on the philosophy of man, the previous two chapters had perforce to gather together and organize his scattered remarks on these two subjects. This chapter faces no such difficulty. Martyr wrote at considerable length on sin, especially on original sin and its consequences for man. As far as possible each major part of this chapter will try to follow Martyr's own order of presentation and to avoid repetition. This will not always be possible, for Martyr wrote several tracts on original sin and on God as the author of sin. There are also passing remarks on these subjects scattered throughout his voluminous writings. His thinking on sinful man possesses great consistency, but the order in which he develops his ideas is not always uniform. Every part of his thinking in this area touches and interconnects with every other part; hence a single straight line of presentation and an absolute avoidance of repetition are impossible.

THE NATURE OF SIN

Martyr's commentary on Romans contains his most important attempt to define and classify sin.[1] He takes up and examines Augustine's definition of sin as every word, act or desire against the law of God. Martyr finds *desire* in Augustine's definition ambiguous. Does *desire* mean only those desires made with full consent of the will or does it also include those pre-reflective urges of incipient lust, anger and so forth? Martyr records that Peter Lombard interprets Augustine so as to exclude these incipient desires. Martyr is by no means willing to exclude them. Martyr also examines St. Ambrose's definition of sin and finds it lacking; he therefore goes back to scripture to reformulate an adequate definition of sin: "sin is whatever is opposed to the law of God."[2] He points out that his Catholic adversaries refuse to

---

[1] *Romanos*, 262-65.

[2] *Romanos*, 263: "peccatum esse quidquid adversetur Legi Dei." Martyr gives the same definition in *Romanos*, 149. Later this chapter will show that when

admit that these incipient desires or first movements of concupiscence are sin. Martyr insists that they fall within scripture's definition of sin and are sins even if they occur in the baptized without any consent of the will. Original sin likewise does not involve the consent of the will but is certainly a sin. These incipient acts are either good, evil, or neutral. They cannot be good since scripture tells man to repel them; they cannot be neutral since the divine law does not leave any part of the soul neutral or uncommitted but commands man to love God with his whole heart and whole soul. Hence these first movements are evil and sinful. Martyr repeats this argument frequently in his writings.[3]

Martyr distinguishes between mortal and venial sin, but his distinction is very different from that traditional in Roman Catholic theology. For Catholics a mortal sin is that which removes or "kills" the presence or life of grace in the soul. Venial sin is sin which does not remove this supernatural quality in the soul. Martyr works out of a different theology of grace which derives from Luther and refuses to see grace as a quality in the Aristotelian sense. Hence Martyr's distinction between mortal and venial sin must shift. For Martyr all sins are lethal of their nature unless the grace of God intervenes. That a given sin does not lead to damnation is due not to its smallness (*levitas*) but to God's mercy. No sin is venial because of what Roman Catholic theologians call paucity of matter. All sins are serious and lethal, but Martyr insists that this does not imply the Stoic doctrine that all sins or vices are equal. For Martyr those sins are mortal which in Pauline terminology "reign" in man, that is, those which are not mortified, which man commits against his conscience without penitence: in short, wanton sin. Paul gives a list of sins that exclude from the kingdom of God—these actions man must cease doing and repent. Martyr defines venial sins as either those major actions which exclude from the kingdom of God but which man has repented and ceased doing, or they are those minor failings which, however much resisted, can never be excluded from human life because of man's inborn weakness and ignorance. Some examples may make Martyr's distinction clearer. Murder, unrepented, is a mortal sin. Slight habitual impatience is a venial sin since it can never be totally overcome,

---

Martyr comes to deal with the problem of God's authorship of sin, he gives a significantly different definition.

[3] *Romanos*, 149, 263-65; *Melachim*, ff. 13r, 15r; *Defensio de Caelibatu*, 357. Martyr's teaching on the first movements gives a rather mechanistic and impersonalistic slant to his whole theology of sin.

given the human condition; but murder which is repented and which a man no longer commits is also a venial sin—it has received *venia*, forgiveness.[4] Martyr is entirely aware that his Protestant terminology in this matter differs from the common and traditional usage.[5] Martyr insists that in principle there is no sin which cannot be forgiven because an unforgivable sin would imply a sin which Christ could not overcome; but elsewhere he does speak of the sin against the Holy Spirit as unforgivable.[6]

Martyr also distinguishes sin into three categories depending on whether it is habitual or actual. First there is man's innate cupidity, second the first movements that arise from this cupidity, and third there are the sinful acts which are done with the consent of the will. The last are actual sins, the first is the depravity of human nature resulting from original sin. Martyr hestitates to classify the first movements either as actual sins or to attribute them wholly to original sin. In so far as man actually does something in these first movements, they have the character of actual sins, but in so far as man undergoes these movements without willing them, they share in the character of original sin.[7]

Martyr discusses the various causes of sin. Strictly speaking there is no efficient cause of sin, only a deficient cause since sin is an evil, a privation, the absence of the good. Nothingness has no cause. Martyr gives a long list of quasi causes: man's intellect and will, his sense appetites, his depraved sense, the apparent good for whose sake man acts, the tinder (*fomes*) of original sin, human weakness, the suggestions of the devil and of evil men, bad example, and other previous sins.[8]

---

[4] *Romanos*, 154, 209, 264, 284; *Defensio de Caelibatu*, 355.

[5] *Romanos*, 263: "... in gravioribus peccatis quae ... vulgo appellantur mortalia." Martyr's use of the term *mortal sin* is consistent but must be read with extreme caution as he uses *mortal sin* in three meanings: 1) in the vulgar, traditional, Catholic meaning of a gravely sinful action; 2) in his own definition—sin reigning, wanton, unrepented sin; 3) in the etymological sense—all sin merits death of both body and soul and every human action is sinful: "Et de his sentiunt nostri cum docent opera hominum, quantum vis sanctorum, non esse absque mortali peccato: quoniam absque hoc genus defectibus nihil agimus. Dicuntur autem huiusmodi defectus mortales esse: quia natura sua merentur mortem. Stipendium autem peccati mors." *Romanos*, 263-64.

[6] *Romanos*, 160, 263.

[7] *Romanos*, 264.

[8] *Samuelis*, ff. 278r, 281r.

ORIGINAL SIN

Martyr's treatment of original sin belongs to the heart of this study. There are treatises on original sin in Martyr's commentary on Genesis and on Romans, the two biblical books most important for the doctrine. This chapter will integrate these two treatises as well as shorter remarks on original sin scattered through Martyr's writings. The order of presentation follows that of Martyr's twenty-five folio page tract in the Romans commentary. Martyr begins by asking whether original sin exists. His question refers, of course, to original sin as transmitted to Adam's posterity rather than Adam's personal sin. Martyr responds that it does exist and points out two groups of adversaries who deny its existence. Martyr erects his proof for original sin on a large number of scripture texts, mostly drawn from the Pauline epistles.[9] Martyr's Genesis commentary argues syllogistically that all men have original sin: "Each individual passes on to the sons he begets that kind of nature that he possesses. . . . But Adam after the fall had a vitiated nature, so he communicated that kind of nature to his offspring."[10] This teaching is open to several objections that Martyr tries to answer. Why does not the man who has been justified procreate another justified person? Martyr counters: justification is only the non-imputation of sin and does not emend nature nor take away its whole vice. Hence the justified man passes on his vitiated nature. Justification and faith cannot be transferred since they are gifts of God's goodness that do not depend upon nature. Martyr confirms his argument with a simile borrowed from Augustine: the farmer must separate the chaff from the seed grain, but the seed grain will produce more chaff when planted and harvested. So too, circumcision had to be renewed with each generation. Besides, Adam must not be looked upon as a private person but as the trunk and shoot and seed-bed of all human nature.[11]

To the objection that all sins are committed by the will, without whose act there can be no sin, Martyr replies that this objection applies specifically to personal sins, but original sin is a different kind of sin, a corruption of nature; moreover, even original sin pertains

---

[9] *Romanos*, 164.

[10] *Genesis*, f. 34r: Primam propositionem ratione ita confirmo: Qualem quisque naturam habuerit, talem procreatis a se filiis largitur quia in generatione perfecta, quam naturales univocam appellant, eadem natura utrique participatur tam a procreatis filiis. At Adamus naturam post lapsum vitiatam habuit. Talem igitur natis ex se communicavit.

[11] *Genesis*, f. 34r; *Romanos*, 151.

to the will in two ways: first because it resulted from the will of man-kind's first parent, second because there is here a matter of a habit, and those who act from habit act voluntarily, as Aristotle's *Ethics* teaches. To the further objection that the evils which nature brings upon man are worthy of pity, mercy and forgiveness rather than punishment, Martyr responds that this is true of an evil of the body, but original sin is not a bodily evil. Besides, it is not for man to decide whether he deserves mercy or punishment since that is God's preroga-tive. Vermigli also rejects the contention that as man receives only his body, which is incapable of sin, from his parents but not his soul, original sin cannot be transferred from parents to child. Against this contention, Martyr urges the close inter-relationship and inter-de-pendence of the body and soul, citing Galen as his authority. Since parents pass on a body corrupted by original sin, is there any wonder that the soul is immediately contaminated with corruption so that man is born with original sin and without original justice? [12]

Having demonstrated the existence of original sin, Martyr moves on to examine its nature. He cites various definitions of original sin and records Peter Lombard's description of those Pelagians who verbally affirmed original sin but emptied it of its real meaning. For them original sin is an obligation or liability to death and damnation but not a real sin or guilt. Martyr then dubs Albert Pighius the reno-vator of this doctrine. Pighius remains Martyr's chief whipping-boy whenever his commentary on Romans touches on original sin, grace, predestination, and justification. Pighius objected that original sin was not a transgression of a law and was not voluntary and therefore could not be sin in the proper sense.[13] Martyr adds that Pighius attributes to man a corrupt nature even before the fall. Martyr denies Pighius's assertion and argues that God gave Adam an integral nature that did not have the passions and desires which might entice

---

[12] *Genesis*, ff. 34v-35r.

[13] *Romanos*, 165, 175. Although Pighius's doctrine of original sin had Pelagian affinities, much of his theology represents an abortive Roman Catholic attempt to come to terms with Luther's doctrine of grace: see Hubert Jedin, *Studien über die Schriftstellertätigkeit Albert Pigges, Reformationsgeschichtliche Studien und Texte*, Heft 55, (Münster i. W.: 1931), especially chapter three: "Pigge als 'Vermitt-lungstheologe'," pp. 96-123. For Pighius's doctrine of original sin, see p. 113. Pighius rejects Augustine's identification of original sin with concupiscence, Anselm's identification with the loss of original justice, and St. Thomas's attempt to combine both these elements. Pighius makes original sin merely God's reckon-ing of Adam's sin against his posterity. Concupiscence is for Pighius merely a natural property that has nothing to do with original sin.

him to act against reason and the Word of God. For Pighius, on the other hand, Adams' fall meant a loss of non-natural gifts and a return to the pristine condition of human nature. For Martyr it meant a new unhappiness which man acquired for himself.[14]

Before proposing his own definition of original sin, Martyr reviews the two classic positions taught by Augustine and Anselm. Augustine identified original sin with concupiscence. Martyr quickly adds that the scholastics interpret this concupiscence as affecting not merely the lower part of the soul but also the will; Pighius distorts Augustine by isolating concupiscence in the lower part of the soul. Augustine thought that the corruption of inherited nature was connected with the carnal passion aroused in procreation, but Martyr sides with "several of the more intelligent scholastics" who say that original sin would be handed down even if no inordinate passion were involved.[15] Original sin is voluntary for Augustine only in the sense that it is not imposed violently and that it was committed voluntarily by man's first parents. On the other hand St. Anselm and many of the scholastics identified original sin with the lack or loss of original justice. Original justice is the right institution of man so that the body obeys the soul and the lower parts of the soul obey the higher parts and the mind itself is subject to God and His Law. This was Adam's original condition and would be man's today had Adam not sinned. Martyr does not share the reluctance of some scholastics to call the lack of original justice sin in the proper sense, but only a source of man's opposition to God's law. Martyr does not advert to the fact that the Council of Trent had shortly before endorsed and adopted the reluctance of these scholastics.[16] Martyr sees no basic difference between the view of Augustine and Anselm; Anselm's terminology simply clarifies what is included obscurely in concupiscence.[17]

Lest the lack of original justice be understood as a mere privation of God's gifts that involves no defect of nature, Martyr proposes his own fuller definition of original sin: "the depravity of the whole man carried over from the fall of the first parent into his posterity by means of generation which judicially imposes on all those born from him nearly infinite evils and eternal damnation unless rescued by the

---

[14] *Romanos*, 168.

[15] *Romanos*, 169: "nonnulli tamen ex prudentioribus scholasticis." Confer Aquinas: *S.T.* I-II, 83, 2 and 3.

[16] *Romanos*, 171; on Trent, see Denzinger-Schönmetzer, *Enchiridion*, n. 1515.

[17] *Romanos*, 173.

benefit of Christ." [18] Although Martyr claims to be the inheritor of Augustine and Anselm and of the attempts by Aquinas and other scholastics to combine their teaching, his definition gives a new centrality and emphasis to total depravity which is distinctly Reformed.[19]

Martyr immediately follows his definition with a discussion of its four causes. The material cause is all man's parts and powers. The formal cause is their depravity. The efficient cause is Adam's sinful will together with the handing down of original sin by generation as an instrument. The final cause and effect of original sin are eternal damnation and the woes of this life. Man's total corruption seems especially clear to Martyr from the fact that, although man is made to seek God as his highest good, he instead does not understand divine teaching, hears with reluctance the promises and commands of God, spurns his rewards and punishments, his body refuses to obey the soul, and his surging passions scorn reason and God's Word.[20]

Original sin obviously differs from actual sins, but precisely how? Does original sin make a man guilty; does it make him liable to punishment? Martyr insists that original sin makes a man guilty and liable to punishment.[21] Guilt and liability are closely connected since guilt confers liability: Martyr uses the matter/form analogy to describe their relationship. That original sin makes a man liable to punishment is perfectly obvious to Martyr from the fact of human death, the frequency of sickness and disease, the conflict of spirit and flesh, man's propensity to sin, his blindness to divine teaching, and the weakness of his faculties in doing good. Guilt and liability are not identical, for they can be separated, as is clear from Paul's assertion both that sin still dwells in his members and that there is no condemnation for those united to Christ Jesus (Romans: 7:23-8:1). The guilt of original sin remains even after justification has removed the liability to punishment.[22]

[18] *Romanos*, 173: Est ergo peccatum originis totius hominis naturae depravatio, a lapsu primi parentis in posteros traducta per generationem quae, nisi beneficium Christi succurrat, omnes inde nascentes infinitis prope malis et aeternae damnationi adiudicat.

[19] *Romanos*, 173: Quod vero totus homo sit corruptus inde liquet, quia in eum finem conditus est, ut Deo tamquam summo bono adhaereret. Iam vero divina non intelligit, promissa scriptuarum impatienter expectat, praecepta Dei moleste audit, poenas et praemia contemnit, affectis tumultuantes rationi et verbo Dei petulanter insultant, corpus animo parere detrectat.

[20] *Romanos*, 173.

[21] *Genesis*, f. 35r: Hoc originis malum secum habet reatum et culpam. Reatum dico imputationem, damnum, obligationem qua aliqui mulcta vel poena addicitur.

[22] *Genesis*, f. 35r.

The greatness of man's guilt and liability can be measured by the greatness of its expiation, the death of Christ, and by the horrible sins which even holy men fall into because of original sin. Original sin removes the original justice which held in check man's bodily drives and sense appetites. Thereby original sin terribly weakens man's resistence to actual sins.[23]

Total depravity is a topic to which Martyr returns frequently with great vehemence. He develops the concept of total depravity in two ways: by cataloguing how it affects all stages, aspects and departments of human life and by describing how it corrupts all parts of the human make-up, body, sense appetites, will, and intellect. In Martyr's view man is the most miserable of all living things; his birth, infancy, childhood, education, and upbringing are filled with tears and pain, moans and labor.[24] Man lacks constancy and courage; even though constantly helped by God, he trembles at every turn and would immediately fall into sin unless borne up by God's grace.[25] Original sin has left man more than half dead and gives rise to evil passions which constantly wax stronger; unless these passions are blunted and mortified, man's whole life brings only increasing corruption of his nature.[26] One sin begets another on an ever increasing chain. Man's concupiscence is so mighty that even man's efforts to curb it often only make it stronger. Concupiscence resembles a horse which rears more viciously whenever the rider digs in his spurs to control it and is like gangrene and elephantiasis which only increase with the efforts of doctors to cure them. Martyr points to this aspect of concupiscence and original sin to explain why St. Paul says that the Law of Moses only resulted in greater sin.[27] Depravity and the other results of original sin are the true causes of all later sins. Although Martyr holds that one sin is often the result of and a punishment for earlier sin and that original sin has so depraved man that he can do nothing but sin, so that all sins are the fruit of Adam's sin, he insists that not all subsequent sins are *simply* the punishment for previous sin.[28] Martyr teaches that the depravity from original sin affects all men, but it does not take the same form in each man. "We are not so stupid that we think

---

[23] *Genesis*, f. 35r.
[24] *Romanos*, 175.
[25] *Genesis*, f. 127v.
[26] *Romanos*, 159, 265.
[27] *Romanos*, 231.
[28] *Romanos*, 159, 231, 265.

the wills of men are the same on all points."[29] The will, desires, and ambitions of men take divergent directions when they reach adulthood; but all men are equal in coming from the same corrupt source, and all are headed toward evil. Individuals act differently and have different temptations according to their varying upbringing, bodies, and occupations, but all are governed by the law of sin due to original sin.[30]

Aside from his Eucharist theology, there is probably no point which Martyr emphasizes more frequently than that the total depravity of man affects all his powers, those of the soul as well as those of the body. Original sin corrupts the irrational appetites, the mind, the will and the nature of the soul itself.[31] He takes up Paul's distinction of the spiritual man (*spiritualis*), the animal man (*animalis*) and the carnal man (*carnalis*). Martyr insists that this Pauline terminology is not based on the distinction of body and soul or even of the lower and higher parts of the soul. Rather it is based on the degree to which a man is ruled by the spirit of God or by sin. Each of these three Pauline terms embrace the whole man, body and soul. In this sense the body in a man ruled by grace is spiritual, just as the soul in a man ruled by sin is carnal. Several other Pauline terms—the external man, the old man, the flesh, the body of sin—also refer to the whole man in so far as he is not regenerate, united to Christ, and directed by God's Law.[32] Martyr seems to have a large number of adversaries in mind when he insists that the will and intellect are also corrupted by original sin, but he names only Albert Pighius and Richard Smith.[33]

---

[29] *Romanos*, 388: Nos autem ita stupidi non sumus ut voluntates hominum undecumque putemus easdem esse.

[30] *Romanos*, 388.

[31] *Genesis*, f. 35v.

[32] Some of the places where Martyr makes this point are: *Romanos*: 35, 174, 205, 240, 275; *Corinthios*, ff. 429v, 434v; *Melachim*, ff. 12v, 13r; *Genesis*, f. 35v; *Defensio de Caelibatu*, 357. A good example of this distinction is *Romanos*, 241; Habemus hoc loco nomina carnis et membrorum et ex altera parte mentis et interioris hominis. Quae distinguenda non sunt penes corporis animique partes. Sed ex uno latere significatur totus homo quatenus non est regeneratus neque adhuc pravitatem naturae perfecte atque in universum exuit. Ex altero item latere totus homo intelligitur quatenus iam regeneratus est et aliquam saltem partem spiritualis regenerationis accepit. Longe falluntur qui opinantur, quamvis in Christum non credamus, tamen in nobis mentem et voluntatem omnino esse integrae naturae. Neque enim meminerunt quid Paulus scribat ad Corinthios: animalis homo non percipit ea quae sunt spiritus Dei. Nam haec verba manifeste indicant intelligentiam nostram multum habere caliginis et vitii, cum ita inepti simus ad spiritualium rerum perceptionem.

[33] *Romanos*, 174; *Defensio de Caelibatu*, 357. Heiko Oberman, *The Harvest of*

Martyr realizes that his teaching on total depravity is open to several objections, so he tries to anticipate them. To the objection that everything God created was good, Martyr responds that man's nature was good as originally created but has been corrupted by Adam's fall. He scorns those who philosophize that if man only develops virtues to moderate his passions, everything would change for the better and man would be perfect. To Martyr these critics grasp neither the grandeur of man's first creation, nor the misery of his present condition, nor the full demands that God makes of man. Martyr argues that his doctrine of depravity does not mean that there are no good acts among pagans. God operates even in pagans and sometimes endows them with marvelous and heroic virtues which check the ravages of original sin and uphold civil society.[34] Martyr adds a rather spurious harmonization of the conflicting theories of virtue proposed by Plato and Aristotle. Plato taught that the virtues were naturally implanted in man, whereas Aristotle insisted that the virtues are developed only gradually. Martyr deems that reason and experience side with Aristotle, but Plato's theory is valid if one looks at human nature as first created by God in His own image.[35]

Medieval Theology: Gabriel Biel and Late Medieval Nominalism, (Cambridge, Mass.: 1963), p. 59, attributes to Biel an opinion very close to that which Martyr attacks, but there is no evidence that Martyr ever read Biel.

[34] *Romanos*, 178.

[35] *Genesis*, f. 35v. Martyr's thoughts on man as the image of God can be usefully summarized here. This theme was very common among the Church Fathers, especially Augustine, and the Renaissance humanists (see Charles Trinkaus, *In Our Image and Likeness: Humanity and Divinity in Italian Humanist Thought*; (Chicago: 1970) I, xiii, xiv. The theme is based on the statement of Genesis (1:26): "Then God said, 'Let us make man in our image and likeness to rule over the fish in the sea, the birds of heaven, the cattle, all wild animals on earth, and all reptiles that crawl the earth.' " The theme is not as prominent in Martyr's thought as might be expected. Klaus Sturm's study, because it rests so heavily on Martyr's Genesis commentary, tends to overstress the importance of the *imago Dei* theme, pp. 205-07, 214, 215. Martyr gives several explanations of why man is the image of God. Both God and man find happiness in action and in contemplation. Man can produce offspring, just as God created the Universe (*Ethicorum*, 1, 2: *Genesis*, f. 23r).

Man is God's image chiefly because he rules over the animals just as God rules over the beasts. Martyr is rather unhappy with Augustine's famous psychological analogy as an explanation of man as the image of God. Augustine saw the three powers of the soul, memory, mind and will, as reflecting the three Persons of the Trinity. The three powers in one soul seemed to represent the three Persons in one nature; Augustine went on from there to try to explain the divine processions of Son and Holy Spirit by the analogy of man's psychological acts. Martyr is much more down to earth and explains that the three faculties of the soul do not so much themselves represent God as they are the sources of man's

Martyr devotes considerable attention to the classic problem of how original sin is transmitted. He points out that original sin is found first in the body as root and principle but flows over to occupy the soul also.[36] He reviews the major theories of the transmission of original sin proposed by earlier theologians. Martyr finds this a difficult question, one not necessary for salvation, and he endorses Augustine's recommendation that man should expend more effort on avoiding the consequences of original sin than on tracing its transmission.[37] Martyr spends no time on refuting the Pelagian view that original sin is not really hereditary but is merely passed on by bad example. Martyr first describes transducianism, the theory that somehow the child receives his soul as well as his body from his parents and that original sin is passed along as part of the soul. This was the view of Tertullian and received considerable support from Augustine. Martyr finds the arguments favoring transducianism probable but not conclusive.[38] Against transducianism is a philosophical difficulty. How can a spiritual substance which is simple be divided so that part of it can be passed over in procreation? Martyr does not see any scriptural arguments that can be raised against transducianism, but still he tends to favor the main alternative hypothesis which taught the direct creation of each soul by God. This view had largely replaced transducianism in the favor of theologians. If the soul is created when infused how

domination over the animals. Even then man's domination mirrors the divine domination only in so far as man is reborn and acts according to God's will. Unless man conforms his will to God, his domination is mere tyranny. Original sin destroyed for Adam and his posterity domination over the beasts and the lordship of creation. Martyr argues, however, that the restoration of grace through justification restores the image of God; it even partly restores man's domination over the beasts, as several biblical examples prove (*Genesis*, f. 6v; *Corinthios*, f. 286r; *Ethicorum*, 293). Even Adam's loss of grace obscures but does not entirely destroy the image of God in man. His natural knowledge remains intact. Man's physical body is in some sense the image of God, although only improperly since God is incorporeal. Bodily action, working as the soul's instrument, expresses similarities to God which lie hidden in the heart. Adam's body was also the image of God because God foresaw that the incarnate Word would have such a body (*Romanos*, 58; *Genesis*, f. 7r). Martyr did not draw from his notion of the body as the image of God those extreme conclusions that Calvin bitterly attacked in Osiander. See *Institutes*, I, xv, 3.

[36] *Romanos*, 179.

[37] *Romanos*, 152; *Corinthios*, 410r.

[38] Martyr wholly repudiates Augustine's view that the pleasure of sexual intercourse is somehow sinful and that this sinful pleasure results in or aids the transference of original sin. Marriage is holy, and sexual pleasure is not sinful *per se*. Original sin manifests itself not only in the disordered use of sex, but also in the desire for wealth, honor, revenge and the like.

does it come to have original sin? There were two explanations to this. According to one view God creates the kind of human soul that fallen man needs: a soul having original sin. Martyr rejects this opinion because it makes God the author of sin absolutely (*simpliciter*), because a soul so created would seem to differ in kind from that of Adam, and because God would contaminate the soul with sin even before it pertained to Adam.[39] For these reasons Martyr prefers the more widespread version of the direct creation hypothesis which taught that the soul is created sinless but becomes contaminated by original sin as soon as joined to a body which descends from Adam. The corruption of the newly created and infused soul flows from two sources. The soul itself does not possess the supernatural gifts with which God originally endowed Adam's soul. Moreover it animates a body which is cursed and which weighs the soul down and whose organs are unsuited to spiritual works.[40] One obvious objection to Martyr's poisition is that the material cannot act upon the spiritual and that therefore the body cannot corrupt the soul. Martyr counters that he does not teach that the body corrupts the soul, but rather that the body, already corrupted by original sin, resists the action of the soul since the soul no longer has the prelapsarian gifts which enabled it to rule the body. Rather the body now rules the soul. Moreover, the teaching of science indicates (*physicae rationes docent*) a sympathy between body and soul; for instance, a man's personality and temperament depends on how much yellow or black bile he has.[41]

Martyr is only marginally interested in how original sin actually affects man's psychological processes in the act of sin. His answer to this question relies heavily on Aristotle's explanation in the *Ethics* of how the incontinent man chooses vice or sin when his mind knows what is right. Aristotle answered that the incontinent man is overly attracted by the singular good which his senses present: the desire for the singular good so impresses the mind that it does not efficaciously consider the true good which it recognized previously. Martyr confirms this by quoting his favorite line of poetry:

Video meliora proboque, deteriora sequor

Man sees the good, yearns for it, and then does the evil because concupiscence blocks man's good aspirations. According to Martyr,

---

[39] *Romanos*, 153; *Samuelis*, f. 263r.
[40] *Romanos*, 153.
[41] *Romanos*, 185.

Aristotle understood this psychological enigma of sin when he wrote that the better part of the soul always urges man to choose the good, and that when man fails to do so, conscience reproaches him.[42]

For Martyr the depravity which original sin produces in man is a privation, not something positive. The privation in man resulting from original sin leaves its subject lamed, deformed. Man's soul retains its powers and actions, but these do not have their due rectitude and are therefore corrupt. Here again Pighius goes astray since he urges that man possesses his natural integrity minus only those supernatural gifts conferred on Adam. For Martyr original sin not only means a privation of nature but also brings a positive propensity for evil.[43]

The most important consequence that Vermigli draws from his teaching on original sin and human depravity is that the unregenerate cannot do acts pleasing to God, that all the acts of the unregenerate are sins, and that without grace man is necessitated to sin. Martyr makes no exceptions—for the unregenerate acts of kindness, of duty, of familial piety are all sinful, even if less gravely so than adultery or murder. For this dour conclusion Martyr gives many reasons. Sometimes his reasons are no more than a scriptual citation which seems to uphold his teaching, sometimes his reasons are ultimately based on scripture but proximately involve some theological reasoning. Martyr finds the ignorance of fallen man a block to performing acts pleasing to God. Moreover, original sin has produced not only an ignorance of the things of God but a positive repugnance to them, even as certain sicknesses pervert the taste so that the sick man cannot judge rightly about food and drink.[44] Besides this, original sin allows the devil to mix his suggestions into man's thoughts so that ethical reflection ceases to be a safe guide.[45] Even those actions which are otherwise good, fallen men credits not to God but to himself and thereby becomes puffed up with pride.[46] Martyr argues from scripture that the unregenerate are slaves of sin and for this reason cannot do

---

[42] *Romanos*, 27: The verse is from Ovid's *Metamorphoses*, VII, 21. Vergil is easily Martyr's favorite poet; he hardly ever quotes Ovid except for this one verse in which he sees a pagan confirmation of St. Paul's teaching in Romans, 7: 14-24.

[43] *Romanos*, 178: Deinde peccatum originis non solum dicimus esse hanc privationem, verum etiam comprehendere positiva: ut propensionem ad malum, naturae impetum contra Verbum Dei, et alia id genus.

[44] *Romanos*, 265, 585; *Corinthios*, f. 52v; *Defensio de Caelibatu*, 250.

[45] *Romanos*, 239.

[46] *Romanos*, 259.

anything pleasing to God; moreover, Christ says that nobody comes to him unless the Father draw him, that is, unless God give him grace.[47]

Martyr rejects the notion of good works preparatory to grace: either they are done after regeneration and are the fruit of the Gospel, or they are performed while man is still the slave of sin, and then their only fruit is death.[48] Martyr feels that the scholastic theologians come close to Pelagianism when they teach that man can by his natural powers keep the commandments as regards their substance even if not as regards the intention of the Lawgiver that they be done out of charity.[49] Martyr's favorite argument to show that all the acts of the unregenerate are sinful is based on the commandment in scripture to love God with one's whole heart and whole soul. In his commentary on Kings, Martyr devotes a seven page scholion to the question of whether man can love God with his whole heart in this life; Martyr concludes that he cannot. Since this is an absolute command touching all man's actions, which man never fulfills, all his actions are against the Law of God and are therefore sinful.[50] Vermigli admits that there are good works in so far as the regenerate have an incipient obedience to God, but even these are evil in so far as they fall short of God's commandments; therefore even the works of the regenerate are good in so far as they proceed from the Spirit working in man but evil in so far as they proceed from man himself. In this life man is never wholly regenerate. Man's partial spiritual rebirth and renovation through grace no more divides along the line of body/soul or inferior soul/ superior soul than does his corruption through original sin. The whole man is corrupted; the whole man is reborn, but not completely reborn —the carnal dynamic, man's propensity toward sin and away from God, is never totally eradicated in this life so that the old man and the new man live on together within the regenerate like water mixed with wine. The persistent concupiscence within man lies deeper than philosophers such as Aristotle ever guessed.[51] "Hence we can gather

---

[47] *Corinthios*, f. 52v.

[48] *Romanos*, 214.

[49] *Romanos*, 191, 276.

[50] The scholion is in *Melachim*, 12r-15r. Note especially f. 12r: . . . nos huic mandata satisfacere non posse. Nunc autem quando hebes est cognitio, amor quoque imperfectior est. Quare dum hic vivitur, non quantum lex exigit Deum amamus.

[51] *Melachim*, f. 13r: Quare dicat Aristotelis de rebus civilibus quicquid libuerit, ad Paulum nihil attinet eius disputatio; eum scribit mentem precari meliora

that there are two forms of carnal men. Some are totally and completely nothing but flesh so that they have nothing whatsoever of Christ. Others, although regenerate, still have even now very much of the flesh and therefore the Corinthians are still called carnal by Paul." [52]

Just as there are degrees of sinfulness among the unregenerate, so the regenerate are not all on the same level. Some strongly resist the temptations of their base passions and avoid crass sins; others put up a more feeble defense and succumb; for instance, David when he fell into adultery. But even the latter belong to the elect and therefore are restored by repentence. Both the regenerate and the unregenerate are beset by evil desires, but the regenerate give way only reluctantly and regretfully, whereas the unregenerate do so spontaneously. Sin reigns in the unregenerate and holds them captive at its beck and call. The justified at least struggle against sin even if they cannot wholly avoid it, but they cannot shake off completely the imperfection of fallen nature.[53] God must give man power both to will and to accomplish. The Pelagians were in serious error in thinking that man can begin a good action. Without God man can do nothing good.[54]

Martyr's teaching is open to an obvious objection: if the law to love God with one's whole heart absolutely cannot be accomplished, why is it proposed to man? Martyr answers that the purpose of the law is not to show what man can do, but what he ought to do. The Law of God has many purposes: to manifest sin, to illustrate real rectitude, to stir up man's conscience. Does God then demand the impossible? As regards the unregenerate, God does indeed demand the impossible. As regards the regenerate, an incipient obedience is possible but perfect obedience remains impossible. Only in heaven will man love God with his whole heart. On earth the remains of original sin will ever hinder perfect love of God. Martyr, of course, rejects the contention that the command to love God with the whole heart means only to love Him above everything else. This can be done, but is not loving with the whole heart.[55]

(sic). Deus longe diversam ab eo sententiam profert ac testatur figmentum humani cordis a pueritia malum esse.

[52] *Melachim*, f. 13r. Unde colligere possumus duplicem esse carnalium hominum formam. Aliqui enim, quanti quanti sunt, nihil aliud sunt quam caro ut qui nihil Christi penitus habeant. Alii vero quamvis renati sunt, attamen etiam nunc permultum carnis habent. Atque ita Corinthii adhuc a Paulo dicebantur carnales.

[53] *Melachim* f. 13r.

[54] *Melachim*, f. 13v: Ea est noster conditio dum hic vivitur.

[55] *Melachim*, f. 13v. Martyr argues that his position on the great commandment

Now that Martyr's thinking on the great commandment to love God has been examined, his understanding of the Law of Moses can be summarized briefly. The Law of Moses, of which the ten commandments are the most important part, is holy in itself but disastrous for man. The Law is holy because it teaches God's truth and has the Holy Spirit for its author. Without the Law man would have a very imperfect idea of true morality. Because original sin has clouded man's ethical thinking and has opened the door for the devil to insert false ethical ideas, reason has ceased to be a firm guide to right behavior. While the Old Testament makes it clear that men had some notion of right and wrong before Moses received the Law, this was very imperfect. Nevertheless the Law of Moses is a law of death and results only in greater sin for mankind, for the greater moral knowledge that the Law provides leads only to greater guilt because the Law provides no means of forgiveness for man's sins and no strength to overcome the weakness and depravity incurred by original sin. The purpose of the Law is not to justify man; rather the Law serves as an inducement to sin because man is evil and takes a special malign joy in doing what is forbidden simply because it is forbidden. Martyr uses a comparison to show how the Law reveals man's deformity: the Law is like a lamp which somebody brings into a dark place where deformed men hide their deformities from sight. The deformed curse the light-bearer, "Get out; do not deform us with your light." Light does not deform, but only manifests deformities already there. So too, the Law only manifests the depravities that already exist in fallen man.[56] Martyr's ideas on the Law largely parallel those of Luther, but the Law/Gospel contrast is not a fundamental category for Martyr's theology as it was for Luther's.

God as the Author of Sin

So far this chapter has made clear that Peter Martyr took a grim view of fallen human nature. But Martyr sees a still deeper level to the mystery of evil and sin. Sin exists in the world because God permits it; he even in some sense wills sin. Martyr does not think that the theologian can completely elucidate the mystery of sin, but the theologian is dutybound to search as far into this dark realm as the light of reason

---

to love God is Augustinian and cites many passages from Augustine to prove his claim. See also *Melachim*, f. 15r.

[56] *Romanos*, 156, 191, 228, 230, 239, 268, 271.

and divine revelation carry. When this light fails, he must fall silent in reverent awe before the majesty of God.[57]

The problem of God's authorship of sin is one that Martyr tackles repeatedly during his scripture commentaries. He first treated it at Oxford when lecturing on the Epistle to the Romans.[58] He returned to it briefly at Strasbourg in his commentary on Judges.[59] When he came to write his commentary on Samuel in Zurich he obviously felt that a much more thorough treatment was necessary. Early in his commentary he inserts a treatise of twelve folio pages entitled, "Is God the Author of Sin?" [60] He seems not to have been wholly satisfied with this effort because later in the same commentary he adds a twenty-one page treatise with the same title.[61] Martyr's last commentary, on Kings, summarizes the ideas developed in the Samuel commentaries.[62]

---

[57] *Romanos*, 35; *Samuelis*, f. 20v.

[58] *Romanos*, 35-37, 381, 480.

[59] *Iudicum*, f. 52rv.

[60] *Samuelis*, ff. 19r-24v: "An Deus Sit Author Peccati?"

[61] *Samuelis*, ff. 275r-285r. Martyr's teaching on this question, predestination, and free will brought him into conflict with the veteran professor Theodore Bibliander soon after arriving in Zurich. Martyr used his lectures on Samuel to attack Bibliander. See Schmidt, *Leben*, 215. Although Martyr's treatises on whether God is the author of sin do not mention Bibliander by name, they reflect Martyr's controversy with him. The controversy resulted in a hearing before the burgermeister that cost Bibliander his chair. There is an unverified story that Bibliander sought to duel Martyr with a double-edged axe! Much the best treatment of the controversy is that of Joachim Staedtke, "Der Züricher Prädestinationsstreit von 1560," *Zwingliana*, IX, 1953, 536-46. On the duel, see 544-45.

[62] *Melachim*, ff. 133rv, 178r. At the end of most editions of the *Loci Communes* there appear three short tracts entitled "De Libero Arbitrio," "An Deus sit Causa et Author Peccati?" and "De Providentia et Praedestinatione". (*Loci*, 989-95). I have not used them in preparing this study, partly because they add nothing new to Martyr's teaching, partly because their authorship is bitterly disputed. Among others, McLelland, *Visible Words*, 264, and Schmidt, *Leben*, 107, 215-16, deny that Martyr wrote them and attribute them to Bullinger. Peter Walser, *Die Prädestination bei Heinrich Bullinger*, (Zurich, 1957), shows conclusively that they cannot be by Bullinger and urges Martyr's authorship. Walser, 204, points out that the definitions of predestination and reprobation given in the disputed tract on providence and predestination, *Loci*, 993, agree almost word for word with those Martyr gives elsewhere, *Loci*, 449, 451. Thomas Brassel in a short note, "Drei umstrittene Traktate Peter Martyr Vermiglis," proclaimed Walser's conclusions as certain: *Zwingliana*, XI, 1962, p. 476. Brassel offered no new evidence and made a number of minor mistakes. These were immediately attacked by Joachim Staedtke, "Drei umstrittene Traktate Peter Martyr Vermiglis," *Zwingliana*, XI, 1962, pp. 553-54, who denied Bullinger's authorship but refused to accept Martyr's as proven and declared the authorship of the disputed tracts an open question. My reading of the tracts has convinced me that their close parallels both in thought and phrase with Martyr's certain writings makes Martyr's authorship unquestionable,

The Samuel commentary presents Martyr's most mature reflections on the subject. It is much longer and more complex than the Romans treatment, which used the literary vocabulary and metaphorical, non-philosophical concepts of the Bible to stress God's sovereignty, even to the hardening of sinners' hearts. The Samuel commentary employs more philosophical vocabulary and exploits certain scholastic concepts, particularly those of privation, concurrence, *causa removens prohibens*, and the distinction between the divine *voluntas signi* and *voluntas bene-placiti*. These additions allow Martyr to stress God's justice and sanctity without down-playing his sovereignty.

The summary here combines the two scholia in the Samuel commentary. The basic thesis is the same in both: "that God is not *per se* and properly the cause of sin: secondly that nothing happens in the world not, even sins themselves, outside his will and choice or providence." [63] Martyr rejects the interpretation of scripture that has God merely permitting sin; on the contrary, when scripture says that God hardens sinners, this should be taken literally: God is the cause of the sinful acts, but the actions are good in so far as they proceed from God, although evil in so far as they proceed from human perversity.[64]

After this general statement Martyr goes down to particulars. He clarifies two preliminaries. First, what is sin? Earlier Martyr defined

---

as I demonstrate in "Three Disputed Vermigli Tracts" which will appear in the forthcoming *Festschrift* for Myron Gilmore.

[63] *Samuelis*, f. 277r: Deum non esse per se et propriam causam peccati; alteram, nihil in mundo fieri nec etiam peccata ipsa praeter illius voluntatem et arbitrium seu providentiam.

[64] *Samuelis*, f. 276rv. *Romanos*, 37, 381, 480. Martyr felt that his doctrine on this question squared with that of the main Protestant spokesmen. After citing statements from Augustine and Ambrose supporting his teaching, Martyr continues: "Alii ab illis non dissentiunt: Zwingli et Lutherus, reformatae religionis heroes, Oecolampadius, Bucerus, Calvinus. Possem alios adducere sed non suffragatoribus ago" (*Samuelis*, f. 285r). Martyr's treatment of God as the author of sin seems dependent on the *De Providentia* of "Zwinglius, piae memoriae, vir doctus et constans" (*Loci*, 103) which Martyr cites repeatedly. Still there is some need of caution in assessing Zwingli's real influence. Martyr wrote these pages in Zurich with an eye to his controversy with Bibliander. The invocation of Zwingli clearly advances a claim to be the true inheritor of the Zurich tradition against a professor who had been teaching there since 1532. After pointing out that most of the leading Protestant divines teach a doctrine similar to his about God's authorship of sin, Martyr points out one theologian who has left the true path on this point: "venerabilem virum Philippum Melanchthon quem amo et suscipio." Martyr cites with approval the teaching on this subject in the earlier editions of Melanchthon's *Loci Communes*, but the later editions have gone astray. *Samuelis*, f. 285r. Obviously Martyr studied Melanchthon's *Loci Communes* carefully.

sin as whatever opposed God's law, but now he offers a new definition that stresses its negative character and eases the problem of explaining God's authorship: sin is the privation of the justice man should have.[65] He points out that a privation, such as blindness, must be distinguished from its subject. Man is born a sinner, a child of wrath, lacking the justice of God.[66]

For Martyr God is the cause of sin only as a *causa removens prohibens*, that is, a cause in the sense of some one or something that removes an obstruction which previously prevented something from happening. Martyr gives the example of a helmsman: when the helmsman is removed, the waves cause a shipwreck. A modern example that might be clearer is somebody who switches on a light. He does not cause the electricity—a generator does that. He merely removes a block in the electrical circuit so that the flow of electricity causes the light to shine. God's grace holds in check man's depraved nature which has a constant propensity toward sin. God, by ceasing to supply man with the grace that keeps him from sin, acts as the *causa removens prohibens* of sin. Nobody has a claim to God's grace; he is free to give it or withhold it just as he pleases. Whatever evils come to man are less than he really deserves since all mankind is a mass of curruption. It is pure mercy that God chooses to save some from the corrupt mass; indeed man would have no just complaint even if God saved nobody.[67] Martyr cites the scholastics' opinion that even if man were immune from sin, still God would not be bound to give man grace.[68]

---

[65] *Samuelis*, f. 19r.

[66] *Samuelis*, ff. 19rv, 276v.

[67] *Samuelis*, f. 19v.

[68] *Samuelis*, f. 19v: Universa humani generis massa corrupta est in Adamo; ex ea Deus aliquos pro sua misericordia eruit, et si neminem inde liberaret, tamen crudelitatis accersiri non potest. Toti enim sunt homines in sua stirpe corrupti. Deinde cum hic vitam exigunt, alia peccata nativae corruptioni adiiciunt. Nihil ergo est cur queramur, cum gratia destituimur, nos indigne tractari. Quin scholastici iam dictis hoc etiam adiecerunt: quod natura nostra etiamsi ab omni peccato esset prorsus immunis, tamen Deum non fore obstrictum, ut nos favore et gratia sua ornaret, sed illos mitto quia me iuvat loqui de rebus ut iam sunt. Quod enim illi fingunt iam esse non potest, ut scilicet natura sit omnis corruptionis immunis. Id vero nobis oportet omnino constare, Deum cum suos electos gratia prosequitur id ex mera puraque misericordia facere et reprobos cum destituuntur, indignos fuisse quos gratia sua complecteretur, cum in ipsis causa sit cur ita reiiciantur ita ut nihil habeant quod possint iuste conqueri.

Martyr's reluctance to entertain considerations within God's *potentia absoluta* should be noted. On this point Calvin is even more vehement. Writing of himself in his *Brevis Responsio Io. Calvini ad Diuendas Nebulonis Cuiusdam Calumnias Quibus Doctrinam de Aeterna Dei Praedestinatione Foedare Conatus Est*, 1557, *Opera Calvini*, IX, c. 259, Calvin notes: "Passim Calvinus commentum de absoluta Dei potentia,

There is another angle from which Martyr must approach God's causality: since God is pure act and the first cause, no creature can act unless the first cause moves it to action. Still, God causes each object to act according to its nature and preserves the integrity of secondary causes. When God causes a good object to act, the object moves with a good act; but when the object is depraved, it moves with a corrupt act. The evil of the action must not be attributed to the highest cause but restricted to the corrupt secondary cause.[69] To illustrate this, Martyr uses the analogy of a man with an injured shinbone who walks with a limp. The limp, in so far as it is an action, comes from the motive power of the soul; but in so far as it is lame and defective it depends upon the injured shinbone. So too God's act of concurrence, when it moves man to act through his depraved soul, is not evil as it comes from God. The evil is confined to the secondary cause.[70]

Martyr further argues that the concurrence from God works differently in good and evil actions. It works only obliquely in the production of evil acts, for what God suggests is good but results in sin because the concurrence operates on evil men. In the production of good acts, God not only suggests but effects the good. Even in evil actions God limits the evil within bounds, for God's providence governs evil as well as good.[71]

Martyr next turns his attention to the act of the human will which produces evil. God does not act simply through the will; the will itself acts. But what does it mean to say that both God and the human will produce the result? Does God produce the whole result, and the will also the whole result, or do each produce part? Martyr responds with a distinction between action and effect. Without God the human will cannot *per se* produce the action. Martyr admits that God in his *potentia absoluta* could cause the total action, but he is concerned about

---

quod in scholis suis ventilant sophistae, acriter repudiat et detestabile esse asserit: quia ab aeterna Dei sapientia et iustitia separari non debeat potestas."

[69] *Samuelis*, ff. 20r, 280v. Nec tamen hoc negari potest Deum, cum sit (ut loquuntur philosophi) actus purus. . . . Itaque omnia perpetuo incitat, movet, et impellit. Sed quamvis motus rerum omnium sit a Deo, attamen singula etiam ex naturae suae principiis moventur. Et cuius rei principia sana fuerint, ea res utique bono et sano motu agitatur, et cuius e diverso fuerint depravata, ea corrupto motu et vitiato permovetur. Neque ad altissimam et primam causam eius motus referenda, verum ad singularia principia corruptioni obnoxia, unde profectus est accommodabitur. *Samuelis*, f. 20r.

[70] *Samuelis.*, 280v. Luther uses the same argument, *De Servo Arbitrio*, *W.A.*, *XVIII*, 709. For the example of lameness, compare *S.T.*, I, 49, 2.

[71] *Samuelis*, 279v.

the real world of God's *potentia ordinata*. God wills to work with creatures as co-agents. Hence neither God nor the creature are the total cause of the *action*. But God and the will each cause the total *effect*, although conjoined in action. For an analogy to show this Martyr calls on his philosophical psychology: in human action both will and intellect work together. The will produces the whole effect, but so does the intellect. The will is proximate cause, the intellect is remote cause. So God and the human will produce the total effect, one as the primary cause, the other as secondary cause. [72]

Martyr's explanation of the causality of sin so far has assigned God and the creature as the cause of the action, but the creature alone is the cause of the evil, the lack of goodness. The concurrence as it comes from God is good, but being received in sinful man produces sin; but this explanation is, as Martyr points out, inadequate to explain Adam's sin since Adam was not sinful as created but adorned with grace. God could have kept Adam from sinning by supplying him with greater grace than he did. Adam had sufficient grace to avoid sin had he acted diligently. Human reason here queries, why does God give some men more, others less grace? Why does God now help a given man more, now less? Martyr answers simply that God is free to distribute grace as he wishes. No reason can be given beyond God's free decision for individual instances of God's uneven distribution of grace, but Martyr

---

[72] *Samuelis*, f. 280v: ... nunc de actu ex voluntate nostra erumpente agimus. Unde recte dicitur privationem rectitudinis non sequi opus voluntatis nostrae et motum eius quatenus est in genere naturae sed ut est in genere motus. Augustinus *De Civitate Dei*, libro septimo, cap. 30 dicit Deum sic administrare creaturas ut illae proprios motus exercere et coagere sinat. Non enim solus agit Deus, sed pravi, ut supra dixi, et diabolus suam malitiam in agendo adhibent. Sed cum dicimus actum ipsum qui postea vitio nostro malus est a causa suprema, id est Deo, et nobis, id est voluntate nostra, produci, quomodo id accipiemus? An quod Deus totum faciat et nos totum? An quod ille partem et nos partem? Atque hic productionem contrahimus ad ipsum actum voluntatis nostrae. Respondetur, si ratio toti (sic: totius) referatur ad causam, uno modo est dicendum; si referatur ad effectum, aliter. Si totum referamus ad causam, ita ut intelligamus voluntatem nostram totam causam actionis esse, ut per se absque Deo possit producere, verum non est. Quia nisi Deus innueret, non posset actionem edere; ita Deus etsi absoluta potentia sua per seipsum opus facere posset, tamen ut est cursus rerum, non vult solus agere, sed vult creaturam coagentem habere. Hoc pacto nec voluntas nec Deus dicuntur tota causa. At si ad effectum ipsum referatur, Deus et voluntas causa sunt plena. Nam Deus et voluntas totum effectum faciunt, licet coniungantur in actione. Exemplo rem ostendam. Ad actionem producendam, voluntatem habemus et intelligentiam; et voluntas totum effectum facit, et intelligentia est causa totius effectus. Sed una est propinqua, altera est remotior. Ita est de voluntate et Deo: ipsa totum facit et Deus totum facit, sed una causa est prima, altera secundaria.

sees certain general arguments why God distributes grace unevenly. Should God help all equally, men would conclude that they acted virtuously due to their own strength and thereby become proud. God wants man to recognize his liberality and wants men to pray for his help. [73]

Martyr interprets the biblical statement (1 Tim. 2 : 4) that God wills all men to be saved not in the sense that God desires every individual's salvation, but in the sense that God wants to save some individuals from all sorts and classes of men. [74] An obvious objection to his teaching is the scriptual statement that God wishes the life and not the death of the sinner. To answer this objection Martyr adopts the scholastic distinction between the divine *voluntas signi* and *voluntas beneplaciti* (also called the *voluntas efficax*). The *voluntas signi* teaches men what to do and what to avoid. But much in reality happens contrary to the *voluntas signi*, whereas nothing happens contrary to the divine efficacious will, or *voluntas beneplaciti*. God wills the life of the sinner and that he not perish with his *voluntas signi*, just as he wills that man keep the commandments and so forth. But the divine efficacious will does desire the death of the sinner. God is the potter who has made some pots for glory, some for ignominy. It is the efficacious will that rules and governs man's wicked desires and sins and that gives man over to his own perversity. [75]

Martyr's last scripture commentary, on the two Books of Kings, returns once again to God's authorship of sin. It summarizes the doctrine found in the Samuel commentary but adds three points. First, it connects the problem of human sin with the problem of how the human will is free. Secondly, Martyr frankly confesses that all men are not given sufficient grace for salvation even though they hear the external preaching of the gospel and are inwardly given some grace. [76] Martyr's denial of sufficient grace gave him a simple, clear, and pure position, but the price was high for it entails what many will deem a very harsh doctrine of predestination. The third new point investigates why the Gospel is preached if it is not to save sinners. The preaching of the Word is for the predestined. They hear it, believe, and are justified. They recognize from the obstinacy of the reprobate who refuse to believe how corrupt human nature is as a result

---

[73] *Samuelis*, f. 20v. *Romanos*, 35.
[74] *Corinthios*, f. 58r; *Samuelis*, f. 282r; *Loci*, 467.
[75] *Samuelis*, ff. 20v-22r. Compare Aquinas, *S.T.*, I, 23, 4 and 3.
[76] *Melachim*, f. 133r.

of Adam's sin. The predestined also recognize that the only reason they too are not obdurate in sin is the grace of Christ, and recognizing this they cultivate modesty and humility and give thanks for the grace they have received. The very obstinacy of the reprobate proves a spiritual help to the elect. Besides this, God wants his Word preached to all because he wishes the elect and the reprobate to live in this world without their being distinguishable by human reason. Human reason finds God's decision to punish rather than to pity the unregenerate an open affront because reason tries to make God's justice parallel with human justice. But there is no parallel or basis of comparison. Sinners are necessitated but not forced to sin (a distinction the next chapter will explain when treating freedom). They sin willingly and rejoice in their wickedness and do not refrain from those sins that lie within their power to avoid.[77]

This chapter has presented Peter Martyr's theological anthropology as it relates to fallen man. The course of this presentation has made clear beyond all doubt that while many specific points in Martyr's theological thought on fallen, sinful man can be traced back to Aristotle and the medieval scholastics, the major elements of his thought are unquestionably Augustinian, but not simply Augustinian. Augustinianism is a sprawling mansion of many wings built up over many centuries. Martyr is in the same wing as Bucer, Calvin, Beza, and Zanchi. His emphasis on total depravity and predestination clearly indicate that he belongs in the Reformed tradition.

---

[77] Melachim, 133v. Martyr also treats God's authorship of sin in *Iudicum*, f. 52rv and *Melachim*, f. 178r. As these passages add nothing, they have been omitted from consideration.

CHAPTER SIX

MAN IN GOD'S SAVING PLAN

The previous chapter traced Martyr's teaching on the human condition enslaved by sin. But God from eternity has determined to rescue some men from their enslavement; these he predestines to eternal life, justifies and aids by his grace, then glorifies and reunites them to their risen bodies. The rest of men he leaves to the consequences of their sin.

Predestination

The most important doctrine in Martyr's theology is his teaching on predestination. Predestination is not the central doctrine of Martyr's theology, as was pointed out earlier, because Martyr himself states clearly that the master truth of Christianity is that Christ suffered for men so that through him they might receive forgiveness of their sins.[1] This master truth, however, is the common patrimony of all Christian theologians in the sixteenth century and gives no distinctive cast to Martyr's theology. Martyr's teaching on predestination is distinctive and affects his whole theology.[2] It exerts an important influence on the

---

[1] *Romanos*, 565. Klaus Sturm (pp. 189-90) insists that during Martyr's first period at Strasbourg predestination was not one of Martyr's fundamental dogmas. This was certainly not the case during Martyr's mature years as a Protestant. Anne Jacobson Schutte has suggested to me that the stress that Italian Calvinists such as Vermigli and Zanchi put on predestination may stem in part from their psychological conviction of having been chosen by God's peculiar favor from the *massa damnata* of the Roman Church in Italy.

[2] It was long fashionable to make predestination the central dogma in Calvin's theology, but most recent scholarship has challenged that view. See Wendel, 265-69, and Wilhelm Niesel, *The Theology of Calvin*, trans. Harold Knight, (London: 1956), 159, 9-20. An important element in this re-appraisal has been greater emphasis on the precise point at which Calvin discusses predestination in the later editions of the *Institutes*. From 1559 onwards Calvin treats predestination after sanctification and justification. See Wendel, 265-69. Otto Gründler finds a strong argument for predestination being Zanchi's central doctrine because he treats it in his doctrine of God. See his *Gotteslehre*, 22, 23. Although Martyr connects predestination with providence, no arguments can be drawn from the position of predestination in the *Loci Communes* since he was not responsible for the order of the *Loci*. His main treatise on the subject originally came after the ninth chapter of his Romans commentary; its position there simply reflects the fact that chapters eight and nine of Romans are the chief biblical passages on predestination.

development of the Reformed tradition; over a century ago Charles Schmidt stated that after Calvin, Martyr did more than anybody else to establish the doctrine of predestination.[3] Chapter VII of this book will assemble evidence to show the influence of Martyr's teaching on predestination.

Predestination is a theme to which Martyr recurs frequently in his writings, but his most important treatise on the subject is a long appendix to chapter nine of his commentary on Romans. It very likely dates from not later than 1552, perhaps from 1551. Martyr describes it in a letter to Bullinger in November, 1553. The treatise did not appear in print until 1558 when the rest of Martyr's commentary on Romans was published.[4]

The most important sources of Martyr's treatise are obviously the Pauline epistles and St. Augustine's anti-Pelagian writings to which Martyr appeals on almost every page. Martyr's medieval and contemporary sources are not so easily pinned down; the only contemporaris Martyr mentions are Pighius and Erasmus who figure as adversaries

---

[3] Schmidt, *Leben*, 106.

[4] "You will perceive the nature of what I have taught [upon predestination], as soon as I shall have published my commentaries on the Romans, which I shall do this year." Martyr from Strasbourg to Bullinger, November 3, 1553. *Original Letters Relative to the English Reformation*, edited by Hastings Robinson for the Parker Society, (Cambridge: 1847), II, 507. According to Schmidt, *Leben*, 106, Martyr began the Romans lectures in 1550; about a year should be allowed for him to have covered the nine chapters which precede the treatise on predestination. It is noteworthy that no specific outside agent forced Martyr to take up and develop the question of predestination as Jerome Bolsec forced Calvin to do. Despite Martyr's pledge to Bullinger, the Romans commentary did not appear until published at Basel by Perna in 1558. The delay was probably because Martyr and especially his friend Jerome Zanchi found themselves at odds with the Lutheran pastors at Strasbourg over the eucharist and predestination. Martyr probably wanted to avoid further trouble. By the time the commentary appeared, Martyr was teaching at Zurich. Martyr's choice of a Basel publisher may be significant, since several of his works had previously appeared at Zurich. Sergio Corda has suggested to me that Martyr chose Basel, where censorship was lax, because of possible opposition to his strong views on predestination at Zurich.

The presentation of Martyr's doctrine of predestination that follows concentrates on the Romans commentary and deliberately ignores the 1561 memorial on predestination that Martyr wrote on behalf of the Zurich divines. Many of these had a less developed and milder view than Martyr, which he had to allow for in the joint memorial. The signers were Martyr, Bullinger, Gualter, Wolf, Simler, Lavater, W. Haller, Wick and Ulrich Zwingli. A full discussion of the history and content of the memorial is given by Peter Walser, *Die Prädestination bei Heinrich Bullinger im Zusammenhang mit seiner Gotteslehre*, (Zurich: 1957), 181-193.

rather than sources. Among medieval theologians Gregory of Rimini is the most likely source. Gregory reasserted the strong and somber views of Augustine against the Semipelagian tendencies in many late medieval scholastics. As has been shown, Martyr was familiar with the writings of both Aquinas and Duns Scotus; both soften a bit the teaching of Augustine, but neither can fairly be called Pelagian since they deny that foreseen merits are a cause of predestination.[5] Several points of agreement with Aquinas, which are probably instances of direct borrowing, will be pointed out in the analysis of Martyrs' doctrine that follows.

Martyr's debt to previous Protestant theologians is difficult to assess. At first blush the obvious source of his teaching would seem to be John Calvin, whose very name suggests a stern doctrine of predestination to the popular mind, but there is evidence that Calvin's influence was not paramount. This evidence is partly a matter of chronology: If Martyr's main treatise on predestination, that in the Romans commentary, was completed by 1552, as I have urged, then it cannot be dependent on Calvin's major treatments of predestination. Calvin wrote the *Congregation sur l'election eternelle* against Jerome Bolsec in 1551 but published it in 1562. In 1552 he attacked Pighius in his *De Aeterna Dei Praedestinatione*, a bit late probably for Martyr to have received and assimilated it in England. The early editions of the *Institutes* contain the main lines of Calvin's doctrine, but its great elaboration and reworking came in the edition of 1559.[6] "While (Calvin) never ceases, in discussions of the most various questions, to repeat the great themes of the freedom of God and his glory and of the divinity of Christ, he only very rarely speaks of predestination except on the four chapters that are devoted to it in the edition of 1559."[7] This does not mean that the main lines of Calvin's doctrine were not available to Martyr. Calvin published a lesser work, *De Praedestinatione et Providentia Dei* in 1550, but this antedated his quarrel over reprobation with Bolsec and the full development of his thought on the subject. Whether Martyr saw it in England is doubtful. Calvin's doctrine of double predestination is present in his *Catechism* and his commentary on Romans. Both were available before 1552, and Martyr

---

[5] Thomas, *Summa Theologiae*, I, 23, 4; Duns Scotus, In Sententiarum, I, dist. 41, 10 and 11. Martyr claims that Aquinas teaches justification by faith alone in his commentary on Galatians, *Loci*, 564.

[6] Wendel, 264-68.

[7] Wendel, 264-65.

even states in the preface of his own commentary on Romans that he has read Calvin's commentary. But neither Calvin's *Cathechism* nor his verse by verse commentary on Romans contains anything like Martyr's elaborate and systematic treatise on predestination. More important than chronology in countering an over-hasty estimate of Calvin's influence are two letters Martyr wrote to Calvin from Zurich, one in July 1557 and the other in April 1558. In each letter Martyr states that he has just read with great joy a work of Calvin dealing with predestination and indicates the close agreement between his teaching and that of Calvin. In the second letter he points out that his own commentary on Romans, containing an extensive treatment of predestination, has been at the printers for several months, but Martyr gives not the slighest hint that his teaching on predestination has been borrowed from Calvin.[8]

---

[8] On July 1, 1557, Martyr wrote to inform Calvin about the opening stages of his quarrel with Bibliander. The previous week Bibliander had taken up the question of predestination and "quaedam auditorio proposuit ab hac veritate plurimum aliena." Martyr used the rejection of Saul by God in the first book of Samuel which he was then lecturing on as a point of departure to answer Bibliander. Martyr also thanks Calvin for sending him a small book or pamphlet on predestination. "Libellum abs te mihi transmissum gratissimo animo accepi et magna cum volutate legi. Nam praeterea quod illa defensio ad honorem Dei et ad orthodoxam fidem tuendam attinet, mihi quoque esse communem sentio. Nam ea in re, quemadmodum in caeteris dogmatis religionis, facio tecum qui fit ut defensio tua meum sit patrocinium." This letter strangely is not printed in the *Opera Calvini*. I have used the text given by Johann H. Hottinger, *Historiae Ecclesiasticae Novi Testamenti*, (Zurich: 1667), VIII, 829. Hottinger's date July 1, 1517 is an obvious misprint; Staedtke, 543, quotes a few lines of the letter and gives the correct date. The second letter to Calvin, April 21, 1558, contains this important passage: "Atque ad hanc meam voluntatem aliud accedit, nempe superioribus diebus summa perlegisse quam edisti lucubrationem pro tuenda aeterna salvifica Dei Opt. Max. praedestinatione. Proinde cum ea lectione fuerim admodum recreatus, par et aequum existimavi gratias tibi agere: nec dubito labori quo ad electos ac praedestinatos ad aeternam vitam a Deo ad cuius gloriam susceptus fuit, iustum uberemque fructum iri. Ego quoque in istam eandem sententiam permulta colligeram in commentario meo Epistolae ad Romanos quem ante aliquot menses imprimendum Petro Pernae Basileam miseram; qui tamen liber iis nundinis absolvere non potuit. Quod idcirco nunc significo, quo tibi fidem faciam, ex animo et iusta causa, me tuo scripto non vulgariter gavisum esse." *Loci*, 1117; also printed in the *Opera Calvini*, XVII, c. 144. A further difficult question arises. Which works on predestination by Calvin do these letters refer to? Schmidt is usually a careful scholar on such questions. He is acquainted with both letters and believes (*Leben*, 216) both refer to the same work: *Calumniae nebulonis cuiusdam, quibus odio gravare conatus est doctrinam J. Calvini de occulta Dei providentia . . . responsio*. In doing this he makes at least two blunders, and his solution is quite unacceptable. He dates the *Calumniae . . . de . . . providentia* 1557, but the last sentence of the work itself names January 1558. He also dates the second letter of Martyr to Calvin as April 21, *1557* instead of 1558 and there-

There are several other Protestant theologians whose influence on Martyr's doctrine of predestination might have surpassed that of Calvin. While Martyr admired Melanchthon, he felt that the later editions of the German's *Loci Communes* were soft on the area of grace and predestination.[9] Martyr certainly read Luther's *De Liberto Arbitrio*, which teaches a strong doctrine of predestination; probably even more influential are Zwingli and especially Bucer. Martyr read with approval Zwingli's *De Providentia* as early as the period of his conversion to Protestantism at Naples, and he praises it in his Zurich writings nearly a decade after the predestination tract in the Romans commentary. The *locus classicus* for Zwingli's doctrine of predestination is Chapter VI of the *De Providentia*. The most recent study of Zwingli's teaching concludes that he was a thorough-going predestinationist.[10] But if the main lines of Martyr's and Zwingli's teaching coincide, there are noteworthy differences. Martyr's teaching generally stands closer to Calvin's than to Zwingli's. Like Calvin, Martyr connects predestination with God's sovereignty, while Zwingli connects it

---

fore inverts the order of the two letters. Since the first letter antedates the *Calumniae ... de ... providentia*, it cannot refer to it. I think it refers to a different work with a similar title but published in 1557 (Geneva: Crespin): *Brevis responsio Joannis Calvini ad diluendas nebulonis cuiusdam calumnias, cuibus doctrinam de aeterna Dei praedestinatione foedare conatus est*. This work has been identified as belonging to Martyr's library: see Ganoczy, *Bibliothèque*, 207. Does the second letter, April 21, 1558, refer to the same work? I think it most improbable. Why two letters months apart thanking Calvin for a brief work of a half dozen pages? Martyr says that he read a work *superioribus diebus* (hence a fairly lengthy book) *pro tuenda aeterna salvifica Dei Opt. Max. praedestinatione* (seemingly an allusion to the title or at least the subject matter). Martyr compares Calvin's work to the treatise on predestination in his own Romans commentary. This can refer to neither of the works above, but dovetails perfectly with Calvin's *De Aeterna Dei Praedestinatione* of 1552. Both Martyr's and Calvin's treatises are their major work on the subject, and both are directed against Pighius. This identification is confirmed by the fact that Martyr's library possessed a copy of Calvin's *De Aeterna Dei Praedestinatione*; see Ganoczy, *Bibliothèque*, 206. The conclusion from all of this is that Martyr did not read Calvin's major treatment of predestination until years after the composition of his own treatise and months after it went to press. Both letters to Calvin express close doctrinal agreement with Calvin, but neither indicates a doctrinal debt to him. Had there been a debt, Martyr would have likely expressed it. This is obviously not an air-tight argument from silence, but it points to a strong probability that the major source for Martyr's teaching on predestination was not John Calvin.

[9] *Samuelis*, f. 285r.

[10] Gottfried Locher, *Huldrych Zwingli in Neuer Sicht*, "Die Prädestinationslehre Huldrych Zwingli", (Zurich: 1969), 105-125. Martyr cites and praises the *De Providentia* in his 1560 lecture on free will, *Loci*, 976, 982. Also *Samuelis*, f. 279r. Martyr read the *De Providentia* in Naples, McNair, 149.

more with His mercy and goodness. There is a tendency, albeit held in check, in Zwingli toward universal salvation; Martyr never experienced that temptation. Zwingli develops his doctrine of predestination as a subordinate part of his teaching on divine providence. Providence is important for Martyr too, but not nearly as important as predestination. Martyr's teaching keeps as close as possible to and seems to arise out of the text of scripture and appeals frequently to the Fathers, especially to Augustine. The whole atmosphere of the *De Providentia Dei* owes more to speculative natural theology than to the Bible. The charges of rationalism that are sometimes hurled against Zwingli usually point to the *De Providentia Dei* as evidence. Only after Zwingli has spent the first four and a half pages of Chapter VI setting out the main lines of his predestination doctrine does he write, "Now we come to the witness of scripture."[11] Scripture seems more a confirmation than the source of Zwingli's teaching.

For these reasons Martyr's teaching on predestination probably owed far more to Bucer than to Zwingli. The preface of Martyr's commentary on Romans implies familiarity with Bucer's commentary on that epistle. The preface to Bucer's Romans commentary gives his most elaborate statement on predestination. The importance of predestination for Bucer is beyond question; the most recent study puts it quite simply: "The doctrine of predestination or election is one that shapes the whole of Bucer's theology. Even where it is not expressed explicitly, its stamp is to be found. The centrality of this doctrine and the way Bucer interprets it distinguish him from Luther on the one hand, and from his catholic and radical opponents on the other."[12] Martyr's doctrine agrees with Bucer's on all basic points, even if emphases vary a bit. Bucer's influence on Calvin's doctrine of predestination has long been recognized.[13] I think that the similarities between Martyr's teaching and that of Calvin result less from any borrowings Martyr made from Calvin than from a parallel development of the heritage they both shared from Bucer as well as from Augustine and Paul.

---

[11] "Nunc ad scripturae testimonia imus." *Hulrici Zwinglii Opera*, ed. M. Schuler and J. Schulthess, IV, 115. My remarks on Zwingli are based partly on Locher, partly on my own reading of the *De Providentia Dei*.

[12] W. P. Stephens, *The Holy Spirit in the Theology of Martin Bucer*, (Cambridge: 1970), 23. The first two chapters of this book provide the best treatment of Bucer's teaching on predestination. Schmidt, *Leben*, 63, also stresses Bucer's influence on Martyr's doctrine of predestination but over-emphasizes Calvin's role.

[13] See Wendel, 264-82, passim.

Martyr's treatise on predestination begins by defending the propriety of discussing predestination at all, since the doctrine that all men are already pre-ordained to heaven or hell might seem to engender apathy or spiritual sloth. Of what use can zeal, prayer, and preaching be if the number of the elect is already fixed? To answer these objections Martyr draws on St. Augustine's *De Dono Perseverantiae* and *De Correptione et Gratia*. A denial of predestination involves a denial of God's foreknowledge. More importantly, the doctrine of predestination makes it impossible for man to glory in himself and leads him to glorify God. Without the doctrine of predestination there cannot be a satisfactory defense either of divine grace against the Pelagian exaltation of human merit or of the gratuity of justification.[14] For Martyr the great themes of Protestant theology, *sola fide* and *solo Deo gloria*, find their logical culmination in the doctrine of predestination. To the allegation that the doctrine of predestination leads men to despair, Martyr retorts that instead it provides rich consolation that should be given to all, learned and unlearned alike, according to their varying capacities. Predestination teaches Christians that their salvation does not depend upon their own feeble strength but upon God's unshakable decree. Predestination increases trust in God and provides great joy.[15]

Martyr points out that no Christian has ever flatly denied the doctrine of predestination, but many have tried to empty it of meaning, especially Albert Pighius. Pighius emphasizes that God lives in an eternal present so that there is no past or future with him; hence God is always foreknowing and predestining, and therefore each person has it is in his power to determine how God will foreknow and predestine him. Martyr utterly scorns this taking refuge in God's eternal present because God is even now predestining men yet unborn.[16]

---

[14] *Loci*, 444-45: While preparing notes on the predestination and justification treatises, I did not have access to the Latin edition of the Romans commentary. I have therefore used the reprint of these treatises in the *Loci Communes*.

[15] *Loci*, 445-46. Melanchthon was one of those who thought that meditation on predestination could lead to despair. See Wendel, 269-70. That the teaching of predestination might involve despair was brought home vividly to the leading Reformed theologians by the case of Francesco Spiera, an Italian converted to the Reformed faith. Apprehended by the Inquisition at Venice, he recanted. After his release he fell into complete despair and considered himself among the reprobate. In this attitude he died. Martyr recounts his case in the treatise on predestination and argues that Spiera's fear of reprobation was groundless and merely subjective (*Loci*, 460). Calvin wrote a whole tract on the Spiera case.

[16] *Loci*, 446-47.

In defining predestination Martyr follows his usual procedure. After discussing the uses and meaning of the Greek word in the Bible for predestination, Martyr refines the concept by distinguishing it from foreknowledge. Predestination differs from mere foreknowledge since it includes the divine will as well as the divine intellect. Predestination also differs from providence: providence directs things to their natural ends, whereas predestination directs men to salvation, a supernatural end. Providence is God's ordination and unchangeable and perpetual administration of all things.[17] Martyr rejects any indentification of providence with fate, at least if fate is understood as some astral determinism. The concept of fate is admissible if understood as a conjunction of secondary causes subordinate to God's will. Martyr provides the scriptural foundation for belief in providence and avers that a denial of providence involves a denial of either the divine knowledge, or power, or goodness. Finally Martyr gives his formal definition of predestination: "the most wise resolve of God by which he has steadfastly decreed before all eternity to call those he has loved in Christ to the adoption of sons, to justification by faith, and finally to glory through good works—a resolve by which they are made conformed to the image of the son of God so that in them may be declared the glory and mercy of the creator."[18] Martyr claims that this definition contains all the necessary elements and that all the elements are rooted in scripture; he then appends a long scriptural proof for each part of his definition and warns against the impudent attitude that relies on the fact that however one lives, predestination will come

---

[17] *Loci*, 448. Martyr's distinction between providence and predestination follows the *Summa Theologiae*, I, 23, 1, as does Zanchi, *Opera Theologica*, II, 478. Calvin treats providence (I, 16) separately from predestination (III, 21) in the *Institutes*.

[18] *Loci*, 449: praedestinationem esse sapientissimum propositum Dei quo ante omnem aeternitatem decrevit constanter eos quos dilexit in Christo vocare ad adoptionem filiorum ad iustificationem ex fide, et tandem ad gloriam per opera bona, quo conformes fiant imagini filii Dei, utque in illis declaretur gloria et misericordia Creatoris. Calvin's definition is much simpler: "the eternal decree of God by which He has determined in Himself, what He would have become of every individual of mankind." *Institutes*, III, 21, 5. St. Thomas defines predestination as "quaedam ratio ordinis aliquorum in salutem aeternam in mente divina existens." *Summa Theologiae*, I, 23, 2. McLelland's "Reformed Doctrine of Predestination" (263, 271) rightly stresses the Christological orientation of Martyr's definition and explanation of predestination. Walter Kickel bitterly criticizes Theodore Beza's treatment of predestination because it lacks a Christological orientation. Kickel attributes this defect to the influence of Aristotle (167-168). Martyr's treatment suggests that Aristotelianism and a Christocentric theology are not quite so antithetical as Kickel imagines.

about. Martyr directs the reader's attention to further facets of pre-destination. It is God's work and is located in the divine mind and not in the predestined themselves. Predestination relates principally to the divine goodness, wisdom, and power: the resolve to save flows from the divine goodness which is seated in the will of God; the divine wisdom is involved in preparing his saving action, for the will can act only where there is first knowledge; finally the execution of God's saving resolve calls into play the divine power.[19]

A real understanding of predestination involves a grasp of its anti-thesis, reprobation. Martyr observes that the distinction between pre-destination and reprobation is also used by the scholastics. Predesti-nation looks to and wills both means and end; reprobation looks only to the end but not the means (sin) because of which man is damned. God does not directly cause sin but uses sin as punishment for earlier sin. God can also remove grace so that man necessarily falls into sin. In discussing man's dependence on God in this connection, Martyr once again introduces the idea of concurrence. God does not directly cause sin, since the sinner has sufficient cause of sin in himself, yet God in some sense wills sin. This brings Martyr to his definition of reproba-tion: "the most wise resolve of God by which he steadfastly decreed from all eternity not to have mercy upon but to pass over those he has not loved, though this be without any injustice on their part; in this resolve he declares by their just condemnation his glory and his wrath toward sin."[20] God is in no way bound to be merciful to anyone—the potter can use his pot as he pleases (Rom 9:20). There can be no question of injustice or unfairness here because all man by their fallen nature are enmeshed in sin. Those God's election passes over are justly punished because they are sinners. Just as foreseen merits have nothing to do with God's decision to predestine some, so foreseen

---

[19] *Loci*, 450. Martyr's point that predestination is in the divine mind and not in the predestined merely repeats statements made by Augustine (*De Dono Perseverantiae*, 14) and St. Thomas (*Summa Theologiae*, I, 23, 2).

[20] Sit igitur reprobatio sapientissimum Dei propositum quo ante omnem aeternitatem decrevit constanter, absque ulla iniustitia eorum non misereri quos non dilexit, sed praeteriit: quo iusta illorum condemnatione iram suam erga peccata et gloriam declararet. *Loci*, 451. Martyr's definition by itself speaks only of a passing over, of a not having mercy upon the reprobate. It does not explicitly state double predestination in the sense of a singling out of individuals for damnation as well as for glory. But that this is what Martyr teaches seems clear enough from his whole explanation of reprobation. God in his efficacious will even laughs at the death of the sinner: "Non enim Deus nolens aut violenter sed sponte sua et alacriter ad perdendos impios adducitur," *Loci*, 476.

sins have nothing to do with the divine decision to reprobate. An individual's sins are not the cause of reprobation, which has existed from all eternity; but they are the cause of his damnation, which follows at the end of time. The ultimate purpose of reprobation is to declare the mighty justice of God. Martyr see reprobation, damnation and sin as a chain of means and ends: God's end is the glorification of his justice, the means to this end is the damnation of the sinner, and the means to the damnation of the sinner are his sins.[21]

Martyr devotes the second part of his predestination treatise to discussing the causes of predestination. The will of God is the cause of predestination just as it is the cause of everything else. Searching deeper one can sometimes assign reasons for God's wishes, although these reasons are not to be understood as causes, especially not as efficient causes since that would be positing something more ultimate than God's will. The scripture gives some understanding of the reasons for God's actions. For instance, God acts on Pharaoh to show his power, on the elect to show his glory. The material cause of predestination is the men who are predestined together with the means of predestination, such as vocation, justification, and glorification. The problem of final causality requires caution. Martyr points to two meanings of final cause or end: first, final cause as purpose or motive in the mind of the efficient cause; second, final cause as some extramental good to be acquired. Men are predestined by God so that they may lead virtuous lives, but not in the sense that their good works operate as merits or as causes which move God to predestine them. Rather, vocation to grace is an effect of predestination, not its cause; in turn, vocation is the cause of justification, and justification is the cause of good works. Good works are, therefore, the means and not the cause whereby God leads to man eternal life. Good works do not cause election, nor do sins cause reprobation; if sin were the cause of reprobation, then nobody could be elected or saved since all men are equally born in sin. The decision to save or reprobate a given man is equally free to God.[22]

---

[21] *Loci*, 451; *Samuelis*, f. 221v.

[22] *Loci*, 451-453. John Calvin does not use the schema of the four causes in his discussion of predestination in *The Institutes* but does so in his commentary on Ephesians (*Opera*, LI, 148-150). For Calvin the divine will is the efficient cause, Jesus Christ is the material cause, the preaching of the Gospel is the formal cause, and the praise of divine grace is the final cause. Clearly Martyr and Calvin are quite independent in the way they assign the causes of predestination. Theodore Beza assigns the causes in a way that comes closer to Calvin than to

Why are not good works the cause of predestination? Martyr answers that the Bible never teaches that good works are the cause of predestination; indeed it rejects this notion. There are biblical passages which might seem to attribute this role to works, for instance 2 Tim 2:21, if read incautiously. But these passages are easily explained; the Bible does say that man must act uprightly if he is to be saved, but that does not mean that ethical behavior is the cause of salvation. God working within man is the cause of salvation. God does not work within man as though man were an inert stick; rather, he so regenerates man that man knows and wishes those sanctifying actions by which God saves man. Martyr also proves that foreseen works cannot be a cause of predestination by working backwards from justification by faith:

> Now consider with me: it is completely contrary to Paul's aim to make foreseen works the cause of predestination. For then works would be the cause of justification, but the Apostle is opposed to that view on every score. I prove this argument solid from the fact that the Apostle makes predestination the cause of vocation, and vocation the cause of justification. But if works are the cause of predestination, then they will also be the cause of justification. The rule of the logicians is firm: whatever is the cause of some cause is also the cause of its effect. Besides, nobody can deny that good works flow from justification, for we are said to be predestined so that we may be holy and guiltless. ... Wherefore if works are the effect of predestination, how may we say they are its causes? [23]

Martyr. See John Stanley Bray, "Theodore Beza's Doctrine of Predestination," 77, 78, 157.

[23] Deinde considera mihi, id Pauli scopo quam maxime adversari, ut opera praevisa statuat esse causa praedestinationis. Ita enim opera forent causae iustificationis: Atqui Apostolus eam doctrinam omnibus modis oppugnat. Rationem firmam esse ex eo demonstro, quoniam Apostolus facit praedestinationem causam vocationis, vocationem iustificationis. Quare si opera sint causae, erunt etiam causae iustificationis. Constans enim est regula dialecticorum: Quicquid causa est causae alicuius, est enim causa effecti. Praeterea nemo inficiari potest, bona opera proficisci ex praedestinatione. Dicimur enim praedestinati ut simus sancti et inculpati. ... Quemobrem si opera sunt effecta praedestinationis, quomodo ea dicemus esse eius causas? *Loci*, 453. Martyr's argument here closely parallels that of Aquinas, *S.T.*, I, 23, 5. Martyr's concern with the cause-effect relationship between predestination, vocation, justification, and good works was shared by Jerome Zanchi. See Gründler, 117. Martyr never reduced this relationship to an illustrated or schematic form; as did Theodore Beza in his *Tabula Praedestinationis: Summa Totius Christianismi, sive descriptio et distributio causarum salutis electorum et exitii reproborum ex sacris literis collecta*, (Geneva: 1555). This work proved very popular and was translated into French, English, and Dutch. It was also imitated, for instance, by William Perkins, *A Golden Chain or the Description of Theologie, containing the order of the Causes of Salvation and Damnation,*

This discussion leads Martyr to the conclusion that the only final cause of predestination is God's good pleasure (*beneplacitum*). Scripture (2 Tim 1:9; Tit 3:4; Rom 11:33) makes it clear to Martyr that works cannot be the cause of vocation any more than of predestination. Paul puts the reason for election in the depth of the wisdom of God. Human reason cannot penetrate further—to try is foolhardy.[24]

Martyr feels that it is the desire to escape facing up to this unfathomable mystery and the desire to satisfy human judgement that lead his adversaries to posit foreseen good works as the cause of predestination. But what can this all-too-human solution answer to the problem of infants who die after baptism? They are saved even though they perform no good works. The claim that God saves these infants because he foresees that they would have done good works does not evade the difficulty; Christ said that Tyre and Sidon would have repented if he had preached to them, yet God destroyed them. The truth cannot be evaded: there is no basis in man for God's saving election, for all men are sons of wrath.[25]

Catholics might be tempted to posit foreseen works as the cause of predestination and justification, but according to Martyr this is no temptation to the true Protestant. The Protestant might be tempted to suggest foreseen faith as a basis of predestination. Martyr thinks that this was in fact the position of Ambrose, Chrysostom, and early Augustine. Martyr answers this theory by adducing several scripture texts which assert that faith is a pure gift of God; hence God does not predestine because of foreseen faith. Martyr develops several arguments with a strong scholastic flavor against either foreseen faith or foreseen works being the cause of predestination. Both faith and works are temporal, while predestination is from eternity; but a cause must pre-exist its effect, therefore neither faith nor works can cause predestination. Again, an efficient cause must be more noble (*dignior, praestantior*) than its effect. Predestination is constant and infallible while human good works are inconstant and proceed from man's un-

---

according to God's Word. Perkins's work, available in both English and Latin and frequently reprinted, contained long extracts on predestination from Beza and Zanchi. Martyr deserves some of the credit for Beza's *Tabula*. Beza wrote for Martyr's advice on it. Martyr responded: ". . . ut etiam tabulis quibusdam pictis eam ob oculos ponas, patefacias ac enodate dilucidas, et laudo et vehementer probo." Martyr advised Beza to buttress his schema and its explanation with appropriate scriptural quotations. This Beza did. Indeed, the quotations make up over half the work. See *Correspondance de Theodore de Beze*, I, 153-55.

[24] *Loci*, 454; *Romanos*, 288; Loci, 983.
[25] *Loci*, 454.

stable will. Martyr claims that his opponents, in their desire to satisfy human understanding and to save free will, do not realize that they are robbing God of his legitimate power and freedom. God is the potter, men are the pots; God does as he wills with his pots and needs to answer to no man for them.[26]

Martyr cites Erasmus as one of those who demand that God elect only those he knows will not act viciously and that he reject nobody except those he foresees will act wickedly. Erasmus considered that divine justice requires God to act so. But Martyr counters, justice is not at issue since all men are sinners. If any are spared, it is due solely to God's mercy. The teaching of Erasmus and those like him leaves the door open for men to boast that predestination depends upon themselves. Martyr contrasts this with the humble gratitude of the true Christian who recognizes that his election to salvation is entirely gratuitous.[27]

Martyr finds great spiritual comfort in the conviction that salvation does not depend upon man. If men had to depend upon themselves for salvation, their instability would lead them to lose heart. The conviction that one's salvation is fixed in God brings great joy. God loves differently than men who love only when they recognize the good qualities in others. God recognizes in man nothing but his own gifts. The recognition that everything good in man comes from God and belongs to him gives man the strength to bear adversity, for all things work together unto good for those who love God. Martyr continues with one of his favorite texts (Eph 1:11): "We are predestined according to the purpose of God by which power He does all according to the counsel of His will." God freely chooses the foolish and sinful to confound the wise and virtuous. Jesus consorted with publicans, whores, and robbers, not with philosophers. Where is the *"ratio meriti"* here? The prophets do not say that God will deliver his people because of their merits, but for his name's sake. The basic purpose of Paul's Epistle to the Romans is to teach the grace of Christ; nothing could be more opposed to this than to attribute predestination to works.[28]

After some reflection on how the incarnation and death of Christ relates to predestination,[29] Martyr turns to answer over a score of

---

26 *Loci*, 454.
27 *Loci*, 454.
28 *Loci*, 455-56.
29 The importance of predestination in Martyr's thought is underlined by

arguments against his theory of the causes of predestination. Some of the objections are scriptual, others argue from the evil results that are alleged to flow from Martyr's teaching. Most of the objections obviously betray Pelagian and Roman Catholic presuppositions; indeed, Martyr attributes over half the objections to Pighius. After several pages of answering objections, Martyr goes on the offensive and attacks Pighius's theory of predestination. This portion of the treatise is extremely dense and only a few highlights can be mentioned here. Martyr considers that the chief objections are that his teaching leads to moral licentiousness, that it implies that God desires sin, that it causes men to hate God as an arbitrary tyrant, that it imposes necessity on man's conduct and thereby destroys the notion of responsibility and guilt, and that it virtually denies the goodness of God since the possibility of salvation is open only to a few men. Regarding this last accusation, Martyr admits that most men will be damned, but the reason for this is an unsearchable mystery buried in God's good pleasure. Martyr's answers to the other objections can be easily surmised fom his positive exposition.[30] In the course of answering these objections and attacking Pighius, Martyr takes some noteworthy theological options. His predestination is supralapsarian; original sin is seen as a means to carry out reprobation and therefore it necessarily follows rather than precedes predestination and reprobation. Martyr scorns the postulate of limbo as a Catholic fable to keep infants who die without baptism out of hell.[31] He considers it absurd to

---

his response to the question whether the incarnation and death of Christ are causes of predestination. He answers that they are not causes but rather the first and greatest effects of predestination. *Loci*, 457, 462.

[30] *Loci*, 457-61.

[31] *Loci*, 460. Martyr's teaching on the fate of those who die in infancy highlights the importance of predestination in his theology. His teaching (*Romanos*, 181; *Genesis*, f. 65v; *Corinthios*, f. 178v; *Melachim*, 73v) may be reduced to a few propositions. Those infants who die after baptism will probably but not certainly be saved, depending on whether they are predestined or not. Those infants who die without baptism but are children of the faithful are probably saved, depending on whether they are predestined or not, since in some sense they pertain to the covenant because they are children of the faithful. Unbaptized children of pagan parents may also be saved if they are predestined. In short, predestination alone is decisive. Baptism and being the child of Christian parents merely indicates a greater likelihood of being predestined. The original sin of the predestined who die in infancy is not imputed to them. The reprobate who die in infancy do have original sin imputed and are therefore damned, but their punishment in hell will be less severe than the punishment of adults who add personal sin to original sin. It is noteworthy that neither faith nor baptism is necessary for salvation. Martyr (*Genesis*, f. 65v) criticizes Augustine and those

teach that God has a universal saving will. He rejects the suggestion of Scotus that Christ would have become incarnate even if Adam had not sinned.[32]

So ends the long section of Martyr's treatise devoted to the causes of predestination. He next turns to the effects of predestination and reprobation. The first and chief effect of predestination is the incarnation, life, death and resurrection of Christ. All other gifts to the elect come through Christ. Other effects of predestination are vocation to grace, justification, glorification, conformity to the image of the Son of God, good works, certitude and confirmation of salvation, and the manifestation of God's glory. Martyr develops the effects of reprobation at greater length. Many men are left in original sin. Man's need to work results from original sin; indeed, for Martyr all the stupendous results of human industry and ingenuity result from original sin. A deep pessimism pervades his view of the accomplishments of fallen man. These may seem to be beautiful but because they proceed from a corrupt principle, they are sins in God's sight. God punishes man's sin with yet other sins; in fact, except for the first sin, all sin has the charater of punishment. The final result of reprobation is damnation and the manifestation of the power and justice of God.[33]

All benefits God confers on the predestined are rooted in grace. Is grace given to all men, or only to certain individuals? Martyr says that God gives grace only to a few, and he tries to break down the scriptural arguments of those who maintain that God gives grace to all men which some men then reject. Martyr insists that God gives grace to some individuals and calls them to himself; others are simply not called to the true way. Those who maintain that grace is offered to all men reduce grace to nature. The unregenerate are too perverted to accept grace; therefore God must make them good. If man were free to accept grace or reject it, he would have something to boast about.

---

commentators on the *Sentences* (surely he has Gregory of Rimini in mind) who consigned the babies of the faithful who die without baptism to hell. This error results from attributing too much importance and efficacy to the sacraments: "Putant enim vi et efficacia operis baptismi peccatum remitti, neque agnoscant sacramentis potius remissionem obsignari quam adulti assequuntur credendo et parvuli fidelium qui ad electionem pertinent, per spiritum sanctum et gratiam iam habent" (*Corinthios*, f. 178v). "Addimus Deum per Iesum Christum suos electos ac praedestinatos mundare ita ut vitium quod sua natura peccatum esset mortale illis mortem non imputetur. Deinde spiritu suo ornat et renovat, postea obsignatio exterioris baptismi adiicitur" (*Melachim*, f. 73v).

[32] *Loci*, 461.
[33] *Loci*, 462-63.

It is an error to suppose that God gives all men sufficient grace to move them. If the grace were sufficient, men would be moved, even as a rock moves when sufficient strength is applied. A really sufficient grace would make even hardened sinners repent, though by suasion and not by force. Roman Catholic attempts to distinguish between efficacious and sufficient grace are mere pussy-footing. Instead, Christians should frankly admit that in some cases God does not wish to be merciful and does not give everybody sufficient grace for salvation. Martyr feels that his opponents allow man to choose God by accepting or rejecting grace, whereas scripture teaches that God chooses man.[34]

Martyr next turns to handle the many scripture texts that seem to say that God wishes the salvation of all men. To take these texts literally is to run the danger of reviving the heresy of Origen. Rather, some of the texts alleged for universal salvation really apply only to the elect; others refer only to the preaching of the message of salvation to all men, but it is only the elect that profit from that preaching.[35] Indeed the reprobate do not generally profit fron the preaching even to the extent of performing the external actions that lie within their power so that an important result of the universal preaching of the Gospel is to render the reprobate inexcusable. Martyr concludes that although his adversaries boast of themselves as the preachers of God's mercy since they open the door of salvation to all men, this is only an illusion; Martyr's own doctrine is the real good news of divine mercy since it makes room for God's grace.[36]

To the accusation that his theory makes God unjust and arbitrary, Martyr replies that his teaching preserves God's justice in predestining and reprobating, but the reason why God predestines or reprobates individual men lies hidden in God's mysterious and ineffable wisdom. In explaining Paul's statement that God wishes all men to be saved

---

[34] *Loci*, 464-65.

[35] *Loci*, 465-66. Martyr is rather insensitive to the problem of the *salus gentium*; the epic geographical discoveries of his age did little to shake his complacency: "Proinde ad modum pauci erant, imo ferme nulli qui vel praedicationem Evangelii non audiverint vel saltem de Christo nobile et insignem famam non acceperint, quamquam successu temporum fieri potest, ut nomen Christi negligentia et incredulitate sit abolitum, ut Lusitani perhibent de locis a se inventis per iter quo navigarunt a Gadibus in Indiam. Unde solent aliqui movere curiosam quaestionem, quid sit putandum de his qui nascuntur aut in sylvis extra hominum coetum aut in his locis ubi Christus non praedicatur et nomen eius non auditur. Quibus dicendum est huiusmodi homines, si qui tales reperiantur, excusari nonnihil neque fore illorum tam gravem damnationem ut eorum qui audiverunt Evangelium et contempserunt." ... *Romanos*, 463.

[36] *Loci*, 465.

(1 Tim 2:4) Martyr follows Augustine and narrows the divine salvific will only to representatives of all nations, eras, social classes and so forth, just as in the same way that God saved all the animals in Noah's ark. Paul's statement to Timothy means no more than the statement that a certain business man serves the whole city; the statement, moreover, can be interpreted as referring to a certain stage in God's will (*de voluntate signi*). That God does not really want to save everybody is evident from the many infants that die without baptism. In this vein Martyr picks his way through a whole gauntlet of difficulties arising from the biblical expressions of God's saving will. Vermigli admits that the reprobate (for example Saul and Solomon) sometimes do good works and that the elect (Peter and David) sometimes sin seriously. But the good works of the reprobate are only temporary; they are neither perfect nor sincere nor pleasing to God and they have only the appearance of good. From this he generalizes that good works sometimes lead to salvation, sometimes to damnation; conversely sin also sometimes leads to salvation, sometimes to damnation. In the reprobate sins lead to hell, but in the predestined they only enhance the divine glory when God rescues the predestined from them since their sins lead the predestined to appreciate better God's benefits.[37]

HUMAN FREEDOM AND PREDESTINATION

At this point Martyr's treatise on predestination takes up its final consideration: the relation between human freedom and predestination. This was not a new problem in reformation polemics. Luther's *De Servo Arbitrio* developed two lines of argument against Erasmus and free will. One line tried to show that God's foreknowledge, providence and predestination were incompatible with human free will.[38] The second line of argument showed that original sin and concupiscence made it impossible for man to perform any acts which lead to eternal salvation without the help of grace. Martyr's Romans commentary deals at length with both these arguments. Although Martyr makes no explicit reference to the Erasmus-Luther controversy on free will, his statements reveal an easy familiarity with their debate. Martyr rejects Luther's unfortunate argument that divine foreknowledge precludes human freedom, as have most Protestant theologians throughout history. Martyr maintains that original sin has so crippled human

---

[37] *Loci*, 466-69; *Corinthios*, f. 58r; *Samuelis*, f. 282r.
[38] W.A. XVIII, 615.

freedom that man can perform no salvific acts of himself. In this he agrees with the main stream of Christian thought from Paul through Augustine, Aquinas, Luther and Calvin down to the present.[39]

Martyr asks three questions regarding predestination and freedom. Do predestination and reprobation impose any necessity on man? If there is a necessity, does it impede free choice (*liberum arbitrium*)? Do God's foreknowledge and predestination destroy the justice by which God renders to each according to his works? The treatise on predestination is by no means the only place in which Martyr's writings discuss free will; three times previously Martyr's lectures had taken up the subject at considerable length.[40] One of these treatments, that in Martyr's commentary on First Corinthians, largely parallels the section on free will in the predestination tract. The presentation here integrates these two parallel discussions, then turns to Martyr's other treatments which consider the problem of human freedom from a different angle.

In order to answer whether predestination imposes necessity, Martyr feels it necessary to review the various kinds of necessities. His review is very intricate and scholastic. There is only one simply necessary being, God. In created reality there are many kinds of necessity, for instance, intrinsic and extrinsic necessity. There are two kinds of intrinsic necessity: mathematical and physical. There are also two kinds of extrinsic necessity, the violent (when something is forced to act against its nature) and the hypothetical (*ex hypothesi*). It is this last which pertains to the problem of predestination. Martyr discusses hypothetical necessity in conjunction with the scholastics' distinction of *necessitas consequentiae* and *necessitas conquentis* and the logicians' distinction of *sensus compositus* and *sensus divisus*. According to Martyr the scholastics use these distinctions to try to solve all the difficulties

---

[39] On the importance of distinguishing Luther's two lines of argument and their quite different status in the history of theology, see Harry McSorley, *Luther: Right or Wrong?* (New York and Minneapolis: 1969), 297-366.

[40] The first time Martyr took up the question of free will or free choice (*liberum arbitrium*) was in his 1545 lectures on Exodus at Strasbourg. These have not survived, but theses extracted from them and proposed to his students for disputation have survived and are printed in the *Loci*, 1025. At Oxford Martyr incorporated a tract mainly dealing with philosophical objections to free will to the end of the second chapter of his Corinthians commentary. Martyr's most important tract on freedom comes after the seventh chapter of his Romans commentary; it deals mainly with the relation of grace and original sin to human freedom and relates closely to the Exodus theses. In his Samuel commentary (279v ff.) Martyr took up the subject briefly in his controversy with Bibliander at Zurich. Both the Corinthians and the Romans tracts were reprinted in the *Loci*.

that arise on the problem of predestination. Martyr, however, proposes a distinction of his own as a solution. He distinguishes the necessity of coaction or coercion from the necessity of infallibility or of certainty.[41] He comes back to this distinction again and again. The human will is not necessitated from an internal principle since by its God-given nature the will is changeable and can choose alternative courses of action. Still it is subject to the hypothetical necessity—it is conditioned by God's foreknowledge and predestination: what God has foreknown and predestined will necessarily take place. The human will has an aptitude to embrace either of alternative courses, but it only does the action which God has foreseen it will do. The necessity lies in the connection of divine predestination with human acts. The scholastics understood this connection according to their notion of *sensus compositus* and according to the *necessitas consequentiae*, that is, man's actions are not necessary when considered in isolation from God and according to their proximate principle, the will. In Martyr's terminology the action is free from the necessity of coercion even though it is immutably predestined and foreknown by God and must happen with the necessity of certainty or infallibility.[42]

The concept of providence likewise implies the necessity of certainty. Most events happen by natural intrinsic necessity, but that is not the issue at hand. What man calls contingents are so only by abstracting from God's foreknowledge and providence, as people generally realize. As long as fate is understood as a chain of causes over which God presides, no objection to this way of speaking should be made, but Martyr feels that there is need for caution lest there be perverse talk of some iron necessity or astral determinism beyond God's power. He asserts that the wiser pagans realized that fate was under God's direction.[43] Vermigli repeats tirelessly that God's action does not subvert the natural order and does not take away man's free nature,

---

[41] *Loci*, 469. Martyr here seems to follow Luther's *De Servo Arbitrio*, *W.A.*, XVIII, 617, 634, 720.

[42] *Loci*, 469.

[43] Martyr was completely untouched by the sixteenth century mania for magic and astrology that affected even such respectable theologians and scientists as Melanchthon and Kepler. He feels that there is no rational basis for the alleged connection between the stars and human events. If the stars control men, why do twins born under the same constellations often have such different lives? Martyr argues that astral determinism logically implies that prayer, piety, and worship are worthless. *Loci*, 470; *Corinthios*, ff. 51v, 61v. For Martyr's attitude toward magic, see *Genesis*, f. 121v.

but he never really explains this claimed compatibility beyond citing scripture texts intended to support its existence.[44]

Martyr's chief adversaries on the question are pagans, especially Cicero in his *De Divinatione* and *De Natura Deorum*. All Christians admit foreknowledge, providence, and predestination. In dealing with Cicero scriptural arguments are useless and the tone becomes more philosophical. Cicero does not reject human free will; rather he argues that free will and divine foreknowledge are incompatible. If everything happens as foreknown, Cicero thinks that law, admonitions, rewards and punishment become meaningless. Accordingly Cicero chooses freedom and rejects foreknowledge. Martyr feels that Cicero's option leads inevitably to atheism since it involves a rejection of all the prophecies in scripture. Martyr insists that the Christian must retain both freedom and foreknowledge. Self-reflection reveals to man his freedom; faith reveals divine foreknowledge, therefore Christians must deny that foreknowledge leaves nothing to the human will. God's foreknowledge itself sees the human will as one of the causes of events just as it understands the other causes; and just as God's foreknowledge does not rob other kinds of causes of their power to bring about their effects, so it does not destroy the factor of human will. Attacking from a different angle, Martyr points out that divine foreknowledge is not constitutive of the human soul. The cause of the soul's actions must therefore be traced back to the nature of the human will itself and not to foreknowledge. Now it is intrinsic to the will that it can do nothing unwillingly or by coercion. Nothing outside the will can coerce it to act.[45]

---

[44] *Loci*, 470; *Corinthios*, ff. 60v-61v. Martyr's emphasis is clearly the opposite of Luther's: *W.A.* XVIII, 615.

[45] *Loci*, 472; *Corinthios*, 58v-61v; *Melachim*, f. 124v; *Samuelis*, f. 279v; *Romanos*, 59; *Genesis*, f. 110r. In the Corinthians tract Martyr cites the refutation of Cicero's objections given by Augustine in the fifth book of the *De Civitate Dei* as the source of many of his arguments. Other than scripture, Cicero, Augustine, Chrysostom, Aristotle and a vague reference to the scholastics, Martyr does not cite sources in his discussion of free will. Almost certainly he had read Luther and Calvin on the one side and Erasmus and Pighius on the other as free will became a battle-field between Protestants and Catholics. The question of freedom was also much discussed by the Italian humanists, often in the framework set by Cicero and Augustine. Did Martyr know the important discussions by the Florentine chancellors Salutati and Valla? His position lies between theirs, but he cites neither Salutati's *De Fato et Fortuna* nor Valla's *De Libero Arbitrio* by name. He knew many of Valla's writings and cites him frequently. Erasmus, Luther, and Calvin all cite Valla's dialogue in their writings on free will. See E. Cassirer, P. O. Kristeller, J. H. Randall, Jr., ed. *The Renaissance Philosophy of Man*, (Chicago: 1956), 153; the same work contains a translation of Valla's

Martyr enlists Aristotle and the scholastics in his fight against Cicero:

> In his *Ethics* Aristotle argues, and does so learnedly as he is wont with every question, whether, when shipwreck threatens, throwing (the cargo) into the sea should be classed with voluntary acts. Although he confesses that some such actions are a mixture of the voluntary and the involuntary, he still concludes that acts of this kind should be considered as pertaining to the voluntary. . . . The scholastics usually call this necessity of consequence and not a necessity of the consequent. Some will jibe: these distinctions will not help us if everything happens exactly as God foreknows it. But these distinctions do help not a little because by them we understand that the human will cannot be forced but desires freely and of itself whatever it wishes.[46]

The problem of foreknowledge and freedom does not perplex only devout Christians and philosophers such as Cicero; it also agitates many worldly people who generally fall into two groups. Some insist on free will, but postulate a God who is unconcerned with the moral behavior of mere mortals; they therefore conclude that they have license to act just as they please. Others so emphasize divine foreknowledge that they deny their own freedom and moral responsibility. Either way the result is moral license. Martyr suggests several analogies to show the compatibility of freedom and foreknowledge: for instance, one can know that a person is coming to visit him without

---

dialogue on free will, 155-82. Only a minute comparison of Martyr's text and those of Salutati and Valla is likely to demonstrate any borrowings. It is quite improbable that Martyr knew Pomponazzi's important discussion of freedom in the *De Fato* since that massive treatise circulated only in manuscript until Vermigli's friend Grataroli published it at Basel shortly after Vermigli's death. A very likely source of Martyr's teaching on free will is Gregory of Rimini. There are clear affinities between Martyr's and Gregory's teaching on free will, though these may stem mainly from a common debt to Augustine. For Gregory's doctrine of free will and the effects of sin, see Gordon Leff, *Gregory of Rimini: Tradition and Innovation in Fourteenth Century Thought*, (New York: 1961), 165-85. For Salutati, Valla and Gregory, see Trinkaus, I, 74-102, 165-68.

[46] *Corinthios*, f. 61r: Porro disputat Aristoteles in *Ethicis*, et quidem erudite, ut solet omnia, num jactura quae fit in mare quando naufragium imminet sit collocanda inter voluntaria. Et quanquam ibi fateatur nescioquam actionem esse commixtam ex voluntario et involuntario, concludit nihilominus eius generis actiones ad voluntarium censum spectare. . . . Soletque appellari a scholasticis ista necessitas non quidem consequentis, verum consequentiae. Dictitant nonnulli: Hae distinctiones certe nos nihil iuvant si quae Deus praescivit omnino sunt eventura. Imo prosunt non mediocriter, quia hinc intelligamus humanam voluntatem minime cogi sed sponte ac ultro quicquid voluerit expetere. Also see *Genesis*, f. 124v; *Romanos*, 379-80.

making that visit less free; knowledge of past events does not imply that the past happened necessarily.[47] So too man's observation of an eclipse does not make it contingent since the sun and moon are operating under the influence of necessary natural causes. So God's foreknowledge does not affect the freedom or the necessity of creaturely operations.[48] God's knowledge is certain but his will accommodates itself to the nature of creatures. "It feeds in food, shines in the sun, produces wine in the vine, and it brings it about in the will of man that they freely and of their own accord will what they will." God so operates in the will that man accepts freely, willingly, and spontaneously the impulses that God inspires.[49]

Martyr also argues that divine omnipotence does not destroy freedom. God moderates his power so that his action in this world dovetails with the nature of created things and their operations.[50]

HUMAN FREEDOM AND THE POWER OF SIN

So much for Martyr's treatise on predestination and for objections against human freedom drawn from divine omnipotence, foreknowledge, providence, and predestination. Martyr does not, of course, open up the modern problems of what role heredity, social and individual environment, or early psychological experience have in determining personality and limiting freedom. But there are other objections to freedom which flow from original sin, personal sin, concupiscence, and grace. These interest Martyr much more than Cicero's philosophical objections. Martyr's controversy with Roman Catholics, Pelagians, and Erasmian Protestants such as Theodore Bibliander over the theological limitations of freedom led him to maintain human freedom in principle but drastically restrict it in practice. Martyr devoted an extensive scholia to the problem in his lectures on Romans.

---

[47] *Loci*, 473; *Corinthios*, f. 60v.

[48] *Loci* 473; Erasmus uses the example of the eclipse to make the same point. D. Erasmi, *Opera Omnia*, (Leiden: 1706), IX, c. 1231.

[49] *Loci*, 473: Verum tamen ista voluntas qua Deus efficit omnia in omnibus sese accommodat rerum naturis. Nam in cibo alit, in soli illustrat, in vite vinum producit, et in voluntate hominum efficit ut sponte ac libere velint quae volunt.

[50] *Corinthios*, ff. 51v, 61v; *Romanos*, 373. Martyr in *Romanos*, 369, writes: "Hic obiciunt: Igitur non erimus domini actionum nostrarum si Deus sit qui opera nostra facit in nobis. Isti non intelligunt Deum creatorem tanta sapientia in omnibus rebus operari ut eas non moveat nisi eo modo quo movendae sunt. Quare, cum nostra voluntas ita sit a Deo facta ut cogi non possit, non adigit eam Deus ut invita quidpiam faciat, sed illi ex se ipso dat ut ultro et sponte faciat. Sumus itaque domini nostrarum actionum quatenus coacti nihil facimus."

His long lecture on free will in 1560 at Zurich was aimed at Theodore Bibliander but does not mention his name. It is printed at the end of the *Loci Communes*. The treatment here follows the Romans commentary, integrating other more scattered remarks where convenient.

Martyr begins by pointing out that free choice (*liberum arbitrium*) is not a scriptural term. He defines freedom as following one's own will rather than another's. Free choice is following the decrees of reason as one pleases; the will is free when it embraces as it wishes what is approved by the understanding. Free choice has its roots in the reason even though it primarily pertains to the will; therefore man must first beware of errors of judgement if he wishes to use his freedom rightly.[51]

After defining freedom, Martyr asks whether man is free. He refuses to give a simple answer. Distinctions are necessary; for there are at least four states of man, and the degree of freedom varies from state to state. The states are: Adam before the fall, sinful man, man reborn in Christ, and the blessed after death. Adam was free before the fall, but even here there is need to speak cautiously. Martyr therefore distinguishes three kinds of actions or categories which vary in freedom. First are certain actions of nature such as eating or cooking. Adam had the power and the freedom to perform these actions. Second there are actions which are right or wrong according to civil or ethical reasoning. Third are actions which please and gratify God. Adam was also free with regard to actions in the second and third categories because he was made in the image of God and a high degree of liberty befitted him. Martyr follows Augustine's opinion that God helped Adam with his grace, but rather differently than he does in the reborn. In the reborn the ability both to will and to accomplish the good depends upon grace, whereas Adam had it in his power to will the good.[52]

The situation of sinful, fallen man is rather different. He is like the man beaten and left half dead by robbers in the parable of the good Samaritan so that he has little freedom left. He has the power and the need to do the action of the first category, the works of nature; he also has some liberty to do civil and ethical actions since these depend upon man's natural knowledge and do not surpass the strength of the human will, although man's passions cause him great difficulty. But with regard to the third category—actions which truly please God

---

[51] *Romanos*, 246; *Corinthios*, f. 196r; *Loci*, 971.
[52] *Romanos*, 247; *Samuelis*, ff. 33r, 279v.

—fallen man has no freedom. He simply cannot do these works. Martyr cites Peter Lombard's statement that after the fall, man is in a situation in which he can sin but cannot avoid sin. Martyr consciously goes beyond Augustine and argues that holy acts depend on both knowledge and desire. But fallen man has neither the requisite knowledge nor the desire; without grace he is not free but a slave to sin. Man's heart is made of rock unless Christ transforms it to flesh. If man could live ethically without grace, he could also be justified by his works; but scripture condemns this supposition.[53]

It is not God's fault, according to Martyr, that fallen man cannot keep the commandments. The commandments perfectly fit human nature as it was first constituted and show how man should behave. Martyr rejects the opinion that there can be no sin where there is no choice. He admits that man clings to sin by necessity, but this necessity implies no coercion.[54] Coercion is the key to Martyr's teaching. Man must necessarily choose to sin, but this necessity is not forced upon him. The opposite of freedom is not necessity but outside coercion. Thus clear truth necessitates man's assent, and the saints cannot stop adhering to God once they behold him in glory. In these cases the necessity involved does not violate the rights of the will. Neither does the necessity to sin.[55] The unregenerate do have sufficient freedom to perform the ethical and the civilly upright. Although necessarily immersed in sin, they can freely choose which sins to commit and which to avoid, but they cannot even hope to do actions pleasing to God.[56]

To clarify his position Martyr defines three concepts: the free, the forced (*violentum*) and the spontaneous.[57] To be free is to be able to choose between two or more courses of action as one pleases. But fallen man is not wholly free since he cannot choose a course of action leading to salvation. To be forced is to be moved to action by an external principle which overcomes one's struggles. To be spontaneous is to have an internal principle which favors the action. Hence spontaneity and necessity are not contradictory but can be joined together as happens when the will necessarily seeks happiness. The will suffers no coercion but freely and gladly seeks happiness. The necessity under

---

[53] *Romanos*, 247-49; *Samuelis*, f. 284r; *Loci*, 972-74.

[54] *Romanos*, 249; *Melachim*, f. 133r.

[55] *Romanos*, 250; Martyr develops this aspect of his teaching more fully in *Melachim*, f. 133r.

[56] *Romanos*, 252.

[57] Martyr's teaching on necessary and spontaneous acts parallels Luther's discussion, *W.A.*, XVIII, 634.

which the unsanctified sin is not absolute or perfect, for it can be changed, seeing that the grace of Christ immediately dissolves this necessity to sin. Martyr agrees with Augustine's argument that the power or possibility of having faith, hope, and charity belongs to man's nature, but their actual possession belongs entirely to grace. Only divine grace can convert that power into actuality. Augustine agreed with Pelagius in attributing this power to nature but disagreed in attributing actual right-living and goodwill to grace. But Martyr feels it necessary to go further and to distinguish this power: he attributes this power to man only if it be understood as a mere possibility, something not involving a contradiction, but he refuses to accept this power if it be understood as a positive capability of acquiring faith, hope, and charity. He considers this last a hellish suggestion. The human will does not look upon good and evil impartially: it can of itself seek evil, but it can only seek good if restored by divine grace, as even the ancient pagans recognized. The older and better scholastics also taught that divine grace was necessary to assist every good action, while the later scholastics claimed that the unregenerate can perform some good works which please God and merit the grace of Christ *de congruo*. After explaining the scholastic distinction of merit *de congruo* and *de condigno*, Martyr points out that Augustine, following Scripture, has shown with crushing arguments that the ethically good works of the unregenerate are actually sins on the sight of God.[58]

Martyr rejects the charge that his condemnation of fallen nature implies blasphemy against its Creator. He quotes Augustine's maxim that behind the praises of nature lurks the enemy of grace. Martyr clearly distinguishes his position from Manichaeism: the evil in man results not from God's fashioning, much less from the workings of an evil god, but from Adam's sin. The loss of man's original freedom is not attributable to God's authorship but to man's vice.[59]

After examining Manichaeism and Pelagianism, Martyr comes to the conclusion that the scholastics of his day really teach Pelagianism despite all the differences they allege between themselves and the ancient heretics. They posit a prevenient grace so that sinners can be said to do some good and should not be considered as dead trees but as budding forth some shoots and able to produce foliage, even if unable to bear true fruit and flowers. But, counters Martyr, this is Pelagian-

---

[58] *Romanos*, 250-251; *Samuelis*, f. 279v; *Ethicorum*, 422; *Melachim*, f. 133r.
[59] *Romanos*, 251-53.

ism. They forget that in the gospel the Lord cursed the tree which bore only leaves without fruit and ordered it cut down and burned.[60]

JUSTIFICATION BY FAITH

Among Martyr's favorite scriptural texts is Romans 8:30, "And it is these, so fore-ordained whom he has also called. And those whom he called he has justified, and to those whom he has justified he has also given his splendor." God calls the predestined to faith and thereby to justification and salvation. Sometimes God calls by the interior working of the Holy Spirit alone, sometimes through the written word, sometimes through the preached word. The word confronts man with the divine teaching and promises, sometimes adding threats and tribulations. This vocation can come at any time in man's life; it is twofold, either to a specific task alone, or also embracing final salvation. For instance, Saul was called to be king of Israel, but he was not called to final salvation. God issues both efficacious and inefficacious calls: when the gospels say that many are called but few are chosen, they refer to an inefficacious call. The efficacious call that St. Paul describes in Romans 8:27-30 always results in the eternal salvation of the elect whom God calls. This efficacious call leads to faith and thereby to justification.[61]

The doctrine of justification by faith alone is crucial for Martyr as for all the Reformers. Luther characteristically emphasized the sense of Christian freedom that the doctrine brings. Calvin stressed how *sola fide* upholds God's sovereignty. Martyr prefers to dwell on how the generosity and kindness of God manifest themselves through justification by faith alone and how man needs to attribute all glory to God alone.[62] Martyr frequently explains his conviction of justification by faith alone, but the doctrine exercises a pervasive influence even where it is not explicitly stated.[63] Martyr's most extended treatment is the tract at the end of the eleventh chapter of his Romans commentary; it is also reprinted in the *Loci Communes* (III, 4) where it covers fifty-four folio pages.[64]

---

[60] *Romanos*, 260. Martyr also argues that the decree of the Council of Trent on justification is thoroughly Pelagian. *Romanos*, 546-547.

[61] *Loci*, 476-79, 980-81, 482.

[62] *Loci*, 553: Nam cum nostris meritis et operibus nihil tribuatur, necesse est gloria universa cedere Deo.

[63] Martyr included short tracts on justification at the end of the first chapter of his First Corinthians commentary and in his Genesis commentary (after commenting on Genesis 15:6).

[64] *Loci*, 510-64.

Characteristically Martyr's tract begins by studying the nuances of the various words the Hebrew Bible uses for justification and for faith. He is struck by an analogy which links the root Hebrew notions for *justify* and *believe*. "*To justify* means to attribute justice in one's judgement or estimate to somebody, but not actually to make him to be just; so also *to believe* is not actually to make somebody's statements or promises certain and solid, but to think or consider them so."[65] Martyr defines faith as the "firm and certain assent of the mind to God's words inspired by the Holy Spirit and leading to the salvation of believers."[66] He shows how his definition includes all four Aristotelian causes. The Holy Spirit is the efficient cause, salvation the final. The formal cause is the assent itself, which takes place in the mind and deals with the divine word—the two-fold material cause. This definition is entirely consonant with that given by the Epistle to the Hebrews, 11:1.[67] Justifying faith primarily believes that God will be the author of man's peace and happiness and will remain faithful to his promises. This is a live faith, not to be confused with the dead faith St. James (2:14-25) rightly condemned. So strong is true faith that it brings along with it trust, hope, charity and good works. By faith the believer grasps God as his ultimate good, hence he necessarily comes to love him. Faith, hope, and charity are distinct, but they are inseparable companions; charity accompanies faith like light follows the sun.[68]

Martyr's tract on justification tries to prove three basic propositions: that good works do not justify, that faith justifies, and that faith alone justifies. Throughout his tract Martyr attacks Albert Pighius, Richard Smith, and the Tridentine Decree on Justification.[69] Martyr starts by pointing out that Smith's *Diatriba de hominis justificatione . . . adversus P.M. Vermelinum . . .* (Louvain: 1550), although its title attacks him by name, was really written against Luther and Melanchthon and seldom mentions him; few of its arguments are original but are borrowed from earlier Romanist apologetes such as Pighius and Johann Eck.[70]

Martyr gives sixty-three reasons, carefully numbered in the margins

---

[65] *Loci*, 510.

[66] *Loci*, 511.

[67] *Loci*, 511.

[68] *Loci*, 512, 495-97.

[69] Pighius is the "Achilles papistarum," (*Loci*, 529, 541). Smith joins himself to Pighius like a Theseus joining Hercules, (*Loci*, 554).

[70] *Loci*, 512. At Oxford Smith attended Martyr's lectures on First Corinthians and hence knew something of Martyr's teaching on justification.

of the *Loci*, why good works do not justify. Most of the arguments show that justification by works opposes the text of scripture either directly or by clear implication. Most of the texts cited by Martyr are from the Pauline epistles, but some are from the gospels and the Old Testament. Martyr's target seems to be Pelagian tendencies in popular Catholicism, for he concludes by saying that some men are so foolish that they attribute justification not only to good works but also to such stupid superstitions as holy water, blessed ashes, and palm branches.[71] This part of Martyr's tract merely tears apart a straw-man since Trent's Decree on Justification (January 13, 1547) condemned the proposition that the good works of the unregenerate justify. Martyr never acknowledges this.[72] More interesting than Martyr's heaping up of scripture texts against justification by works are his statements in answer to several objections. He insists that Paul's attack on justification by works is not restricted to the ceremonial works of the Jewish Law, but also reaches to morally good works of all kinds.[73] Nor do the Christian sacraments confer grace—they put before man by word and visible sign God's promise in Christ, but man lays hold of this profferred grace only by his faith.[74] Martyr rejects the idea that a general grace is granted all men by which they can perform good works; this old error of the Pelagians confounds nature and grace.[75] All the works of unbelievers are sins and therefore contribute nothing to justification. Vermigli also rejects any sort of confused faith in God which allows those who do not as yet believe in Christ to perform works that please God and advance them toward justification; on the contrary, Scripture insists that only faith in Christ pleases God.[76]

Martyr next turns his fire on the "sacred anchor" of the Catholics: the distinction between congruous and condigned merit. He defines congruous merit as that which is due moral actions, which of their nature do not really merit salvation, except in so far as salvation is promised out of a certain goodness of God. Condigned merit is a reward strictly owed, such as that owed the good work of the regenerate. Martyr rejects this distinction: not only is it not found in Scripture, it opposes the clear teaching of Scripture that the sufferings of

---

[71] *Loci*, 520.
[72] Denzinger-Schönmetzer, nn. 1532, 1551.
[73] *Loci*, 521, 524.
[74] *Loci*, 521.
[75] *Loci*, 523.
[76] *Loci*, 522.

this time are unworthy of comparison with future glory (Romans 8:18). Martyr claims that his adversaries have maliciously fabricated this destinction to avoid the arguments of the Reformed.[77] Martyr also rejects the notion of works that prepare man for justification: none are needed since God gives salvation freely; but if man prepares himself for salvation, then he has grounds for pride and self-congratulation, contrary to the teaching of Scripture. Christ saved prostitutes who were without good works, but he did not save the scribes who performed them.[78] God's predestination is the true cause of man's happiness.[79] Martyr repeats tirelessly that God's Law only increases the knowledge and therefore the guilt of men without faith. Could man perform unaided the works of the Law, he would be justified by them, but he cannot; only the justified can perform works pleasing to God.[80]

After refuting these various objections, Martyr turns to the teachings of the Church Fathers. He feels this necessary because his adversaries, more patrologists than real theologians, cull out isolated quotations from the Fathers to impress the uneducated. In fact, the Fathers agree with Martyr in rejecting justification by works. Martyr cites passages from Basil, Gregory Nazianzus, Augustine, Chrysostom, and Cyprian to show that works do not cause justification; he quotes Origen, Basil, Chrysostom and Augustine who teach that justification is freely given *ex mera Dei gratia*.[81] He then turns to the statements of the Church Councils, which must be carefully measured against Scripture and not accepted uncritically. Martyr quotes with approval the fourth and fifth canons of the Fifteenth Council of Carthage (May 1, 418).[82] He also quotes and explains Canons 4, 5, 6, 7, 8, 13, 17, and 25 of the Second Council of Orange (July 3, 529).[83]

Martyr's remarks on the early councils serve as an introduction to

---

[77] *Loci*, 524. In fact the distinction antedated the Reformation. See Oberman, *Harvest*, 44, 67-74. Elsewhere Martyr attributes the distinction to the later scholastics, *Loci*, 156.

[78] *Loci*, 524.

[79] *Loci*, 528. Vera enim causa foelicitatis nostrae est quod simus electi et praedestinati a Deo ad aeternam illam haereditatem.

[80] *Loci*, 525-30.

[81] *Loci*, 531-33.

[82] *Loci*, 534. Until recently there was a great deal of confusion about the history of this council. Martyr attributes its fifth canon to "Concilium Aphricanum" and its fourth to "Concilium Milevitanum." For scholarly references and the text of the canons see Denzinger-Schönmetzer, nn. 226, 227.

[83] *Loci*, 534-35. For the text of the canons, Denzinger-Schönmetzer, nn. 374-78, 383, 387, 395. All these canons condemn aspects of Pelagianism.

his attack on the Council of Trent and its Decree on Justification. He singles out its fifth chapter which treats the preparation for justification. He summarizes it and exclaims: "Could Pelagius have said anything else were he alive?" [84] Martyr then tries to show how Trent opposes the teaching of the Council of Orange, particularly since the earlier council stated that the human mind does not obey the call of grace unless it has been changed from unbelief to faith. He seems especially upset by Trent's insistence that man does not do absolutely nothing in the process of justification and has the power to receive grace, even though this ability depends upon a previous action of grace. Martyr argues that Trent misuses Scripture when it illustrates man's role with Zechariah 1:3, "Be converted to me, and I will be converted to you." This verse, he argues, has nothing to do with interior justification but refers only to external good works. In short, Trent claims to uphold grace but its teachings are consonant with Pelagianism. [85] Martyr also attacks the sixth and seventh chapters of the Tridentine decree which deal with the preparation for and causes of justification. There can be no preparation since all human actions before justification are sins and so increase man's alienation from God. [86]

The second major thesis in Martyr's justification tract maintains that justification comes by faith. Should man attain justice by his works, the justice of God would not be manifest, and man would boast of his efforts and zeal. "The most important thing God requires of man is that he have nothing to boast of." [87] Martyr's God is a jealous God who will not share his glory with another. In the process of man's salvation outlined in Romans 8:29-30, Martyr discerns five stages: foreknowledge, predestination, vocation, justification, and glorification. Between vocation and justification only one thing intervenes, faith. There are no preparatory steps. Vocation confronts man with God's promises of salvation; by believing the promises man lays hold of his salvation. [88] Martyr gathers over fifty biblical texts to show that man is justified by faith, drawing particularly on Romans and Galatians, but ranging over the whole Bible. [89]

Most of the objections against justification by faith that Martyr

---

[84] *Loci*, 535. Denzinger-Schönmetzer, n. 1525.

[85] *Loci*, 535-36.

[86] *Loci*, 536-37.

[87] *Loci*, 537.

[88] *Loci*, 538. Man does not merit justification by his faith; it is God's free gift. *Loci*, 488.

[89] *Loci*, 537-41.

answers come from Pighius, Smith, and Erasmus. Pighius argued that faith and charity can be separated since many Christian believers clearly live scandalous lives and therefore possess neither charity nor God's favor. Martyr responds by recalling his definition of faith. True faith is a firm assent which entails joy, love, and good works. Those passages in the Bible (Matthew 7:22; 1 Corinthians 13:1; James 2:14) which seem to show faith separated from justice, charity, and works refer to a dead faith. Dead faith relates to true and justifying faith in the same way a dead body compares to a live person. A corpse is not a man. Dead faith is not truly faith and hence does not justify. This distinction plays a crucial role in Martyr's answer to objections raised by his adversaries.[90]

Martyr does not hold the doctrine of the perseverance of the saints as interpreted by many later Calvinists, that once man has received justifying faith he never falls from grace and justification. On the contrary, Vermigli teaches that man can fall into sin and thereby lose justification, but as often as he truly assents to God's promises he recovers justification.[91] The man who commits serious sins does not have true faith and is alienated from God even though he believes in the existence of God and the articles of faith. There can be no true faith without good works. Faith and love for God always accompany each other but faith has a logical priority.[92] Martyr never uses Luther's phrase *simul justus et peccator*, not only because paradoxical expression is foreign to his mentality, but also because it does not square with his understanding of justification by faith alone. Klaus Sturm points to the double justification theories popular in Italy among Martyr's friends in the decade before Trent and stresses their continued influence on his early Strasbourg statements on justification. He shows that Martyr developed a more fully Protestant stance in the Romans commentary and took considerable pains to distinguish his teaching from that of Trent. Nevertheless, as Sturm rightly points out, his teaching retained many Catholic nuances which Luther and Calvin left behind.[93]

---

[90] *Loci*, 541-44, 495-500. Martyr also calls dead faith *fides signorum* and *fides historica* (*Loci*, 543, 549) and *inanis, temporaria et vana* (*Loci*, 485).

[91] Cur autem Deus repetere voluit illas promissiones, non est obscurum; ita enim infirmus est animus noster ut nisi repetantur et identidem inculcentur verba Dei, facile resiliat a fide. Neque vero iustificatio semel tantum apprehenditur sed quoties promissionibus divinis vere atque efficaciter assentimur: nam quum assidue labamur et incidamus in peccata, opus habemus subinde repetita iustificatione. *Loci*, 545; also, 491.

[92] *Loci*, 546-47.

[93] Sturm, 62-68, 254.

How can man be sure that his faith is true faith, and not merely a dead, historical faith? True faith which comes fom the Holy Spirit is certain, firm, and efficacious. It changes a man's heart and leads him to holy living. The Spirit testifies internally to his spirit, the Scriptures explain it, and man's own good works prove the transformation worked within him. In contrast, the works-righteous do not have the confirmation of the Spirit and are opposed by the teachings of the Bible. Even their good works are a sham, just as were the virtues of the old pagans.[94] Martyr buttresses his case for justification by faith with five pages of patristic quotations.[95]

Martyr devotes less space to his third basic proposition, that justification comes from faith alone. He admits that the word *alone* is not found explicitly in the pertinent scripture passages, but the real meaning of these passages necessarily implies that man is justified by faith alone. This is the thrust and only possible interpretation of all the passages which assert that salvation is given *gratis*.[96] Smith objected precisely to this identification of *gratis* with *sola fide*. Martyr answers that *gratis* means without price or cause; after all, when Paul says that man is justified by faith he quickly adds, "without works" (Romans 3:28).[97] If works intervene, then they are the cause or price which earns justification. In fact charity, hope and good works do accompany justifying faith, but they do not have the power to justify. Otherwise man would have grounds for pride and self-congratulation, whereas Paul teaches that we have nothing but what we have received. To attribute the power to justify to hope, charity, and the works that accompany faith is as foolish as attributing the sun's power to warm to its roundness.[98] Martyr concludes his long treatise on justification with a catena of quotations from and references to eleven Greek and five Latin Fathers plus a distinguished group of medieval theologians including St. Bernard, St. Thomas, and Nicholas of Lyra.[99]

HOPE AND UNION WITH CHRIST

The internal witness of the Spirit and their own good works assure the justified that God will be merciful to them in Christ. Conscious of their faith they are certain that God's promise of forgiveness applies

---

[94] *Loci*, 549, 552.
[95] *Loci*, 555-59.
[96] *Loci*, 559.
[97] *Loci*, 559, 561.
[98] *Loci*, 560.
[99] *Loci*, 563-64.

to them individually and in this very act of believing they obtain forgiveness; they do not and must not doubt that they belong to the elect.[100] The Christian faces life with both fear and joy. His fear arises from the coruption, weakness and tendency to evil he finds still operating within him, but his fear is a filial fear of offending God rather than a servile fear of punishment. Filial fear always accompanies true faith; servile fear never does. But the Christian is also joyful because he trusts in God's goodness and constancy to check his own tendency toward evil. Were he to trust his own efforts rather than God's steadfastness, he would quickly fall into despair.[101]

This joy and trust are the foundation of hope, which is the mean between desperation and that false security which is the contempt of God's justice and the root of all impiety.[102] Martyr rejects Peter Lombard's definition of hope since it included a partial reliance on man's own merits; [103] rather he defines hope as "the faculty given by the Holy Spirit by which we expect with certainty and calmness that the salvation begun in us through Christ and realized through faith shall eventually be perfected in us by God's mercy and not by our own merits." [104] Faith gives birth to hope because the things hoped for are not clear and their final attainment depends on faith. Since the objects of hope are difficult to attain, Martyr contrasts supernatural hope with the natural hope found in animals and men as they struggle to obtain the difficult. This natural hope pertains to the *vis irascens*, whereas supernatural hope is a virtue of the soul. It is worth noting that, while Martyr insists with the whole Reformed tradition that justifying grace is merely *favor Dei* and not a metaphysical habit or quality in the soul, he has no hestitation in following Aquinas in understanding hope as such a habit.[105]

Hope is crucial for holy living. "The sum of gospel living is this, that we are utterly convinced that God loves us and will ultimately make us happy." This is no easy conviction—even the saints waver because in this life man remains imperfect and beset with weakness, but such waverings are not intrinsic to faith and hope in themselves.

---

[100] *Loci*, 491, 549, 552. Marvin Anderson examines Martyr's teaching on hope, "Peter Martyr on Romans," *Scottish Journal of Theology*, XXVI, 1973, 407-413.

[101] *Loci*, 491, 506-07.

[102] *Loci*, 494.

[103] *Loci*, 505.

[104] *Loci*, 507.

[105] *Loci*, 507: Sic Deus in animi nostri parte nobiliori constituit spem. Compare this passage with St. Thomas, *S.T.*, I, 80, 2; II, II, 18, 1.

Mathematics remains a certain science, even though a beginner often encounters hesitations and uncertainties in working out its problems. So too the Christian vacillates because his faith and hope are not yet as perfect as they should be. Nevertheless hope rests on faith and faith rests on God's sure promise of mercy in his revealed word; hence man must trust that God will deliver him from danger and temptation or, should he fall, that God will restore him and lead him to life everlasting.[106]

Clearly the Christian must be convinced of his own election, but what should his attitude be toward the election and salvation of his fellow men, particularly his fellow believers? He does not have the internal witness of the Spirit for others as he has for himself, so he cannot know the sincerity of their faith. Still he can observe their union with the Church and their good deeds. Because he knows that God addresses his general promise of mercy, revealed in the Scriptures, to all believers, he should be optimistic about their salvation, even though he can never know with certainty who are among the predestined or the reprobate. Such knowledge is not helpful toward salvation, otherwise God would have revealed it; therefore man must not worry about or pry into hidden mysteries of God's will.[107]

For Martyr justification brings man into a new relation with Jesus Christ. Since the incarnation there has been a material union based on the Word's assumption of human nature. Christ shares flesh and blood with all men, but the justified achieve a higher union with Christ, a union by insertion into Christ. Paul describes this union when he speaks of the marriage of Christ with the Church in Ephesians 5:23; but Martyr prefers to dwell on the Johannine imagery of the vine and the branches which live and grow by a commom sap and life. Jesus Christ is man's salvation so that those who are joined to him run no danger of condemnation; they are led by his spirit and seek only his glory. Indeed, Martyr claims that a close analysis of this union by the four Aristotelian causes reveals a four-fold sharing common to Christ and the justified. This union which comes through faith causes the Christian to be reborn and makes him a son of God. The unique cause of this adoption as sons is God's free election and predestination; there is no cause on man's side. So too Christ and the Father come to dwell within the regenerate in many ways, but the principal way arises strictly from predestination. Martyr's grounding of union with Christ

---

[106] *Loci*, 508.
[107] *Loci*, 480, 552.

in predestination plays a crucial role in his ecclesiology: in all other visible societies and associations men work together toward a temporal end, but the communion of saints, the Church, is ordered toward everlasting life. Participation in this society depends not only upon the union of the members with one another, but also on their union with Christ. As only the regenerate are united with Christ, only they are truly in the Church: the unregenerate may participate in the Church's external activities, but they are not united with Christ and therefore not really members of the Church.[108]

GRACE

Martyr finds that Scripture assigns two meanings to *grace*: it is primarily God's benevolence for man and the gratuitous favor with which he regards the elect; secondarily grace is the gifts God freely confers on man. The first is justifying grace, the second actual or helping grace.[109] Grace in its primary sense remains solely in God; properly speaking man is not given grace but received by God into his grace and favor and becomes the object of his good will. Vermigli defines grace as "God's free benevolence by which he holds us dear in Christ Jesus, forgives our sins, gives us the Holy Spirit, upright living, and eternal happiness." [110] Together with almost all Protestant theologians he rejects the scholastic definition of justifying grace as a habit or quality inhering in the soul. "They seem to have dreamed up grace as a sort of garment hanging in the air which anyone who wants can put on." [111] Martyr singles out Aquinas for criticism on this point and traces the scholastic theory of justification by inherent grace to the pagan philosophical notion of a habit which enables its possessor to perform actions he otherwise either could not do at all or could accomplish only with difficulty. Since the scholastics have no scriptural basis for their theory, Aquinas and the others offer some flimsy rational arguments, which in fact involve various contradictions.[112]

---

[108] *Loci*, 501-502. Qui autem agunt eius spiritu, affectus et incitationes cupitatum non sequuntur. Ex his apparet quomodo fideles homines et pii sunt in Christo, idque per omnia causarum genera. Materiam enim habeamus eandem, inchoationes etiam formae easdem; donati enim simus eisdem notis, proprietatibus et conditionibus quas ille habuit. Efficiens causa qua impellimur ad agendum, est idem spiritus quo ipse agebatur. Postremo finis etiam idem est, nimirum ut illustretur gloria Dei. *Loci*, 502.

[109] *Romanos*, 193; *Loci*, 479.

[110] *Loci*, 479-80.

[111] *Romanos*, 195; also see *Loci*, 479; *Samuelis*, f. 58v.

[112] *Romanos*, 193, 158; *Loci*, 479.

Martyr also attacks the scholastics who say that grace comes first, but man has the power to accept or reject it. If that were so, man's salvation would depend on himself, whereas Paul and Augustine teach that salvation depends on God and not on man. In the actual process of justification, man's role is passive under the saving action of God. To explain this Martyr draws on two analogies from his scholastic heritage. In a substantial change prime matter remains passive as it receives new substantial forms under the action of the efficient cause. Secondly, the soul has what the scholastics call an obediential potency to justification, that is, a built-in aptitude for God's healing action (although this is a passive capacity rather than an active power within the soul) since man is a rational being created after the image of God.[113] Once man has been justified and reborn, his will should not lie idle and do nothing; it must co-operate with grace so that what God has begun alone can be carried forward by God and man, for now the regenerate have been made sons of God, apt for good works, and directed by the impulse of the Holy Spirit.[114]

Is grace irresistible in Martyr's theology as it was for many seventeenth century Calvinists? Martyr's answer is highly qualified. As far as they can, the unregenerate try to resist grace, but in the actul process of justification their will is passive. Man does not have the power to accept or reject justifying grace. In the regenerate there are various degrees of divine help and grace. The stronger graces absolutely bend the human will, although Martyr insists this involves no forcing of the will but only a gentle yet efficacious conversion so that the will falls in freely with the divine impulse. Sometimes the grace is less strong; if man applies his will and does not fight against grace, he will follow its impulse. But when man does not apply himself, he can be said to resist grace and hence he falls into sin. The variation in the intensity of grace results partly because man's negligence in using grace earns (*commereatur*) this fluctuation in God's help, partly because God

---

[113] *Loci*, 984, 478, 481. ... Materia prima per transformationem suscipit novas formas et movetur ab efficienti. Confert autem subiectum: nam subiicitur illis motibus, deinde habet potentiam seu habilitatem quandam ad has formas; ita mens humana subiectum est passivum istius conversionis atque sanationis; deinde potentiam quandam habet vel habilitatem, non quidem activam, sed passivam: idque dum comparatur Deo, quod possit ab eo active commutari. Sumus enim creati rationales ad imaginem et similitudinem Dei. Et sane haec potentia passiva huius generis, possit dici more scholasticorum potentia passiva: quia sumus capaces divinae immuntationis, cum Deus illam efficere voluerit. *Loci*, 984.

[114] *Loci*, 481.

wishes thereby to show man that he is directed by the divine will rather than his own designs. Hence some actual graces are irresistible, others are not. Adam in the state of integral nature could keep the commandments with even a weak grace, provided that he exerted himself. Regenerate man with effort and zeal can offer an incipient obedience when given a weak grace, even though he cannot obey consistently and perfectly.[115]

Like the scholastics before him, Martyr conceives of actual or helping grace as a particular kind of concurrence that God sends to men. God's concurrence with human acts differs from his concurrence in the operations of inanimate objects, plants and animals because it operates according to man's intellectual and volitional nature by illuminating the intellect and strengthening the will so that man acts in accord with the divine will.[116]

Martyr has little use for most of the elaborate terminology and distinctions invented by theologians for describing grace. All helping grace is the same; it is distinguished only by its effects. Particularly he rejects the scholastic distinction of *gratia gratis data* and *gratia gratum faciens* since all grace is gratuitous. Moreover *gratia gratum faciens* implies an inherent habit rather than God's pure justifying favor. Grace is necessary at every stage of man's spiritual growth; Martyr compares it to the sun which causes the various stages of growth from the first planting of the seed until the production of fruit. So grace first heals man's will so he begins to will the good, then to carry it out, then to persevere in doing good until finally God crowns man's perseverance with eternal happiness.[117]

Besides the imputed justice that the Christian has through faith independent of works, there is a second inherent justice which consists of faith, charity, and good works and is nourished by grace. Although this second justice never perfectly fulfills God's law, it strives to obey the commandments. Martyr finds that this second justice is taught by the Scriptures (Ephesians 4:24; Hebrews 11:33) no less than imputed righteousness.[118] In teaching a second justice or sanctification Martyr fits easily into the mainstream of Protestant tradition.[119]

---

[115] *Loci*, 478, 481, 474; *Iudicum*, f. 113v. McLelland, "Predestination," 259, denies that Martyr teaches irresistible grace.

[116] *Romanos*, 210, 195.

[117] *Loci*, 482; *Romanos*, 196.

[118] *Loci*, 500.

[119] Martyr's doctrine on sanctification compares closely with Calvin's as summarized by Wendel, 242-45.

Here is the point where Martyr's teaching on Christian morality and the pursuit of holiness links up with his theology of man and grace. His teaching on these subjects, rich and fully deserving investigation, seems to flow from a deep personal piety which his prayers on the Psalms reflect and to which his friends testify: but this broad area lies outside the scope of the present study.[120]

RESURRECTION AND GLORIFICATION

Predestination and justification reach their climax with the resurrection of the elect unto life and glorification. Reprobation and the intrinsic dynamic of fallen human nature realize their finality in the resurrection of the reprobate unto damnation and punishment. Martyr's doctrine of the resurrection not only forms an intrinsic part of his theological anthropology but also offers insight into his theological method. References to the resurrection are scattered through all Martyr's scripture commentaries and are particularly rich in his comments on the final chapter of First Corinthians. Martyr presents his most systematic examination of the resurrection as a scholion in his commentary on the Second Book of Kings.[121] The presentation here follows that scholion.

As a preliminary Martyr advances two arguments for the resurrection, although he considers neither argument apodictic. God decrees the resurrection to make His elect happy since there is no happiness in this life in which all human actions, whether theoretic or practical, are imperfect. Man's theoretic or knowing operations are weak for numerous reasons: for example, memory lapses are frequent, and education remains the prerogative of an elite. No less do men fall short of perfection in their practical activities, for passion seethes and tosses men about so that they cannot devote themselves to right doing. Disease and wounds, heat and cold, poverty and hunger all beset man's body and weigh down his soul. The human condition tends to frustrate man's in-built drive for happiness at every turn. Hence another life is necessary if the elect are to reach happiness.[122]

At this point Martyr digresses to fend off dualists who see the soul as good and the body as evil. If that were the case, happiness could hardly result from the reunion of body and soul, but only from the

---

[120] Peter Martyr, *Preces Sacrae ex Psalmis Davidis Desumptae ...*, (Zurich; 1567). Sturm treats regeneration in Martyr, 203-216.

[121] *Melachim*, ff. 214v-233r.

[122] *Melachim*, ff. 214v-215r.

freedom of the soul from the burden of the body. Martyr first singles out the early heretics Marcion, Basilides, Valentinian and the Manicheans. These thorough-going dualists set up two Gods: the good God creates spirit, the evil God creates matter. Man's spirit can only achieve happiness by liberation from its bodily prison. Martyr then broadens his attack to include mitigated dualists who see the body/ soul relationship as analogous to that of sailor and ship, or mover and object moved. Small wonder that the mitigated dualists find the resurrection objectionable since nobody desires to reassume a burden once he has laid it aside. Martyr answers the mitigated dualists by rejecting their understanding of the body/soul relationship and re-asserting his Aristotelian position. The soul is the form and perfection of the body so that the two together constitute a single hypostasis or person. Hence, after death the soul retains a strong propensity to reunite with its body. Martyr fails to name any of the mitigated dual-ists and then does something strange indeed. He calls Plato and Pythagoras as witnesses against mitigated dualism since they argue for metempsychosis, which at least involves reunion of body and soul, albeit a new body. Martyr cites no passage in Plato's writings, but he must have had in mind the myth of Er which concludes the *Republic*. This deference to Plato is the more striking because Plato is the most prominent exponent of the mitigated dualism that Martyr is attack-ing.[123] Martyr compounds his error thirty pages later by again calling on Plato as a witness favoring the resurrection.[124]

Martyr also bitterly criticizes the Stoic theory of the great year or great cycle of renewal which taught that every 36,000 years according to some, every 40,000 years according to others, every event would exactly repeat itself down to the smallest detail. Martyr first attacks the mathematics behind this theory, basing himself partly on the pre-suppositions of the Ptolemaic system, partly on biblical chronology (Martyr calculated the age of the world at somewhat under 6,000 years). "Either opinion (36,000 or 40,000 years) is truly ridiculous and inept and is refuted by Aristotle who vehemently asserts that it is impossible that what has happened can return as numerically identical, however long a space of time you wish to postulate." The resurrection

---

[123] *Melachim*, f. 215r.

[124] *Melachim*, 230v: Because Porphyry attacks Christian belief in the resurrec-tion, Martyr accuses the famous Neo-Platonist of departing from the teaching of Plato "qui posuerit reditum animorum ad pristina corpora." In doing so, Martyr probably reflects St. Augustine, *De Civitate Dei*, XXII, 24.

of the dead depends upon God's power and not on the movement of the stars. Moreover the Stoic concept provides only a sham "resurrection" since the "resurrected" will shortly undergo their original death all over again.[125]

Having dealt with these adversaries against his first argument for the resurrection, Martyr develops his second argument very briefly: God must manifest his justice, but as divine justice is little manifested in this world where the wicked often prosper and the upright suffer, another life is needed.

After these preliminary remarks, Martyr attempts to define the resurrection. As usual he starts with a thorough discussion of the Greek and Hebrew words for the concept, then moves onto more philosophical ground. The resurrection pertains to the predicament of action. The resurrection surpasses created power, hence God alone is its efficient cause.[126] After discussing the Aristotelian classification of kinds of action, Martyr finds that the resurrection defies the traditional categories. It is unique and totally transnatural. Martyr compares the resurrection to a new birth rather than to the act of creation, since creation is a coming to being out of nothing. The soul communicates to the body existence and all the human properties. Risen man will be essentially the same as before, but with accidental differences. With these considerations in mind, Martyr defines the resurrection as a new joining of the soul to the body by the power of God so that the whole man can stand before the last judgement and receive reward or punishment in accord with his past life.[127] He than explicates the four causes contained in his definition. The material cause is the body and the soul; the formal cause is their new union; the efficient cause is God's power, and the final cause is that the whole man may be judged.[128] The exemplary cause is Christ's own resurrection which

---

[125] *Melachim*, f. 215r: "Ridicula vero et inepta est utraque opinio et confundatur ab Aristotele qui affirmat vehementer fieri non potest ut quae interciderunt redeant eodem numero, quanto spatio temporis volueris interposito." Strange as it seems, at least one Italian philosopher of the time did teach this theory: see Umberto Pirotti, "Aristotelian Philosophy and the Popularization of Learning: Benedetto Varchi and Renaissance Aristotelianism," in *The Late Italian Renaissance*, ed. Eric Cochrane, (New York: 1970). 196.

[126] *Melachim*, ff. 215v-216r. Cumque in actionibus duo praesertim expendantur, nimirum agens et subiectum ipsum in quod ab agente actio transfunditur, efficientem causam huius actionis ponemus Deum: quia nulla causa in natura nec vis in ullis creaturis potest reperiri quae resurrectionem valeat afficere. . . .

[127] *Melachim*, ff. 215v-216r.

[128] *Melachim*, ff. 216v, 217r.

provides a model for the general resurrection of the dead.[129] The resurrection is natural in the sense that body and soul have a natural affinity for each other, but it is miraculous and non-natural in its efficient cause and the means which bring it about, for these are a special intervention of divine power.

Vermigli next returns to the question whether there are rational arguments for the resurrection. He gives a qualified answer. Since the resurrection lies beyond any power in nature, there can be no apodictic or necessary arguments for it. There are several suasive, probable arguments. After a rather long comment on the difference between apodictic and probable arguments, Martyr lists several philosophical reasons which he thinks have only probable value in themselves, but which become apodictic for the Christian when grounded in God's written revelation.

The first reason for the resurrection argues that something imperfect is incapable of perfect happiness. Without the body the separated soul exists as mutilated and imperfect and therefore must be rejoined to the body if it is to enjoy perfect happiness. Martyr finds this argument open to two philosophical objections. The soul by nature supplies perfection to the body and receives no perfection or utility from the body; therefore separation from the body cannot be an obstacle to the soul's happiness. Besides, the soul's perfect happiness requires only that the soul have the ultimate good present, understand it perfectly, and embrace it with highest pleasure. For this the body is unnecessary.

The second argument for the resurrection urges that nothing can be permanent and eternal that runs counter to nature. The soul, as it does not die with the body, is eternal. But the soul is by nature the form of the body, and therefore it is unnatural for it to be separated from the body; consequently body and soul must eventually reunite. Martyr finds that this argument also lacks apodictic conclusiveness because it assumes the immortality of the soul as a certain premise. He points out that many eminent philosophers, such as Aristotle, Alexander of Aphrodisias, and Averroes, have doubted the personal immortality of the soul. Martyr raises a second objection drawn from Avicenna's *Metaphysics*: the soul is joined to the body so that it may use the senses to gain knowledge of the universe, but once it has acquired this knowledge there is no need for a second union with the body. A third objection admits that an unnatural separation cannot be permanent but

---

[129] *Melachim*, f. 222v: In his commentary on Romans (p. 280) Martyr develops at some length the idea of Christ as the model for the resurrection of the dead.

contends that this holds true only if the principles of a restitution remain in existence. But if these principles or roots are totally destroyed, then a restitution should not be expected since the in-built "desire" of the soul for the body cannot be directed toward the impossible. Again Martyr admits the strength of these objections of the *ethnici* and *philosophi* before the court of pure reason.[130]

Martyr suggests a third reason for the resurrection based on God's justice. In this life the body and the soul co-operate in doing either evil or good. Therefore both body and sould be rewarded or punished in the after life, not just the soul. To this the philosophers object that it is not clear that God so rules the universe as to reward or punish human individuals. There may be a providence watching over the movements of the spheres and the conservation of the species, but this providence does not extend to settling accounts with individuals. Also, virtue and vice have their in-built reward and punishment since virtue brings the joy of good conscience and vice the inescapable gnawing of bad conscience. The philosophers also point out that the soul is the principal cause of upright or sinful deeds and the body is only its instrument. The craftsman and not his tools rightly receives praise or blame for his products. Martyr does not entirely accept this objection because the body is a conjoined instrument and its relation to the soul differs from the relation of the craftsman to his tools which are only separated instruments. Martyr concludes that the three major arguments for the resurrection are only probable if taken in isolation from scripture. There are many other arguments, suggestive and poetic, but with even less probative force. Trees, for instance, seem dead in winter but revive. The seed dies, then sprouts to life from the earth.

Having examined the probable arguments and analogies for the

---

[130] *Melachim*, f. 217rv; Martyr covers this same ground in *Corinthios*, f. 417v and again anchors his whole argument in scripture and not in philosophical reasons: "Quandoquidem animus non est perfectus vel absolutus absque corpore. Non enim totus et integer homo est, sed potius dimidius, nisi Platonici velimus agere. Neque propterea in illorum scholasticorum sententiam inclino qui aiunt, si datur animorum immortalitas, probari posse resurrectionem mortuorum. Nam inquiunt: Cum anima sit forma corporis, non potest absque sua materia sive subiecto perpetuo esse, nam separatio eius a corpore putatur vi contingere. Illis autem satis confessum videtur absurdum ut aliquod violentum perpertuo duret. Sed mea ratio verbis Dei eiusque promissionibus innititur. Dixit enim se velle Deum esse fidelium et credentium in Christum. Proinde illos servabit. At si ab eo perfecte servandi sunt, hoc non tantum fiet quoad animos, verum quoad corpus. Deus autem servat suos ex toto, non ex dimidio."

resurrection, Martyr goes on to show that it is strictly an article of faith. For Martyr what is believed cannot be known naturally. The Christian's faith in the resurrection depends upon the word of God which promises that God will raise the dead. God can do anything that does not involve a contradiction. God is omnipotent, so any difficulty against the resurrection must arise from the side of the body which seems to be totally destroyed. But death does not reduce the body to nothingness but only to prime matter. Hence God's power can remake the body from prime matter.[131]

Much the longest part of Martyr's resurrection tract presents a scriptural proof for the doctrine. Martyr's treatment of the Old Testament texts on the resurrection suffers from the same defect that has been observed regarding his scriptural proof of immortality. Because he had little notion of doctrinal development within the Old Testament, he reads the resurrection into many texts which do not teach it and elaborately twists and explains away texts which assert that death is the end of human existence.[132]

Martyr next discusses the qualities and endowments (*dotes*) of the risen body. He explicitly accepts the teaching of the scholastics in this matter since he finds it in agreement with scripture. The risen bodies of the elect will possess immortality, incorruptibility, light and brightness, agility, impassibility, and subtlety. Martyr gives a long, routine explanation of these qualities and endowments. More interesting is his shorter exposition of the qualities and endowments of the risen bodies of the damned. The damned will share the qualities of immortality and incorruptibility with the elect. Their bodies must be inseparably reunited to their souls so that they can undergo judgement and its eternal consequences as total men. But the bodies of the damned will have endowments (*dotes*) antithetical to those of the saints. Martyr obtains his list of the endowments of the bodies of the damned by applying to them the exact opposite of the endowments attributed to the elect, but he always tries to undergird these deductions with scripture. The bodies of the damned will lack light and brightness but possess darkness, for as Christ proclaims, the damned will be cast out into exterior darkness. Instead of impassibility the damned will be open to every kind of bodily torture and pain, to tears and to the gnashing of teeth. Far from being agile, they will be fettered hand and

---

[131] *Melachim.*, ff. 217v, 218r.

[132] *Melachim*, ff. 219r-227r. Martyr deals with the Old Testament objections against the resurrection in *Melachim*, ff. 231v, 232r.

foot and thrown into hell where the fire is not extinguished. Their bodies will be gross rather than subtle. All these are accidental changes, and the risen damned will retain their human substance.[133]

In the course of his discussion of the endowments of the risen body Martyr singles out four chief adversaries for attack: strict Lutherans, Moslems, chiliasts, and Origen. Each deserves a brief comment here.

Martyr observes with considerable glee that neither sacred scripture, nor the ancient Fathers, nor the scholastics ever attribute ubiquity to the risen body of Christ or the saints. Against the Lutherans he cites the teaching of the scholastics and especially of Thomas Aquinas that the blessed in heaven have a definite habitation. As has been seen, Martyr admits the distinction so important in scholastic thought, especially of the later period, between God's *potentia absoluta* and *potentia ordinata*, but this distinction exerts little influence on his thinking. The Lutheran case for ubiquity partly depended upon an appeal to its possibility within the *potentia absoluta*. Martyr makes short shrift of this appeal. He finds no evidence for ubiquity in scripture and no instance of it in nature. He refuses to entertain appeals to God's power —he cares not a fig for a power that is shown never to have gone into act. "Wherefore the voice of nature, which has God Himself as its author, must be heard."[134]

According to Martyr the Moslems err in attributing too gross a character to resurrected bliss. As risen man is incorruptible, there will be no need for food and drink; still less will there be the use of sex since the risen saints will be like angels of heaven. Risen man will retain intact his digestive and reproductive systems, but these will have no function to perform. Martyr agrees with Avicenna's explanation of why the Koran painted a sensual picture of heavenly pleasure: the original followers of Mohammed were a rude and primitive people; the Koran therefore used vivid, earthly concepts suited to their limited understanding, but such passages should be interpreted allegorically. Martyr also considers as gross the chiliastic views of some of the early Fathers and of certain Protestant radicals that Christ would come to found a thousand year earthy kingdom. This error comes from too literal an interpretation of a few biblical statements.

---

[133] *Melachim*, ff. 228v, 229r.

[134] *Melachim*, f. 230rv: "Quare audienda vox naturae, quae Deum ipsum habet authorem. . . . Caeterum isti (the Lutherans) dicent, 'Cum rogemus de potentia, tu de facto respondes.' Ad hoc dico me nihil morari eam potentiam quae numquam erupuisse in actum ostenditur."

Martyr dismisses the Moslems and chiliasts quickly enough. Not so Origen who erred in the opposite way by spiritualizing man's risen body. According to the Alexandrian the risen saints will have a body but not flesh. Martyr rejects this as second-hand Platonism, opposed to the teaching of scripture.[135] Martyr's attack on Origen may also have been aimed at Lelio Sozzini who held similar ideas.[136]

Having refuted these false notions of the resurrection, Martyr turns to answer the objections of those who reject the resurrection root and branch. The first objection comes from the Neo-Platonist Porphyry who argued that as the destiny of the soul is true happiness, which consists in knowing divine reality, the soul could only be impeded by the body which weighs it down. Martyr replies that the body is not a tomb, but was created by God as the soul's helper; the body becomes a hindrance only through sin. Even in this life, in which human nature has been depraved by original sin, the body is not useless provided that man uses it properly and with faith. At the resurrection the body will be repaired and improved so that it will enhance man's happiness.[137]

To the argument that the body has been so thoroughly destroyed and dissolved into its elements that its restitution is impossible, Martyr responds that this objection underestimates God's power. He who created the world can restore man's body. Besides, it is man's form, his soul, which provides unity and continuity to the human person. Even in this life the body is constantly being destroyed and renewed while the soul perdures through these changes. Even in the extreme case of a corpse eaten by cannibals, God can use the other matter that constituted the body years before its death to restore the body at the resurrection; should anything be missing, divine power can supply it. A further objection urges that death destroys not only the body but also the lower parts of the soul, for instance the sense faculties, the sense appetites, and the digestive and procreative faculties. Martyr answers that death blocks the use of these faculties but does not destroy them since they are preserved integral in the soul, even when separated from the body. The resurrection restores the use of the powers of the lower part of the soul, except the digestive and procreative faculties.[138]

---

[135] *Melachim*, f. 229rv.

[136] George H. Williams, *The Radical Reformation*, (Philadelphia, 1962), 508, 569.

[137] *Melachim*, ff. 230v, 231r. In contrast, Calvin (*Institutes*, III, 9, 4) accepts the Platonic comparison of the body with a prison.

[138] *Melachim*, f. 231v.

This chapter has dwelt at considerable length on Peter Martyr's teaching on predestination, freedom justification, hope, and the resurrection of the dead. All are aspects of God's plan to save man that was formed before creation, achieved in principle by Christ's death and resurrection, worked out through the justification of individual men living under both covenants, and will find full realization at the end-times when the fabric of this world crashes, the dead rise, and God gathers his elect into the new heaven and the new earth. The detailed analysis of Martyr's doctrine has revealed clearly that his conversion to Protestantism and his long teaching career north of the Alps by no means obliterated or rendered useless his earlier training in Aristotelian philosophy and scholastic theology, that in fact this training put into his hands a powerful tool to supplement the usual Protestant emphasis on the Bible, the new literal exegesis, and mastery of the biblical languages. It now remains to suggest ways that Martyr influenced the direction of Reformed theology and to gather together the conclusions of this study.

CHAPTER SEVEN

THE INFLUENCE OF MARTYR'S THOUGHT

Assertions abound that Peter Martyr Vermigli exerted an important influence on his own time and the next several generations. Several scholars consider him the greatest and most influential Italian Protestant theologian.[1] His biographer, Charles Schmidt, states that he did more to establish the doctrine of predestination within Reformed Protestantism than anybody else except John Calvin.[2] Some have pointed out his contribution to the development of Reformed scholasticism, or his sacramental theology or his writings on marriage; still others emphasized his contribution to political thought and others his influence on specific theologians and writers. Nobody has attempted to draw all these threads together and try to give a complete and composite picture of Martyr's influence, perhaps because it is a difficult task which would require an encyclopedic yet precise knowledge of dozens of theologians from 1550 to 1650. Here I attempt only an outline.

Aside from this general requirement there are four specific obstacles to assessing Martyr's impact. Firstly, his impact was geographically diffuse. After the completion of his student days at Padua, his longest stay in any one place was his last six years at Zurich. Martyr's travels spread his influence but also deprived it of a single geographical focal point or center of radiation such as Calvin enjoyed at Geneva or Bullinger at Zurich. Moreover, in four important spheres of his activity, his work was subject to systematic uprooting—by the Theatines and Jesuits at Naples, by the Inquisition at Lucca, by Mary Tudor in

---

[1] "His name was joined with Calvin's in the defensive polemics of the Reformation and together they gave positive shape to Reformed theology." McLelland, vii. "Pietro Martire Vermigli è generalmente considerato come il più grande riformatore italiano del secolo XVI." Augusto Jahier, *Riformatori e Riformati del Secolo XV° e XVI°*, (Florence: 1925), 52. "Pietro Martire Vermigli, la testa teologica più forte di tutti l'emigrazione italiana," Francesco Ruffini, *Studi sui Riformatori Italiani*, (Torino: 1955), 418. T. F. Torrance writes in his Forward to McLelland, vi, "Peter Martyr was undoubtedly one of the finest scholars and ablest theologians of his generation and must be ranked close to Calvin himself. . . ." According to Gordon Huelin (p. 178), J. Scaliger considered Calvin and Martyr the two most excellent theologians of the sixteenth century and noted Martyr's ability to use scholasticism to refute the older scholastics.

[2] Schmidt, *Leben*, 106.

England, and by Johann Marbach and the Lutherans at Strasbourg. The second obstacle to examining Martyr's influence is the complex and encyclopedic character of his learning and his writings, for Martyr was not a man of one idea, and different readers and students took different things from him. The third obstacle is the reluctance of sixteenth century writers to cite precise sources when they borrow ideas from contemporary or near contemporary authors. The fourth and greatest obstacle is that Martyr was not a theological lone wolf but rather an esteemed member of a circle of theologians, led by Calvin, who were developing similar ideas and cross-fertilizing one another's theology at roughly the same time. Martyr's teaching on such subjects as predestination, the Eucharist, and the relation of Church and state differs from that of Calvin, Bucer, Bullinger and others mainly in emphasis and nuance. Most of those who read Vermigli's writings also read those of the other Reformed theologians, often without much advertence to the individual stress of each author. This makes it difficult to take the writings of a later writer, for instance Zacharias Ursinus or William Perkins on predestination, and parcel out so much to the influence of Calvin, so much to Martyr, so much to Beza. The influence of the theologians of Calvin's and Martyr's generation on the following generation was mainly cumulative and overlapping rather than distinct and idiosyncratic.

The single most impressive index of Martyr's popularity as a writer is the wide diffusion of his books. In the hundred years or so after his conversion to Protestantism there were about 110 separate printings of his writings.[3] Save for a few short pieces in Italian, all his works were originally in Latin and intended for the educated of Europe. Most make demanding reading. His most important works are unquestionably the massive scripture commentaries and the polemical writings, but some of his writings reached a more popular audience, for instance his first publication, *Una sempliche dichiaratione sopra gli XII articola della Fede Christiana*. While not among the great or more popular catechisms of the sixteenth century, it did enjoy translation into Latin and English. Almost certainly Martyr's *Preces Sacrae ex Psalmis Davidis Desumptae* were mainly expressions of private devotion and piety, but after his death they were published ten times between 1564 and 1604, including translations into French, English, and German. Easily the most influential of Martyr's works was the *Loci Communes*,

---

[3] Robert Kingdon and I are preparing a scholarly bibliography of Vermigli's works for the *Corpus Reformatorum Italicorum*.

a compilation made by gathering extracts (overwhelmingly from the scholia of his scripture commentaries) and arranging them systematically according to the order of Calvin's *Institutes*. Martyr seems always to have been a bit reluctant to publish his lectures; only those on Corinthians, Romans, and Judges appeared during his lifetime. The idea of gathering a sort of commonplace book was suggested to him, but rather characteristically he replied he might do it when he got the time.[4] Shortly after Martyr's death Theodore Beza urged the project in a letter to Bullinger.[5] Beza's suggestion did not bear immediate fruit, and when the *Loci* appeared in print it was not at Geneva or Zurich but in distant London in 1576. The editor was Robert Masson, pastor of the French congregation in London. There were a number of causes for the delay, particularly the sheer size of the work, over one thousand folio pages. The compilation of the *Loci* had to await the publication by Froschauer of Zurich of Martyr's manuscript Old Testament commentaries. Samuel appeared in 1564, Kings in 1556, and Genesis in 1569. The *Loci Communes* utilizes all these commentaries as well as the incomplete commentary on Aristotle's *Ethics* published in 1563, a year after Martyr's death. In the fifty years following the first edition, there were thirteen more printings of the *Loci* at London, Basel, Zurich, Geneva, and Heidelberg. The final printing came at Amsterdam in 1656.

Books were not the only way that Martyr's influence spread. Perhaps equally important were his personal activity and that of his students and disciples. There were four places where this activity was most important: Lucca, England, Zurich, and Heidelberg. Our discussion will take up and center on each of these places.

At first glance Martyr's career as a Protestant evangelist in Italy might seem to have been wholly abortive, but the seed he sowed bore fruit and the Inquisition was unable to root it up entirely. At Naples, where he was probably already a Protestant by internal conviction by 1540, Martyr preached a sermon which germinated in the heart of Galeazzo Caracciolo and eventually led him to Protestantism, exile, and the leadership of the Italian community in Geneva.[6] Much more

---

[4] See the third page of Robert Masson's unpaginated "Epistola Nuncupatoria" which introduces the *Loci*.

[5] Beza to Bullinger, July 1, 1563; after suggesting the compilation of a *loci communes*, Beza continues: "Nam ego ipse fortassis huic operi manum admoveo." Beza *Correspondance*, IV, 162.

[6] McNair, 154-56; Benedetto Croce traces Caracciolo's life in *Vite di avventure di fede e di passione*, (Bari: 1936), 179-281.

important was Martyr's activity at Lucca. The seed of Protestantism had been sown there years before Martyr's arrival,[7] but Martyr so watered and cultivated the sprout that it grew into a healthy sapling that survived over a decade of persecution after Martyr's flight to Zurich and Strasbourg. Under Martyr's discreet leadership Lucca became the most Protestant city in Italy.[8] During the 1540's and 1550's the Inquisition tightened its grip on the city and many of its citizens fled beyond the Alps to escape persecution or the suffocating pressure to external conformity. The Lucchese fugitives became the core of the numerous and flourishing Italian community in Geneva.[9] In fleeing to Switzerland the Lucchese were following not only Martyr's example but also the advice which Martyr gave in one of his most important letters to the flock he left behind. The long "Letter on Flight in Time of Persecution" presents a classic statement and defense of one of the basic strategies forced on groups and individuals persecuted for conscience during the sixteenth century.[10] Although most of the fugitives were laymen, there were many former canons of Martyr's monastery among them. Three men closely associated with Martyr in Lucca became prominent in the Italian Protestant Diaspora. Count Massimiliano Celso Martinenghi da Brescia became the pastor of the Italian church in Geneva. Even more important were Jerome Zanchi and Emanuel Tremellius, both of whom will be discussed later in connection with Heidelberg. Martyr also played a crucial role in the decision of Bernardino Ochino to flee Italy.[11] It is noteworthy that Martyr's Lucchese converts, in contrast to many Italian Protestants, became staunchly orthodox upholders of the Reformed faith.[12]

---

[7] See Renzo Ristori, "Le origine della riforma a Lucca," *Rinascimento*, III, 1952, 269-91.

[8] McNair, 206-68, gives a thorough account of Martyr's apostolate in Lucca.

[9] The role of the Lucchese is a thread running through several articles in the commemorative volume edited by Delio Cantimori, *Ginevra e l'Italia*, (Florence: 1959). The great Genevan theologians of the seventeenth century, Jean Diodati and the three Turrettini, were Lucchese.

[10] *Loci*, 1073-83. Schmidt, *Leben*, 50-57.

[11] McNair describes in detail Martyr's relations with Ochino, Martinenghi, Zanchi, Tremellius and some other less important future fugitives, 222-31, 281-83.

[12] Ruffini, 418-20. In the last year of his life Martyr made one last and rather bizarre Italian convert to Reformed Protestantism in the person of Antonio Caracciolo, who had known Martyr many years before in Naples. Meanwhile the Neopolitan had become bishop of Troyes, France. Martyr's words at the Colloquy of Poissy so impressed him that he sought Martyr out and brought him back to Troyes. He openly embraced Protestantism and tried to bring over his whole diocese to the Reformed faith. He is the first bishop in the history

Martyr developed his theology during his first stay at Strasbourg, 1542 to 1547, and he soon rivaled Bucer in popularity as a lecturer. According to Johann Sturm, Martyr so impressed Bucer that the veteran Reformer would undertake no serious step regarding the Strasbourg Church and academy without his advice.[13]

Martyr's nearly six years in England were the most fruitful of his career. He was at the height of his intellectual powers. The formative period was over, and his literary output increased sharply over his previous years at Strasbourg. Martyr was only one of the many continental Protestants that the Goverment and Cranmer invited to England after the death of Henry VIII opened the way to full doctrinal Protestantism, but Martyr ". . . was of all the refugee clergy probably to have the most telling effect on the spiritual history of England and the diffusion of staunchly Protestant doctrine."[14] Martin Bucer was a stronger personality, better known, and a more original theologian than Martyr, but he had less than two years on English soil before death intervened February 28, 1551. Significantly, more of Martyr's books were translated into English than into any other vernacular.

Not only was Cranmer responsible for Martyr's invitation to England and his appointment as Regius Professor of divinity at Oxford, but it was through the Primate that Martyr exerted considerable influence on official church policies and documents.[15] As soon as Martyr arrived in England he repaired to Lambeth palace and spent several months with Cranmer. They immediately became friends. Their training, deep patristic erudition, outlook, and temperament were similar. Of all the continental scholars, Martyr got to know Cranmer best and to esteem him most. Martyr's first stay at Lambeth played an important part in the development of the Archbishop's eucharistic thought away from his earlier Lutheran views. Bishop

---

of the French Reformed Church. Martyr described his role in the whole affair in a letter to Beza, Beza *Correspondance*, III, 209. Also see McLelland, 64; Schmidt, *Leben*, 272-73.

[13] Sturm in a letter to Marbach; Zanchi, *Opera Theologica*, VIII, *Liber Epistolarum*, II, 163. Klaus Sturm gives an account of Martyr's first Strasbourg years, 13-38.

[14] W. K. Jordan, *Edward VI: The Young King*, (Cambridge, Mass.: 1968), 191; Smyth, 117, is of the same view. Philip McNair is working on a full scale study of Martyr's English career.

[15] Cranmer was not Martyr's only entree to the centers of power. Lord Protector Somerset was a convinced Calvinist; Martyr's published letter to him evinces more than passing acquaintanceship. The young King gave Martyr an audience at Richmond with great cordiality and read his works with interest. Young, I, 432; McLelland, 23.

Ridley had earlier urged the Reformed view on him, but it was Cranmer's conversations with Martyr that seem to have convinced him.[16] This was of momentous importance for Anglican theology since Cranmer was the chief author of the revised *Book of Common Prayer* and of the forty-two articles which, with changes, became normative for Anglicanism under Elizabeth as the thirty-nine articles.

Both sets of articles reject not only Catholic transubstantiation but also the Lutheran real physical presence and the *manducatio impiorum*. Both teach a eucharistic theology wholly consonant with Martyr's teaching.[17] A strong case can be made that Martyr's influence on Cranmer was felt in the composition of the forty-two articles. At the end of 1549 a series of anti Government uprisings broke out; the streets of Oxford rang with cries of "Death to Peter Martyr." The Regius Professor prudently retired to London where he drew up two sermons against sedition; Cranmer used them as raw material for an important sermon of his own on the uprisings.[18] In March 1552

---

[16] McLelland, 16, 17; G. W. Bromily, *Thomas Cranmer Theologian*, (London: 1956), 5, 6; J. I. Parker writes in his introduction to *The Works of Thomas Cranmer*, ed. G. Duffield, (Philadelphia: 1965), xxxviii-xxxix, "Cranmer, Martyr, and Bucer seem all to have held substantially the same eucharistic doctrine, but not all in the same way: Bucer held it dialectically as a thing of checks and balances . . .; Cranmer and Martyr held it as the direct working out of what they took to be the biblical and patristic idea of the nature of sacraments—namely, that they were (to quote the title of McLelland's valuable book on Martyr) 'the visible words of God,' significant signs of God's presence and power and instruments of His gracious action, just as the preached word is."

[17] See articles XXVIII and XXIX. The final revisor of the thirty-nine articles under Elizabeth was Martyr's dearest friend, John Jewel, Bishop of Salisbury. Jewel wrote to Martyr in Zurich regarding the thirty-nine articles: "as to matters of doctrine, we do not differ from you by a nail's breath; for as to the ubiquitarian theory, there is no danger in this country." *The Works of John Jewel*, edited for the Parker Society by John Ayre, (Cambridge: 1850), IV, 1246. Jewel was Martyr's friend and disciple at Oxford, then followed him to Strasbourg and Zurich where he lived with Martyr almost as a son. Upon Elizabeth I's accession he returned to England and became the best theologian on the bishops' bench. His affectionate and extensive correspondence to Martyr in Zurich has been frequently printed: his *Works*, the *Zurich Letters*, Burnet's *History of the Reformation*. Martyr's impact on Jewel's theology centers chiefly on the eucharist and the importance given to patristics. Jewel's treatment of ubiquity in his *Reply to Harding*, *Works*, I, 480-506, compares closely with Martyr's *Dialogus*. Mastery of patristic literature became an enduring characteristic of the best Anglican theology and derives partly from Jewel and Martyr. Jewel's teaching on doctrinal authority compares closely with that of Martyr. See W. M. Southgate, *John Jewel and the Problem of Doctrinal Authority*, (Cambridge, Mass.: 1962), especially 20, 63, 178.

[18] McLelland, 23.

Martyr was again back in London for a protracted stay to help the Primate with the revision of English canon law. During 1551 Cranmer had unofficially circulated some articles of faith to several of the bishops. In May 1552 he received a command to submit the drafts he had been preparing to the Royal Council for examination. There were minor retouchings later in 1552. Martyr was, therefore, in consultation with Cranmer during the gestation period of the articles, and, as will be shown, Cranmer frequently asked for and deferred to Martyr's judgement on religious questions. Anglo-Catholic writers have been at some pains to minimize Martyr's influence on the articles, yet his influence seems considerable.[19] It was felt most importantly in the articles on the eucharist, but Martyr almost certainly had a direct hand in Article XVII (adopted without change as article XVII of the thirty-nine articles) which treats predestination. In so far as the article avoids the crucial issue of reprobation, it cannot be called Vermiglian. But the definition itself of predestination in the article seems nothing more than an expansion of the definition given by Martyr's tract on predestination which was written just about the same time.[20]

---

[19] McLelland, 40-42.

[20] The similarities between article XVII and Martyr's definition of predestination are best seen by comparison:

Article XVII	*Martyr's Definition*
Praedestinatio ad vitam est aeternum Dei propositum, quo ante iacta mundi fundamenta, suo consilio, nobis quidem occulto, constanter decrevit, eos quos in Christo elegit ex hominum genere, a maledicto et exitio liberare, atque ut vasa in honorem efficta, per Christum ad aeternam salutem adducere: Unde qui tam praeclaro Dei beneficio sunt donati, illi spiritu eius opportune tempore operante, secundum propositum eius vocantur: vocationi per gratiam parent: iustificantur gratis: adoptantur in filios; unigeniti Iesu Christi imagini efficiuntur conformes: in bonis operibus sancte ambulant: et demum ex Dei misericordia pertingunt ad sempiternam foelicitatem.	praedestinationem esse sapientissimum propositum Dei quo ante omnem aeternitatem decrevit constanter eos quos dilexit in Christo vocare ad adoptionem filiorum, ad iustificationem ex fide, et tandem ad gloriam per opera bona, quo conformes fiant imagini filii Dei, utque in illis declaretur gloria et misericordia Creatoris.

Martyr's definition is in the *Loci*, 449; for article XVII see Philip Schaff, *The Creeds of Christendom*, (Grand Rapids: 1966) III, 497. Article XVII is much longer and more formal, but follows that order of Martyr's definition and has frequent verbal echoes. The differences may come from Cranmer or later revisions of the article, or may even be from Martyr's own suggestions to suit a more

Martyr's influence on the *Second Book of Common Prayer* is also the subject of controversy, but more direct evidence is available for this than for the forty-two articles. Cranmer asked both Martyr and Bucer for their judgment of the proposed revised version. Since Martyr could not read English, the noted classicist John Cheke made a Latin translation of parts of the proposed *Prayer Book* for Martyr's use. On the basis of this translation Martyr drew up his Annotations and forwarded them to the Archbishop. Shortly afterwards Martyr read Bucer's *Censura* on the *Prayer Book*, which was based on a more thorough and complete knowledge of the *Prayer Book* than was available to Martyr. After reading the *Censura* Martyr wrote the Archbishop backing up Bucer's recommendations, and he continued to urge them after Bucer's death. Martyr's own Annotations have not survived, but there does exist the letter Martyr wrote to Bucer immediately after reading the *Censura*, and from that Martyr's views become clear.[21] On two specific points Martyr's views were especially important. He successfully urged that when communion was given to the sick, the important parts of the Lord's Supper should be repeated by the minister in the sick room.[22] Against the extreme Swiss party lead by Bishop Hooper and John Knox, Martyr argued that the practice of receiving communion while kneeling involved no superstitious adoration but only respect. Cranmer accepted this view and cited Martyr's name when urging it on the government.[23] One important passage in the *Book of Common Prayer* is a translation from Martyr.[24] More important than any specific passages or practice is the all-over direction of the liturgical and sacramental theology which

---

formal situation. One would not expect Martyr simply to urge a page taken from his lecture-notes on the Archbishop, but the lecture notes probably provided a point of departure. Sometime after I had noticed the similarities between the two definitions, I discovered that this had been pointed out by E. Daniel years ago in his *The Prayer-Book*, (London: 1913), 605. Calvin's definition of predestination (*Institutes*, III, 21, 5) is very different.

[21] McLelland, 28-40, gives a full discussion of Martyr's influence on the second *Prayer Book* and prints Martyr's letter to Bucer, 29-30. Also see Francis Procter and Walter Frere, *A New History of the Book of Common Prayer*, (London: 1902), 71, 77.

[22] McLelland, 30, 31; Procter and Frere, 77; Huelin, 90.

[23] Procter and Frere, 83-85. Martyr also considered the use of vestments as adiaphora and helped to moderate the extremism of Hooper on this point. C. Hopf, *Martin Bucer and the English Reformation*, (Oxford: 1946) 131-32, 146-47; Jasper Ridley, *John Knox*, (Oxford: 1968), 167; McLelland, 25-27.

[24] Alan Beesley, "An Unpublished Source of the *Book of Common Prayer*: Peter Martyr Vermigli's *Adhortatio ad Coenam Domini Mysticam*," *Journal of Ecclesiastical History*, XIX, 1968, 83-88.

Martyr gave to Cranmer and several later Elizabethan bishops and which through them found expression in Anglican liturgy and theology through the centuries.[25]

Peter Martyr also played a part in two other important English ecclesiastical documents. Elizabeth I distrusted the puritan emphasis on preaching, partly from a realistic appraisal of the limitations of her clergy. She preferred that fixed sermons be read from the official *Book of Homilies* which she had her bishops revise. One of these sermons treats drunkenness and gluttony; although attributed officially to Bishop James Pilkington, most of it is a translation from Martyr's commentary on Judges.[26] More important were Martyr's contributions to the revision of canon law undertaken by a large committee commissioned by the goverment for the task. As usually happens when a large committee undertakes a task, the real work devolves on a few individuals, in this case mainly Cranmer, ably seconded by Martyr.[27] Martyr's work involved a protracted stay in London with the Archbishop. Martyr described in glowing terms to Bullinger what a marvelous opportunity this was to purge the English church of the vestiges of popery.[28] Martyr was responsible for the whole of the seventh chapter on Prescriptions.[29] Edward VI's premature death prevented the passage of the *Reformatio Legum Ecclesiasticarum* into law; after the Marian interval the government of Elizabeth refrained from taking up anew the whole prickly business, so that the Anglican church continued to use medieval canon law, with minor revisions, for two more centuries.

---

[25] "We submit therefore, that Peter Martyr's doctrine . . . is the doctrine which Cranmer accepted as at least standing in agreement with the Prayer Book and the Articles of Edward's reign; which John Jewel and his friends considered their own theological position during Elizabeth's time; and which, although not receiving definite expression by any group in the subsequent history of the Church of England—since Puritanism, for example, cannot be called validly the true inheritor of this theology of Martyr and Calvin—yet was one whose influence is evident throughout the history of the Church of England . . ." McLelland, 39.

[26] The sermon is in the *Second Book of Homilies*, 298-310. For Martyr's authorship, see J. W. Blench, *Preaching in England in the Late Fifteenth and Sixteenth Centuries*, (Oxford: 1964), 101.

[27] McLelland, 40; James C. Spalding, "The Reformatio Legum Ecclesiasticarum of 1552 and the Furthering of Discipline in England," *Church History*, XXXIX, 1970, 162-71. Huelin, 84-88.

[28] *Original Letters Relative to the English Reformation, 1531-58*, edited for the Parker Society by Hastings Robinson, (Cambridge: 1847), II, 503.

[29] Gilbert Burnet, *The History of the Reformation of the Church of England*, revised by E. Nares, (New York: 1842), III, 313.

Martyr's legal expertise is especially evident in his handling of the question of marriage in the *Loci*. His treatment of the seventh commandment, which forbids adultery, contains about two hundred references to canon and civil law. One of the key areas of legislation in the *Reformatio* was marriage and divorce, and on these questions Martyr exerted an important influence on English Protestant thought even though the *Reformatio* never became law.[30] Thus Thomas Becon in his *Book of Matrimony* (1562) reviews the opinions on divorce of many continental Protestants but singles out Martyr for special praise: "that precious pearl and marvelous marguerite."[31]

The division of the English Church into Anglican and puritan wings did not reduce Martyr's influence because both sides read his works and appealed to his authority.[32] Early in Elizabeth's reign, controversy over the use of vestments flared up anew; Archbishop Matthew Parker, speaking for the hierarchy and the Government, defended their use against the charges of the puritan Robert Crowley. Both appealed to the authority of Peter Martyr. At least three pamphlets on vestments quoted at length from Martyr's letters and commentaries.[33] Later in the reign the leading puritan theologian, Thomas Cartwright, recommends Martyr "for singular and much reading" in his "For Direction in the Study of Divinity." Cartwright's great opponent Archbishop Whitgift refers to Martyr's writings over thirty times and is acquainted with nearly all his scripture commentaries.[34] John Rainolds, the puritan president of Corpus Christi College, Oxford, from 1598 to 1607, advises divinity students to employ the

---

[30] Reginald Haw, *The State of Matrimony*, (London: 1952), 56-58.

[31] Quoted by Chilton L. Powell, *English Domestic Relations, 1487-1653*, (New York: 1917), 75.

[32] "Peter Martyr . . . was an acknowledged authority on sacramental theology . . . respected by Anglican and Puritan alike." John F. H. New, *Anglican and Puritan: the Basis of their Opposition, 1558-1640*, (Stanford: 1964), 59. Also see McLelland, 39, 40. New finds the eucharistic theology of William Perkins often "a carbon copy of Martyr's," p. 60.

[33] For the Parker-Crowley controversy, see Leonard J. Trinterud, editor, *Elizabethan Puritanism*, (New York: 1971), 77, 78, 95. Trinterud reprints *The Fortress of Fathers*, 1566 by J. B. (probably John Barthlet or John Browne), who quotes extensively from Martyr commentaries (pp. 95-100). The opposite side was argued from Martyr's letters in two anonymous pamphlets published at London without date by Richard Iugge, the Queen's printer: *A Brief Examination for the Tyme* . . . and *Whether It Be a Mortal Sinne to Transgresse Civil Lawes* . . .

[34] *Cartwrightiana*, edited by Albert Peel and Leland Carlson, (London: 1951), 113, 114. *The Works of John Whitgift*, edited for the Parker Society by John Ayre, (Cambridge: 1853), III, xxxii, 646.

commentaries of Calvin and Martyr, "who have written best on the most part of the Old Testament."[35] Through the late sixteenth and early seventeenth century, Martyr remained one of the most popular Continental divines with English readers; his commentary on Romans was particularly popular in English translation and was used as a text-book.[36] The greatest of all puritan writers, John Milton, considered Peter Martyr "a divine of foremost rank" and probably used Martyr's Genesis commentary in preparing to write *Paradise Lost*.[37]

Martyr also retained a high reputation through most of the seventeenth century in puritan New England. John Cotton counted Martyr as one of the leading Protestant theologians along with Luther, Calvin, and Melanchthon.[38] Cotton Mather recommended Martyr's writings in his *Manducatio ad Ministerium* [39] and himself had seven folio volumes of Martyr's scripture commentaries. In fact more copies of Martyr's writings have been counted in the possession of seventeenth century Harvard divinity students than of Calvin's works, although the sample is too small to have much significance.[40]

Martyr's appointment as Regius Professor at Oxford put him directly into the eye of a theological hurricane, for unlike Cambridge, Oxford retained a strong and vocal Catholic party which subjected Martyr to petty harassment such as catcalls and broken windows.[41] Opposition to Martyr's teaching crystallized around his eucharistic

---

[35] Quoted from Rainolds' "Advice for the Study of Divinitie," 1613, by Mark Curtis, *Oxford and Cambridge in Transition, 1558-1642*, (Oxford: 1959), 207.

[36] Huelin, 139-159. Joan Simon, *Education and Society in Tudor England*, (Cambridge: 1966), 380. H. S. Bennett, *English Books and Readers, 1550 to 1603*, (Cambridge: 1965), 88.

[37] Milton's statement is from his *Tenure of Kings and Magistrates*, (Works, V, 25, 26), cited by Arnold Williams, "Milton and Renaissance Commentaries on Genesis." *Modern Philology*, XXXVII, 270; the article urges Milton's use of Martyr's commentary in preparing his epic.

[38] Cited by Perry Miller, *The New England Mind: the Seventeenth Century*, (Cambridge, Mass.: 1963), 104.

[39] Giorgio Spini, "Riforma Italiana e mediazione ginevrine nella nuova Inghilterra puritana," in Cantimori, *Ginevra*, 477.

[40] Samuel E. Morison, *Harvard College in the Seventeenth Century*, (Cambridge, Mass.: 1936), I, 273.

[41] Gordon Huelin gives a good summary of Martyr's duties as professor at Oxford, 73-79. The leading historian of Edward's reign overstates somewhat Martyr's impact at Oxford: "... the appointment of Martyr, with this towering reputation, had tipped the balance at Oxford ... to Protestantism." Jordan, I, 331. Martyr was indeed to have a towering reputation, but it is doubtful that he had one on his appointment since his only publication up to that time were two short works in Italian. The reputation was won at Oxford.

doctrine and led to the famous Oxford disputation of May, 1549, in which Martyr debated the eucharist for several days against three Catholic professors after the original challenger, Richard Smith, the former Regius Professor ousted to make room for Martyr, fled to the Continent. Most accounts of the disputation are pro-Martyr and award him an easy victory. The Government quickly had printed an account of the disputation and a tract by Martyr on the same subject. Martyr's Catholic opponents were not allowed to print their account.[42] Martyr's victory achieved a sort of canonical status among later English Protestants when John Foxe's immensely influential *Book of Martyrs* devoted six columns to a summary of the disputation.[43]

More important than the Disputation or his lectures were the many friendships which Martyr established at Oxford with the younger generation of English Protestants. A good half dozen of these became bishops during Elizabeth's reign and continued to look to Martyr for advice and encouragement. Many of them fled England during the reign of Mary Tudor and kept in close contact with Martyr at Strasbourg and later at Zurich. For instance, on Mary's death two important future bishops, John Jewel and Edwin Sandys, were living in Martyr's home at Zurich.[44]

Martyr spent the last six years of his life in Zurich. The theological situation in Zurich into which Martyr moved was very unlike that of Edwardian England, which was in many ways a theologically under-developed country, at least as regards learned expositions of Protestant dogma: hence Cranmer's desire to attract and place foreign divines in key positions in the English universities. In contrast Zurich was one of the earliest cities of Europe to become Protestant and had developed a vigorous indigenous theological tradition, first under Zwingli, then

---

[42] All of Martyr's biographers dwell on the Oxford disputation, as it is probably the most colorful incident in his life, and they award him the palm of victory: McLelland, *Visible Words*, 17-23; Schmidt, *Leben*, 89-100. A more neutral writer finds the outcome far less clear: Charles Edward Mallet, *A History of the University of Oxford*, II, *The Sixteenth and Seventeenth Centuries*, (London: 1924), 90-92.

[43] John Foxe, *Acts and Monuments of Matters most Special and Memorable . . .*, (London, 1583), 1373-1376.

[44] Huelin devotes a chapter to Martyr's work with the Marian exiles (95-115) and to Martyr and the Elizabethan Settlement (116-138). Christina Garrett, *The Marian Exiles: A Study in the Origins of Elizabethan Puritanism*, (Cambridge, 1938), 8, 49. A great deal of the correspondence of English prelates with Martyr in Zurich is printed in the Parker Society's *Zurich Letters*, ed. H. Robinson, (Cambridge: 1845,1846), I, 2, 15, 18, 21; II, 13, 25, 32, 38, 47, 57. Particularly important is John Jewel's correspondence with Martyr, *Works*, IV, 1196-1256 passim.

under his able successor Heinrich Bullinger. The Zurich theological academy boasted several scholars with European reputations. In this situation the addition of even so distinguished a professor as Martyr was unlikely to result in a theological sea-change, quite aside from the fact that Martyr chose to come to Zurich precisely because he knew that his eucharistic doctrine, which he refused to cloak in ambiguous language for the sake of a facile harmony, would find encouragement in Zurich.

In 1549 the Zurich and Genevan churches had hammered out a doctrinal agreement, the *Consensus Tigurinus*, which almost all the other Swiss Protestant churches accepted. The most important clauses related to the eucharist and asserted the real spiritual presence of Christ in the sacrament. Although Geneva might give greater stress to the *real*, and Zurich to the *spiritual*, the agreement was solid and lasting. Significantly Calvin and not Bullinger took the lead in defending the doctrine of the *Consensus* from Lutheran attack. The vexed question of what Zwingli really taught about the eucharist is of no import here; certainly the Zurich church during Martyr's residence did not support a *nuda signa* doctrine.[45] The Genevan leaders felt closer to Martyr doctrinally than to the other Zurich theologians, and the chief effect of Martyr's Zurich years was to foster the already growing doctrinal concord between the most important centers of Reformed theology.[46] The *Consensus Tigurinus* brought agreement on the Eucharist but it did not unite the two churches on the equally crucial question of predestination.[47]

Zwingli's teaching on predestination varied, but the *De Providentia Dei* written at the end of his life taught a rather strong doctrine of predestination, one that Martyr agreed with. There was a strong humanist element in the thought of many of the leading Zurich divines, starting with Zwingli himself. This found its fullest expression in Theodore Bibliander, who after Zwingli's death openly taught a doctrine of predestination that recalled Erasmus and looked forward to Arminius.[48] Bullinger's thought seems to have been moving slowly closer to that of Calvin throughout the 1550's, even before Martyr's arrival. Still, Bullinger's theology had a strong pastoral orientation

---

[45] On the *Consensus Tigurinus* see Schaff, I, 471-473; André Bouvier, *Henri Bullinger: le successeur de Zwingli*, (Paris, 1940), 110-163.

[46] See Beza's letters to Calvin, July 17, 1557, and January 18, 1558: *Correspondance*, II, 76, 166.

[47] Schmidt, *Leben*, 215.

[48] Staedtke, "Prädestinationsstreit," describes Bibliander's doctrine, 539.

with little inclination toward developing the speculative aspects of predestination to their ultimate conclusion. Bullinger knew Martyr's position on predestination and invited him to Zurich fully conscious that he and Bibliander would probably disagree.[49] Martyr realized the delicacy of his position at Zurich, for in his inaugural address he went out of his way to praise Bibliander, and he tactfully published his Romans commentary with its strong treatise on predestination at Basel rather than at Zurich. The peace was short-lived because Bibliander was soon attacking Martyr's teaching in his lectures. In his lectures on First Samuel, Martyr quickly found verses suitable as a point of departure for presenting his own teaching; and his lecture *De Libero Arbitrio* of 1560, which is reprinted at the end of the *Loci Communes*, is another outgrowth of the struggle. Martyr's victory and Bibliander's dismissal unquestionably marked an important stage in Zurich's adhesion to a full Reformed teaching on grace and predestination.[50]

A further stage resulted from Jerome Zanchi's controversy at Strasbourg with Johann Marbach and gnesio-Lutherans over predestination and related teachings.[51] Zanchi sent out a flood of letters eliciting support from friendly princes, theologians, and academies. At Strasbourg a few years earlier, Martyr had been Zanchi's chief support during the opening phases of the controversy, and he continued to support his disciple by letter, as did Bullinger. Zanchi even made a circuit of Swiss cities trying to drum up support; while at Zurich he spent eight days in Martyr's house. Bullinger and the other Zurich divines commissioned Martyr to draw up a memorial or letter of recommendation which they signed and sent to Strasbourg. The letter evades some disputed points, softens others, but generally supports Zanchi's teaching.[52]

---

[49] Staedtke, 541; Walser, 168-181; Hottinger, VIII, 719.

[50] McLelland, "Predestination," 265-267; Martyr's praise of Bibliander, *Loci*, 1063; for the *De Libero Arbitrio*, *Loci*, 971-989. I am convinced that the Bibliander controversy also provided the circumstances for Martyr's writing the three short tracts ("De Libero Arbitrio," "De Providentia et Predestinatione," and "An Deus Sit Author et Causa Peccati?" *Loci*, 989-995) whose authorship is so much disputed. See Chapter V, note 62.

[51] Walter Sohm, *Die Schule Johann Sturms und die Kirche Strassburgs in ihrem gegenseitigen Verhältnis, 1530-1581*, (Munich: 1912), 179-235; Jürgen Moltmann, *Prädestination und Perseveranz: Geschichte und Bedeutung der reformierten Lehre "de perseverantia sanctorum,"* (Neukirchen: 1961), 72-109. The whole seventh tome of Zanchi's *Opera* relates to the Strasbourg controversy.

[52] Schmidt, *Leben*, 277-278. Hottinger, VIII, 843-847, prints the text of the

Martyr's years in Zurich from 1556 until his death in 1562 definitely witnessed a growing unity between Zurich and Geneva which culminated in the Second Helvetic Confession of 1566, but there is considerable disagreement among scholars about the degree to which Martyr was responsible for this development. Joachim Staedtke insists that in the Bibliander affair Vermigli aimed at and achieved the triumph of Calvinist doctrine in Zurich.[53] Peter Walser's careful study of Bullinger's doctrine of predestination tends to play down Martyr's role and stress Bullinger's own gradual theological development. He emphasizes that Bullinger's support for Zanchi was less a personal doctrinal commitment and more an official act in support of a hard-pressed but staunch upholder of the general Reformed position.[54] His assessment fails to weigh one important fact: shortly thereafter Zanchi was the first choice of Bullinger and the Zurich divines as Martyr's successor. As Bullinger knew full well, Zanchi carried the doctrine of predestination even beyond the teaching of Martyr and Calvin.[55]

Charles Schmidt advocates a middle position, which I also prefer. The controversy at Strasbourg over predestination was of great importance because it established that Lutheranism and Calvinism would split henceforward over the theology of grace as well as over the eucharist, despite the fact that Luther and Calvin differed mainly in their emphasis on predestination. The Zurich memorial for Zanchi, together with Bibliander's dismissal, marked a decisive victory of the Calvinist doctrine of grace which the Zurich church had not accepted earlier.[56] Otto Ritschl, whose view falls between that of Schmidt and Walser, recognizes Bullinger's personal disinclination to carry the doctrine of predestination to extreme conclusions and suggests that his gradual acceptance of the Calvinist position resulted from his intimacy with Martyr.[57]

---

memorial. On its contents and Martyr's authorship, see Moltmann, 100-103; Walser, 188; McLelland, "Predestination," 267-269.

[53] Staedtke, "Prädestinationsstreit," 543. He concludes that as a result of Bibliander's dismissal on February 8, 1560: "Zürich hatte sich an diesem Tage für Calvin entschieden": 546. Alexander Schweitzer attributed even greater importance to Martyr's role in bringing Zurich to a full Calvinist view. Walser quotes and summarizes Schweitzer, 184.

[54] Walser, 182-183 and *passim*.

[55] For Bullinger's invitation to accept Martyr's chair, December 16, 1562: Zanchi's *Opera*, VIII, *Liber Epistolarum*, II, 126. Zanchi declined the offer: Schmidt, *Leben*, 291.

[56] Schmidt, *Leben*, 215, 274.

[57] *Dogmengeschichte des Protestantismus*, (Göttingen: 1926), III, 248-249. For Ritschl's evaluation of Martyr's teaching on predestination, III, 268-270.

In the last year of his life, Martyr attended the Colloquy of Poissy, which Catherine dei Medici sponsored in a vain attempt to find doctrinal agreement between Protestants and Catholics and thereby ward off civil war. Vermigli and Beza headed the Protestant delegation of theologians, and their co-leadership aptly symbolized the growing unity between the French and the German-Swiss Reformed churches.[58] Martyr died shortly after his return to Zurich. During his last days he made a final contribution to unity between Zurich and Geneva; Bullinger discussed with him and gained his approval for the first drafts of what became the Second Helvetic Confession of 1566.[59] Almost all continental Reformed churches eventually adhered to this long confession which became, with the exception of the *Heidelberg Catechism*, the most important Reformed doctrinal statement.[60] Even after Martyr's death Bullinger frequently deferred to his writings and recommended his opinions in letters of counsel to English Protestants.[61]

The most important center for the spread of Peter Martyr Vermigli's ideas and influence after his death was Heidelberg, a University at which he never taught in a city he never visited. To understand this development we must recall some historical background.

The only important Calvinist state in Germany in the period from the Peace of Augsburg in 1555 to the outbreak of the Thirty Years War in 1618 was the Rhenish Palatinate.[62] The Calvinist Electors Palatine adopted a foreign policy of aggressive anti-Catholicism which constrasted sharply with that of the Lutheran princes of the Empire, whose chief aim was maintaining the status-quo of the Peace of Augsburg. This aggressive policy culminated in Elector Frederick V's foolish acceptance of the Bohemian Crown in 1618. The infuriated Hapsburg smashed the Bohemians and their winter's King, while the Bavarian-led Catholic League occupied the Palatinate, thereby ending an era of German history and starting the Thirty Years War.[63]

The Electors Palatine matched their foreign policy of fostering

---

[58] Bouvier, 314-315.

[59] Bouvier, 318; Schaff, I, 394.

[60] Bouvier, 316; Schaff, I, 392.

[61] *Zurich Letters*, I, 345-347.

[62] During the interval 1576-1583 the Elector Ludwig reversed the policies of his father Frederick III and favored Lutheranism, but his early death enabled his brother and successor John Casimir to re-instate Calvinism.

[63] Claus Peter Clasen, *The Palatinate in European History, 1559-1660*, (Oxford: 1963), 1-32.

Calvinist movements abroad with a policy of encouraging Calvinism at home. They built a minor provincial university in their capital, Heidelberg, into the most renowned Calvinist seat of learning of the era. Students and professors came from every land where Calvinism struck roots, especially from France, the Netherlands, Italy, and Poland. The pride of the University was the theology faculty.[64] The theology faculty, especially during the period of its greatest brilliance, 1560-76, became a focal point of Vermigli influence and disciples.[65] In 1558 the Elector Otto Henry reformed Heidelberg University along Protestant lines; outstanding professors were recruited regardless of nationality. His son Frederick III continued this policy. Twice invitations came to Peter Martyr at Zurich to join the Heidelberg faculty. Calvin urged him to accept the post.[66] Twice Martyr refused on grounds of old age and declining health. In his stead he recommended his young Silesian student, Zacharias Ursinus, who was accepted.[67] At Heidelberg he joined Caspar Olevianus, with whom his name is always linked; both were former students of Calvin at Geneva, and both were former students of Martyr at Zurich.[68] Soon the two young men working together produced the most important statement of all Reformed Protestantism, the Heidelberg Catechism of 1563.[69] Olevianus was the more eloquent of the two but a less profound theologian; he made his mark mainly as a counsellor of the Elector rather than as a writer, so that specifically Vermiglian influences on him cannot be pinned down.[70] Ursinus had been for several years a student of Melanchthon's at Wittemberg, and while Melanchthon's influence always remained strong, his later studies under Martyr led him away from Melanch-

---

[64] Clasen, 35, 36; Ritschl, III, 258.

[65] "At this period the University of Heidelberg, with a distinguished faculty that included Ursinus, Boquin, Erastus, Zanchi, and the Jewish Christian Biblical scholar Emanuel Tremellius, attracted advanced students from many countries." John T. McNeill, *The History and Character of Calvinism*, (New York: 1967), 273. All of the above mentioned professors were linked to Martyr, as will be seen.

[66] Erdmann K. Sturm, *Der Junge Zacharias Ursin: Sein Weg vom Philippismus zum Calvinismus (1534-1562)*, (Neukirchen: 1972), 232-233.

[67] McNeill, 269; E. Sturm, 233; Daniel John Toft, "Zacharias Ursinus: A Study in the Development of Calvinism," (Unpublished M. A. thesis, Department of History, University of Wisconsin, Madison, 1962), 22.

[68] Bizer's introduction to Heppe, xxxv, xxxvii.

[69] For the text of the *Catechism*, see Schaff, III, 307-355; for its historical background and importance, Schaff, I, 529-553.

[70] Martyr shows his affection and concern for Olevianus in a letter to Beza, October 4, 1559: *Calvini Opera*, XVII, cc. 651-54.

thonian synergism to a full and explicit Reformed theology of grace and man's fallen state.[71] Ursinus also developed a theology of predestination which reflected the teaching of Martyr's Romans Commentary.[72] Ursinus' most important work, his very lengthy *Commentary on the Heidelberg Catechism*, develops predestination in terms of the Aristotelian causes.[73] As has been shown, Martyr uses the Aristotelian causes throughout his theology and specifically regarding predestination. This seems an instance of the scholastic orientation of Martyr's theology affecting another major exposition of Reformed dogmatics. Martyr's theology cannot properly be called federal (*foedus*) or covenantal, but he does discuss the idea of covenant: Ursinus picked up the notion of convenant in Martyr, Musculus, and Bullinger and developed it further. This theme of covenant was picked up and elaborated still further by puritan theologians in England and New England were federal theology enjoyed great vogue through the seventeenth and early eighteenth centuries.[74]

Just as Theodore Beza played the leading role in excluding Peter Ramus from teaching at Geneva because of Ramus' hostility to Aristotle, so for the same reason Ursinus led the Heidelberg theologians in their successful attack on Ramus' appointment at Heidelberg and their defense of the Protestant scholastic tradition of Melanchthon, Vermigli, and their own colleague Jerome Zanchi.[75] Ursinus' studies with Martyr reinforced the scholastic bent of Ursinus' thought that originated with Melanchthon. The attitude of Ursinus toward philosophy was almost a mirror image of Vermigli's. Nature is the reflection of God, and the knowledge of nature taught by philosophers is a necessary tool of the Christian theologian.[76]

---

[71] E. Sturm, 169-170; Toft, "Ursinus," 39-41; McNeill, 270.

[72] E. Sturm, 3, 170, 189, 210-212; Toft, "Ursinus," 39-47, who also urges (p. 5) that earlier studies overstressed Melanchthon's influence on Ursinus and under-rated that of Vermigli and Bullinger. Ritschl, III, 259-268 repeatedly emphasizes Melanchthon's influence.

[73] Toft, "Ursinus," 45-46.

[74] E. Sturm, 258; Toft, "Ursinus," 70-76; Althaus, 160.

[75] Toft, "Ursinus," 36-37.

[76] Bizer, *Frühorthodoxie*, 16, summarizes Ursinus' attitude toward philosophy: "Denn die wahre Philosophie widerspricht nicht der Theologie und ist nicht einfach Lüge, wie die Lehre der nichtchristlichen Religionen, sondern sie ist Wahrheit und gleichsam ein Strahl der göttlichen Weisheit, die den Gemütern der Menschen in der Schöpfung eingeprägt wurde. Denn sie ist eine Lehre von Gott und von den Kreaturen und anderen dem Menschengeschlecht nützlinchen Dingen, von weisen Männern aus dem natürlichen Licht und aus den von Natur bekannten Prinzipien errichtet. Daher ist es den Christen nicht nur

Martyr's influence at Heidleberg did not die out with the death or departure of the first generation of professors who were friends and pupils. In the twenty years preceding the outbreak of the Thirty Years War Heidelberg suddenly became the leading center for the republication of Martyr's writings.[77] Martyr's friends and pupils passed on his teaching to their own pupils at Heidelberg. This is best illustrated in the case of Martyr's political thought. Martyr's political theory has two notes that distinguish it from the political theory of Calvin and Beza: a pronounced borrowing of terminology and ideas from Aristotle [78] and a greater emphasis on the powers of the state over the ministers of religion. Both these characteristics recommended Martyr's political thought to another former alumnus of Padua, Thomas Erastus (whence Erastianism). Erastus became a warm admirer of Martyr and was responsible as a counsellor of Frederick III for Martyr's invitations to Heidelberg.[79] Martyr's political theory was also taken up at Heidelberg by Ursinus and Zanchi.[80] It obviously fitted the needs of an aggressive but dedicated Reformed prince better than the political theory of Calvin and Beza, which attributed to the state less power over the Church and which consequently found more favor with the many Calvinists who were in opposition to princely regimes. Vermigli's political theory allowed no room for religious

---

erlaubt, sondern auch nützlich sich mit der Philosophie zu beschäftigen, ..." This can be compared with Martyr's statement in a letter to Peter Sturm, May 24, 1562: "... deinde si naturam audimus, ubi sermonibus Dei nihil repugnat, nihil facimus christiana theologia indignum. Habetque siquidem natura Deum authorem ac vindicem...." Printed in *Zanchii Opera, VIII, Epistolarum Liber I,* 107-09.

[77] The first publication of a work of Martyr's in Heidelberg came in 1593; there were further publications in 1599, 1603, 1606, 1609, 1612, 1613 (two), 1622. Most were editions of the *Loci*; the frequency of reprints suggests that the *Loci* may have been used as a textbook at the University.

[78] The Aristotelian character of Martyr's political thought has been pointed out by Ruth Wesel-Roth, *Thomas Erastus,* (Lohr/Baden: 1954), 115-16; by Robert Kingdon, *Consolidation,* 216-19.

[79] E. Sturm, 232; Wesel-Roth, 17, 33. On Erastus's esteem for Martyr, see his *Explicatio Gravissimae Questiones utrum Excommunicatio ... mandato nitatur Divino* ... (Pesclavii: 1589). The place of publication is false; the book was really published in London, indicating that Elizabeth I's government preferred Erastus's views on excommunication to those of his adversary Beza. On page 172 Erastus quotes "doctissimus aetatis nostrae theologus, Petrus Martyr, in comm. in cap. 8, Lib. I Samuelis" on the proper subordination of ministers to the civil magistrate.

[80] Daniel John Toft, "Shadows of Kings: The Political Thought of David Pareus, 1548-1622," (unpublished dissertation, history department, University of Wisconsin, Madison, 1970), 150-51, 171.

toleration: the prince must not only give the faithful the possibility of converting unbelievers and prevent the contrary, but he must also constrain unbelievers to undergo instruction and embrace the true religion.[81] This is precisely the policy which the Electors Palatine followed aggressively in foreign and domestic affairs.

How Martyr's influence was passed on to a second generation at Heidelberg is exemplified in David Pareus, an important theologian and political philosopher at Heidelberg during the late sixteenth and early seventeenth century. He studied under Zanchi and especially Ursinus, whose *Commentary on the Heidelberg Catechism* he saw through the press after the author's death. His teachers led him to study Melanchthon and Martyr and the whole Aristotelian tradition of early Protestant scholasticism. A recent study of his political thought returns again and again to his debt to Martyr.[82] Pareus took over and used "most strikingly Vermigli's Aristotelian separation of function in the performance of ministries." [83] Martyr's thinking on church-state relations enjoyed an important and curious extension when Johann Gerhard, the greatest of the Lutheran scholastics and the acknowledged originator of Lutheran church law, took over Pareus's formulations with little alteration and no acknowledgement.[84]

Martyr's greatest contribution to the development of Protestant scholasticism and to Heidelberg University dated all the way back to his Lucca apostolate. This contribution was the conversion of Jerome Zanchi to Protestantism. As will be urged in the next chapter, Vermigli was a bridge between Calvin and the mature Reformed scholasticism which Zanchi exemplifies. Zanchi was born (1516) and raised in and near Bergamo where he entered the Augustinian canons in 1531. He received most of his philosophical and theological training at Bergamo and Padua.[85] Zanchi's training was even more heavily

---

[81] Carlo Ginzburg, *Il nicodemismo: Simulazione e dissimulazione religiosa nell' Europa de '500*, (Torino: 1970), 192. No recent writer is as hostile to Vermigli as Ginzburg: "Questa tesi duramente intollerante..." "...avrebbe generato a sua volta inevitabilmente nuove simulazione e nuove ipocrise." "...con una fredezza e un realismo in cui sembrava vibrare l'eco della lezione machiavelliana." 192-193. There is no evidence that Martyr ever read his fellow townsman Machiavelli.

[82] Toft, "Pareus," 79, 144, 157, 161, 162, 171, 230, 247, 275, 278.

[83] Toft, "Pareus," 157.

[84] Toft, "Pareus," 172.

[85] There is an appendix dealing with Zanchi, especially his Italian years, in Luigi Santini's *La comunità evangelica di Bergamo: Vicende storiche*, (Torre Pellice: 1960), 228-239. Zanchi's life and teaching need a great deal of further study.

Thomist than Martyr's and left an even deeper impression.[86] In 1541 Zanchi was sent to Lucca and came under Martyr's influence. Martyr's preaching turned Zanchi's primary interest away from Aristotle and the medieval scholastics to scripture, the Fathers, especially Augustine, and to various Protestant exegetes, as Zanchi relates in a letter to Philip of Hesse. Although Martyr secured Zanchi's inward conversion to Protestant doctrine, for nine years after Martyr's flight to Switzerland Zanchi continued to live as a nicodemite Protestant and to preach his real convictions only cautiously. After his dear friend of sixteen years, Martinenghi, who was also a fellow canon and convert of Martyr's, was forced to flee persecution due to his less cautious preaching, Zanchi decided to break openly with Rome. He fled to Switzerland in October, 1551. After a year's study in Geneva, Zanchi was about to join Martyr in England when he was offered a professorship at Strasbourg in 1553 where Martyr joined him on the faculty later that year.[87]

Both Italians taught theology and both taught Aristotle, Zanchi handling the physical works one week, Martyr lecturing on the *Ethics* the next week.[88] Both soon came into conflict with Marbach and the Lutheran pastors who objected to their teaching on the eucharist and predestination. Their common struggle brought the two Italians even closer together. Zanchi developed his teaching on predestination in close consultation with Martyr.[89] When Martyr left Strasbourg rather than face further harassment, Zanchi was almost prostrate with grief, as he explained in letters to Calvin, Beza, and Musculus.[90] So close were Martyr and Zanchi linked that Bullinger does not hesitate to coin

---

[86] For Zanchi's Thomism, see my article, "Calvinist Thomism," which will appear in *Viator*, 1976. The Thomistic strains in Zanchi's doctrine of God are explored at length in Gründler's *Gotteslehre*. For the general revival of Thomism in northern Italy in the sixteenth century, see Kristeller, *Thomisme*.

[87] Santini, *Bergamo*, 230; McNair prints the text of his letter to Philip, 228.

[88] See Santerenziano's unpaginated preface to Martyr's *Ethicorum*.

[89] Martyr to Beza, March, 1555: Beza *Correspondance*, I, 153. Martyr to Calvin, May 9, 1554: "Nos hic quoties rogamur cum publice tum privatim partes et veri et tuas pro virili tuemur, praesertim Zancus et ego": *Loci*, 1092. Martyr to Calvin, March 8, 1555: "Dumque Zanchus et ego, qui coniunctissime vivimus, ita pergimus, erroribus in schola non datur locus": *Loci*, 1094. Martyr to Peter Sturm, February 15, 1561: "De doctrina porro cum etiam tunc Argentina mecum non semel contulit, contulit autem libere admodum atque amice. Quod autem ab eo (Zanchi) dicebuntur attente ac diligenter observavi et animadverti eum de predestinatione ac electione divina ... nihil diversum sentire quam divinae literae tradant, Augustinus doceat, Lutherus ac Bucerus scripserint": *Loci*, 1131.

[90] Zanchi to Calvin: *Calvini Opera*, XVI, 245-246; to Beza and to Musculus: Beza *Correspondance*, II, 47, 49-50.

a new word to describe his teaching: *Martyrizet*—he witnesses to Martyr's teaching. Zanchi was certainly his most ardent and influential disciple.[91] After leaving Strasbourg under pressure in 1563, Zanchi spent several years as a pastor at Chiavenna, then went to Heidelberg and later Neustadt as a professor. Among the students of Ursinus and Zanchi at Neustadt was Franciscus Gomarus (1563-1645) who became the chief theological spokesman for the Counter-Remonstrant or Gomarist Party in the Netherlands in the controversy over Arminianism. There is, therefore, a line running from Martyr through Ursinus and Zanchi to the Synod of Dort in 1619 which made the extreme interpretation of predestination normative for Reformed orthodoxy.[92]

Two other prominent theologians on the Heidelberg faculty of the 1560's were friends of Martyr. Pierre Boquin, a former French Carmelite, joined the Strasbourg faculty shortly before Martyr in 1542.[93] Far more closely linked to Martyr was the learned Jew Emanuel Tremellius. He studied at Padua through the 1530's and was converted to Catholicism, probably by Cardinal Pole. In 1540 he was baptized in Pole's house at Padua with the Cardinal as godfather. The next year Martyr secured his services as teacher for Lucca and converted him to Protestantism. When Martyr fled to Strasbourg, Tremellius followed and taught Hebrew at the Academy. Like Martyr he went to Edwardian England, but to Cambridge rather than Oxford.[94] His Old Testament commentaries were long prized, and he collaborated on an important translation of the Bible into Latin. Otto Ritschl links him with Zanchi and Martyr as constituting a separate theological school.[95]

Only in a few instances have we been able to trace later developments in Reformed theology directly to the scholastic elements in Vermigli's thought. This is not really surprising. Scholasticism was only one side of Martyr, although an important one. The development of Reformed scholasticism in the late sixteenth century was due to many factors, several of them far more important than Martyr's contri-

---

[91] Bullinger to Zanchi, August 30, 1556: "Amorem plane ferventem intellexi ex literis tuis, venerande Zanchi, quo ardes, imo flagras erga Martyrem nostrum . . . Zanchius insidet cordibus nostris, licet Argentinae Martyrizet": Zanchi, *Opera*, VIII, Liber Epistolarum, II, 184. Zanchi describes to Calvin how he always looked on Martyr as his father and teacher and always relied on his advice: *Calvini Opera*, VIII, c. 712.

[92] On the Synod of Dort, see Schaff, I, 508-523.

[93] Ritschl, III, 258.

[94] McNair, 224.

[95] Ritschl, III, 268.

bution. The most important factor was the continued teaching of Aristotle as the basis of philosophical education, indeed of most under-graduate education, in the vast majority of academies and universities, whether Protestant or Catholic. Martyr himself lectured on Aristotle at Strasbourg. He discontinued his lectures at Zurich, not because of any hostility to Aristotle there but because the distinguished Conrad Gesner was already teaching Aristotle.[96] The kind of curriculum Martyr's students underwent is well mirrored in a letter which John Ab Ulmis wrote from Oxford to Rodolph Gualter in Zurich in 1550. "In the morning then, immediately after morning prayers, namely from six to seven o'clock, are read the eight books of Aristotle on Physics; from seven to eight, the common places of Galen upon diseased parts; from eight to nine the books which he (Aristotle) wrote upon morals, and his Republic or treatise on civil government; from nine to ten Peter Martyr lectures upon the epistle to the Romans; from ten to eleven Galen's treatise upon natural qualities is lectured upon. These subjects occupy us till dinner time; but at twelve o'clock some questions in moral and natural philosophy are proposed for our dis-cussion. On Mondays and Wednesdays the masters (of arts) hold disputations; and on Thursday the students in divinity, physics and law dispute among themselves in regular and alternate turns." [97] Most of the students listening to Martyr's lectures brought a similar grounding in Aristotle. What would have been more natural than for Martyr to build on this background in developing his theology? The Aristotelian slant in many of his lectures would go almost unnoticed by his students and his later readers, not because it was esoteric or bèyond their grasp, but because it must have sounded utterly com-monplace. In the sixteenth century, to think as an educated man was virtually to think as an Aristotelian. Even the weapons with which sixteenth century anti-Aristotelians attacked some part of the heritage of the Greek philosopher were taken from other parts of the great arsenal provided by his works.[98]

---

[96] See Santerenziano's preface to Martyr's *Ethicorum*.

[97] *Original Letters*, II, 419. In similar letter to Bullinger dated May 28, 1550, he expresses his warm regard for Vermigli; II, 410.

[98] Charles B. Schmitt, "Aristotle as a Cuttlefish: the Origin and Development of a Renaissance Image," *Studies in the Renaissance*, XII, 1965: "Even to oppose an Aristotelian viewpoint meant very often nothing but to over-emphasize another equally Aristotelian notion. Examples of this abound throughout the Renaissance." p. 72. Lewis White Buck, *Early German Philosophy*, (Cambridge, Mass.: 1969), 118-123.

For all that Luther rejected and Calvin avoided the use of Aristotelian and scholastic concepts in theology, they did not achieve, indeed they hardly attempted, the systematic up-rooting of the Aristotelian undergraduate curriculum that pervaded European education. This on-going tradition continued to mould the minds of educated men well into the seventeenth century.[99] Neither Luther, nor Calvin, nor the humanist opponents of scholasticism such as Erasmus had a systematic, coherent alternative with which to replace Aristotle in the undergraduate curriculum. Peter Ramus came closest to offering a substitute, but Ramism failed for two main reasons: first, it was shot through with internal defects which Walter Ong has abundantly illustrated;[100] secondly, Ramism was a pure logic, or better a rhetoric and a topography of knowledge. Since Ramism offered neither a physics nor a metaphysics Aristotelianism survived into the seventeenth century when it succumbed to the twin assault of Galileo with a new physics and Descartes with a new philosophy.[101]

Other scholastic currents powerfully supplemented the undergraduate training in Aristotle. The medieval scholastics continued to be read, as a cursory examination of authors cited in almost any seventeenth century Protestant scholastic will reveal. In addition the second half of the sixteenth century brought a very considerable revival of scholastic philosophy and theology in Spain and Italy which was soon felt in northern Europe. Suarez and Zabarella were the most influential contemporary philosophers in Protestant Germany and the Netherlands in the early seventeenth century. A young Protestant theologian of the period would be singularly lacking in curiosity if he spent many

---

[99] The pervasive influence of Aristotle and scholasticism in various Protestant countries is well portrayed by Wm. T. Costello, *The Scholastic Curriculum at Early Seventeenth Century Cambridge*, (Cambridge, Mass.: 1958); Peter Petersen, *Geschichte der Aristotelischen Philosophie im Protestantischen Deutschland*, (Leipzig: 1921); Paul Dibon, *La philosophie néerlandaise au siècle d'or*, I, *L'Enseignement philosophiques dans les universités à l'époque précartésienne*. (Paris: 1954). For New England, see the works of Morison and Miller already cited.

[100] Walter J. Ong, "Ramist Method and the Commercial Mind," *Studies in the Renaissance*, VIII, 1961, 155-172, especially pp. 155, 169-70. For a full scale critical study of Ramism, see Ong's *Ramus, Method, and the Decay of Dialogue*, (Cambridge, Mass.: 1958).

[101] A much higher evaluation of Ramism than that of Ong is given by Bizer in his introduction to Heppe, xxvii. Bizer regrets that leading Reformed theologians such as Beza rejected Ramus. Since Ramism was without a metaphysics, its adoption by Reformed theologians would have allowed them to build theology on revelation alone without any contamination from philosophy. In Bizer's view, this would largely have prevented the whole unfortunate development of Protestant scholasticism.

years cutting his teeth on Suarez's metaphysics but never looked into the Spaniard's theological works, which were as thoroughly scholastic as those of the medievals but set forth in far better Latin. The reading of scholastic authors from Thomas to Suarez was bound to affect the style and method of Protestant theologians.

Martyr, Beza, and Zanchi did not bring about Reformed scholasticism. The sixteenth century Aristotelian and scholastic tradition was responsible for its development. What then was the contribution of Martyr and his friends to the origins of Reformed scholasticism? Martyr provided a sanction and he provided an example. He provided a sanction because he was universally respected in Reformed circles as a scholar and as a man of God, even as a sort of Protestant saint and doctor of the Church. He was the first important Reformed theologian to incorporate a large amount of scholastic terminology and method into his theology.[102] In so doing he set a sign of approval on this theological approach which was distinctly different from that of Calvin and Luther. Because his own Reformed orthodoxy was utterly beyond question, because the conclusions he reached were generally further removed from the teachings of Rome than those of Luther and even Calvin, there was no danger that the scholastic elements in his theology could be lightly dismissed as the vestiges of popery from which Reformed theology must be protected and purified.[103] Quite the contrary, far from being something intrinsically redolent of popery, Aristotelian philosophy was for Martyr not even a neutral instrument to be used alike by Catholic and Protestant in the construction of theological argument. Rather, Aristotle was the ally of Protestantism.[104] For Martyr sound metaphysics was an invaluable and trusty tool which Reformed theology could and should use. His works attempt to use it again and again. In doing so Martyr provided not only sanction but an example of the Reformed use of the scholastic tradition. In fact, the more polemical Martyr is against Catholics or Lutherans, the more scholastic he is apt to be. The sanction and example that Martyr provided no doubt affected subsequent writers mainly on a semi-conscious level;

---

[102] Martyr was seventeen years older than Zanchi and twenty years older than Beza. Zanchi's most important theological works were published after 1570. Beza's works appeared earlier but only gradually took on a more scholastic tone.

[103] Martyr's theological position lies between that of Zwingli and of Calvin, especially as regards the eucharist and his attitude toward ceremonials, not between Luther and Calvin, as Benedetto Croce supposes: *Vite*, 253.

[104] *Ethicorum*, 265.

and many of them went far beyond him in their use of scholasticism. They were not likely to make explicit in their works this particular aspect of their indebtedness to Martyr, but it is not less real for that.

Martyr's example of the use of scholasticism was influential partly because it was timely and met a felt need. By 1550 Protestant polemics required a new approach. Many early attacks on Roman Catholicism were rhetorical and scatter-gun. The best example of this is Luther's *Appeal to the Ruling Classes of the German Nation*, which submits dozens of Catholic practices and doctrines to scathing fire but does not pause long enough on any one target to pulverize it thoroughly. As the century wore on, polemics tended to concentrate on fewer but more important issues and to handle them with great thoroughness. A good example of this is Martyr's *Defensio* against Gardiner which devotes most of its over 800 folio pages attacking transubstantiation. After a generation of polemics the scatter-gun approach was unlikely to carry much conviction, at least among the educated, since stock answers were ready to repel stock objections. Only a determined assault such as that of Martyr on Gardiner could expect to carry a position. Such an attack had to be confined to the theologically critical places in an enemy's defenses. A full scale attack against papal annates, for instance, might be very impressive, but overwhelming such a minor outpost of the Roman position would hardly be decisive or worth the effort. As time went on, two other traditional sources of Protestant polemics became less effective. First, attacks on moral turpitude within the Roman Church became less telling as the Catholic Reformation remedied some of the more glaring abuses. Moreover, as Protestantism became more institutionalized, it became ever more open to the simple retort, "*tu quoque*." Secondly, scriptural argument became less decisive, for both sides has long since hurled their scriptural thunderbolts and exhausted their arsenals, yet the enemy remained standing. This is well exemplified by the Marburg colloquy at which Luther and Zwingli tried for days to reach agreement on precisely what Christ meant by "This is my body." Both insisted that scripture was the sole norm of dogma and that its meaning was clear; both were great scriptural scholars, yet in the end they could only agree to disagree.

To be fresh and telling, polemics had to take new directions by 1550. One direction was a more extensive use of the church fathers, and Martyr used this technique widely and well. Another new direction was greater rigor, subtlety, sophistication, and elaboration in argument. Since scripture alone had in fact settled few arguments, it became important to show that the opposite doctrine contained logical flaws or led to philosophical absurdities and contradictions. This was Martyr's main argument against Gardiner. A variation on this approach was to show that the opponent's doctrine logically implied an ancient heretical teaching repudiated by the early Church. For instance, Martyr's *Dialogus* sought to show that Brenz's Christology was monophysite. The use of these kinds of arguments inevitably involved a more scholastic theology. Beyond question Martyr's most scholastic work was the *Defensio* against Gardiner, both as regards the form of the work as a whole or the content of the individual arguments he developed. Martyr's *Dialogus* was in a humanist rather than a scholastic literary genre, but as Schmidt has observed: "It is a very learned but very scholastic discussion of an essentially scholastic question." [105] Martyr's scripture commentaries with their many scholia on controverted subjects answered to the same polemical needs and set an example of how biblical studies and scholasticism could be combined in the defense of Reformed dogmatics.[106]

---

[105] Schmidt, *Leben*, 239: "Es ist eine sehr gelehrte, aber sehr scholastische Erörterung einer wesentlich scholastischen Frage."

[106] "Protestantism, recoiling before the victories of the Counter-Reformation, had to defend itself with the weapons of its adversary. Aristotle, dethroned by Luther, began again to master biblical theology among the followers of the first reformer. The theological readjustments of the decade 1550-60 cut deeply into the biblical studies of the period." Basil Hall, "Biblical Scholarship: Editions and Commentaries," in *The Cambridge History of the Bible*, III, *The West from the Reformation to the Present Day*, ed. S. L. Greenslade, (Cambridge: 1963), 77. In addition to the works of Bizer, Heppe, Liedtke, Gründler, Armstrong, Ritschl, Kickel, Althaus, Wundt, Liedtke, and Pelikan already cited, some further studies of the impact of philosophy on the development of Protestant scholasticism are E. Weber, *Der Einfluss der Protestantischen Schulphilosophie auf die orthodoxlutherische Dogmatik*, (Leipzig: 1908); Josef Bohatec, *Die Cartesianische Scholastik in der Philosophie und reformierten Dogmatik des 17. Jahrhunderts*, (Hildesheim: 1966); and Robert P. Scharlemann, *Thomas Aquinas and John Gerhard*, (New Haven: 1964). Scharlemann's introductory chapter gives a lucid English summary of much of the research which is otherwise only available in German. Unfortunately it is largely restricted to Lutheran scholasticism.

CHAPTER EIGHT

FROM PADUA TO ZURICH:
THE LIMITS OF MARTYR'S SCHOLASTICISM

The introductory chapter of this book pointed out that the most important development in Protestant theology during the second half of the sixteenth century was not the introduction of new teaching but a change in the method of presenting and defending the conclusions already reached by Luther, Zwingli, and Calvin. Several scholars have suggested that Peter Martyr Vermigli played a crucial role in this development, which is usually termed Protestant scholasticism. The introductory chapter proposed that this hypothesis be tested by an examination of Martyr's teaching on man and grace. The next two chapters examined the sources of Martyr's teaching and his theological methodology and concluded that he applied the mastery of Aristotle and the scholastic theologians that he gained at the University of Padua to the elaboration and defense of Reformed dogmatics. The following three chapters presented Martyr's philosophy of human nature, his teaching on sin and its effects, and on God's saving plan to rescue man from the power of sin and the weakness of fallen human nature by predestining him to justification, grace, and glorification. Vermigli's development of these questions clearly owed a considerable debt to Aristotelian philosophy and medieval scholastic theology. Finally, the previous chapter outlined the impact of Martyr's life, teachings, and writings on sixteenth century Calvinism.

We are now in a position to answer the question posed by the introductory chapter: Was Peter Martyr Vermigli a Protestant scholastic theologian?

This is a basic question, but not an easy one since scholasticism is a very complex phenomenon which includes a number of elements.[1] Scholasticism is primarily a method and approach rather than a set of doctrines. Every sixteenth century theologian exhibits some traces

---

[1] Maurice de Wulf devotes thirteen pages to showing the difficulties in defining scholasticism and to pinpointing insufficient definitions. Interestingly, he does not conclude his discussion by hazarding a definition of his own. *History of Medieval Philosophy*, trans. E. C. Messenger, (London: 1951), I, 5-17. Bray, 245-246, discusses the failure of an acceptable definition of Protestant scholasticism to emerge.

of scholasticism in his teaching, but not all are thereby scholastics. The crucial consideration is the relative density of elements associated with scholasticism within a theologian's thought. The degree to which Martyr can be termed a scholastic theologian largely depends upon the definition given to scholastic theology. Perhaps the degree to which Martyr is and is not a scholastic can be best illustrated by measuring his theology against two definitions of scholastic theology, the first formulated primarily to describe medieval scholasticism, the second to describe the fully developed Protestant scholasticism of the seventeenth century.

The first definition is that of M. A. Hotze.

> The particular treatment of theology (especially dogmatic theology) that seeks to understand revealed truths by applying human intelligence is called scholastic theology. Relying upon divine revelation and upon the power of human reason to attain objective truth, it combines positive and speculative theology. Cultivating a spirit of harmony between faith and reason, it borrows methodology from scholastic philosophy and systematizes its matter under the influence of philosophical principles. Aristotelian logic and metaphysics are applied to unfold meanings, show relationships, to deduce theological conclusions, and to defend truths proposed by the teaching authority of the Church.[2]

If *Bible* is substituted for *Church* as the last word of the definition, Martyr's theology fits rather neatly within the terms of the definition. Martyr does apply human reason to deepen his understanding of the truths he finds revealed in scripture. He believes both divine revelation and human reason lead man to attain objective truth with certainty. Martyr's theology is both positive and speculative, that is, it seeks to determine what are the contents of revelation and it seeks to synthesize these into a coherent, reasoned ensemble. He does admit a high degree of harmony between faith and reason, although he clearly subordinates reason to faith and insists that faith attains truths which are beyond the range of reason. His use of the syllogism and his penchant for constructing definitions according to the schema of the four Aristotelian causes are only two examples of his borrowing methodology from scholastic philosophy and systematizing theological materials under the influence of philosophical principles. He uses Aristotelian logic and metaphysics to unfold meaning, to show

---

[2] Article on scholastic theology, *The New Catholic Encyclopedia*, XII, 1153.

relationships, and to deduce theological conclusions. For example, when treating the eucharist, he shows logical flaws in Gardiner's argument and draws out the metaphysical absurdities that his teaching implies. He also shows that the Aristotelian notion of *esse-in-loco* cannot be squared with Brenz's doctrine of ubiquity. His understanding of actual grace as a species of divine concurrence from the prime mover and first act presupposes the Aristotelian doctrines of act and potency. In short, he defends and elaborates revealed truth with the aid of Aristotle. Going beyond Hotze's definition, we can also point to Martyr's use of literary forms that recall those of scholasticism. He uses both the commentary and the *quaestio*, although he tends to combine them. The bulk of his literary output is commentary, either on the Bible or on Aristotle. Within the commentaries are the scholia, many posed as questions and structured after the pattern of a medieval *quaestio*. Martyr never wrote a *Summa*, but his most widely circulated and influential work, the *Loci Communes* compiled from his writings after his death, comes very close to being a Protestant *Summa*. In sum, if one accepts Hotze's definition, Martyr is a scholastic theologian.

Still, caution is needed. There are limits to Martyr's scholasticism which must be stressed. The first chapter of this book quoted the descriptive definition which Brian Armstrong based on his study of fully developed Protestant scholasticism during the seventeenth century.[3] Armstrong's description can be broken down to five characteristics:

1. It aims at a logically coherent and defensible system of belief based on syllogistic deduction from given assumptions.
2. It is based on Aristotelian philosophy.
3. It allows reason to assume at least equal standing with faith and revelation in dealing with religious matters.
4. It sees in Scripture a unified, comprehensive account that can be reduced to a credal statement which then serves as a measuring stick for orthodoxy.
5. It shows a strong interest in metaphysical and speculative questions, especially those relative to God and his will.[4]

---

[3] Armstrong, 32.

[4] Martin Grabmann gives an excellent discussion of the problem of defining scholastic method and offers an insightful definition. I have not employed his definition here because it raises the same questions as does Armstrong's description, and I wished to avoid repetition. *Die Geschichte der scholastischen Methode*, (Berlin: 1957), I, 28-37, especially 36 and 37.

Of these five characteristics only the second is clearly found in Martyr's theology, for he does use Aristotelian logic, physics, metaphysics, philosophical psychology, and theory of knowledge to enrich and defend his theology, just as did the medieval scholastics. Only the third of the characteristics is clearly rejected by Vermigli, for he never allows reason to attain a status equal or superior to faith, nor did he ever tolerate any conscious jettisoning of the authority of revelation. In this he is far from those seventeenth century Protestant scholastics who paved the way for eighteenth century rationalism. Both in theory and practice his loyalty to the Protestant principle of *sola scriptura* is beyond question, yet he does assign reason a larger role in theology than did Bonaventure and Occam, who were certainly scholastic theologians.

Armstrong's other three characteristics are only partially verified in Vermigli. He rightly considered his theology as defensible and coherent. Still he does not really present it as a coherent body in which the parts interlock and re-enforce each other as parts of a chain of deductive ratiocination. Had he lived to write the *Loci* himself, he might have made more explicit the inter-relationships between the various parts of his teaching. Still, I think, Martyr's primary stress is that each part of his theology derives from scripture, and as scripture is self-consistent, so the doctrines drawn from scripture dovetail and reinforce each other in an *analogia fidei*. The truth value of each doctrine derives primarily from its scriptural origin rather than its congruence and place within an over-arching deductive ratiocination. Martyr would claim his teachings are true primarily because they are biblical and only secondarily because they are consistent.[5] He never attempts to present an extended part of his theology as a chain of syllogistic deductions from given premises; rather his use of the formal syllogism is usually restricted to single arguments. Very clearly, the formal syllogism as a type of argument and a method of presentation has far less importance for him than for later Calvinist scholastics such as Zanchi and Pierre du Moulin. For instance, the second, third, and fourth tomes of Zanchi's *Opera Theologica* state hundreds of theses; the theses are then regularly proved by a formal syllogism, which is in turn explained and defended at great length. Martyr comes closest to this thesis method in his *Defensio* against Gardiner.

Martyr certainly thought that Scripture contained a unified and

---

[5] Klaus Sturm comes to a similar conclusion: 55, 74, 75, 247, 248.

intelligible account, even if the human mind could never understand it exhaustively. He felt that the main themes in the scriptural account could be gathered and expressed in a credal statement that could serve to measure orthodoxy and check heterodoxy; indeed, he aided in the composition of several such credal statements, but he always insisted that they cannot replace Scripture and have value only to the extent that they reflect the teaching of Scripture.

Vermigli was not indifferent to metaphysical questions, as the chapter on his philosophy of man made clear, and he was quite willing to relate metaphysics to theology, but his interest is pragmatic rather than speculative. He is interested in using metaphysics to deepen his understanding of revelation or to answer objections, but he has little interest in metaphysics for its own sake, nor does he try to develop a rational theology. Like Calvin's *Institutes*, Martyr's *Loci Communes* and his other writings simply do not contain an extensive speculative tract *de Deo uno*, such as Aquinas includes at the beginning of the *Summa Theologiae* (I, 3-26). Later Protestant scholastics gloried in such tracts; Zanchi, for instance, devotes 586 folio columns to his treatment of the divine attributes, over four times as much space as the *Summa Theologiae* gives to the same material.[6] Nevertheless, when Martyr does attempt to explore the Godhead, his interest falls on the divine will, particularly its sovereign freedom in the act of predestination; in this interest he foreshadows the emphasis of later Calvinist scholastics. Perhaps it is significant that Martyr once planned a major work defending the Trinity against Michael Servetus, but no less significantly he never carried out his plan in the face of other pressing demands on his energy and talent.[7]

To sum up, Peter Martyr represents a transitional stage between the humanist and biblical orientation of Calvin and the developed scholasticism of the seventeenth century. His thought has many of the characteristics of the later Calvinist scholasticism, but other traits are either absent or are found only in a limited and incipient way. His theology served as a stepping stone between Luther and Calvin on the one hand and seventeenth century Protestant scholasticism on the other. It should not be forgotten that humanistic influences continued to play a role in Martyr's thought, even though this study has not explored them in depth. Martyr lectured on Cicero's *Tusculan Disputations* and

---

[6] *Opera*, the whole second tome.
[7] *Calvini Opera*, XIV, 707; XV, 3.

on Homer as well as on Aristotle; [8] his writings quote Cicero and
Virgil more often than Peter Lombard and Thomas Aquinas. In the
sixteenth century scholasticism and humanism were different and
distinct, but no more intrinsically opposed than the sciences and
humanities are today. The tension between humanism and scholasticism was keenest early in the century, but with the passage of time
many men mastered both. Melanchthon was both more the humanist
and more the scholastic than Luther. Beza was both more the humanist
and more the scholastic than Calvin. So too Peter Martyr combined
the mastery of the three classical languages and broad reading in the
literature of antiquity with skill in Aristotelian philosophy and the lore
of the medieval schoolmen to produce a theology at once humanist
and scholastic.

Does Martyr's scholasticism have affinities to any particular medieval school? Yes. Martyr cannot fairly be called a Thomist, yet his
scholasticism stands far closer to Thomism than to any other major
school of the Middle Ages. His training was mainly Thomistic; he
cites Aquinas far more often than any other scholastic except Lombard;
he cites more individual works of Thomas than of any other non-
patristic theologian; and on innumerable specific points his teaching
coincides with that of St. Thomas. [9]

I have been at some pains to emphasize Martyr's affinities with
Thomism and the relatively little influence exerted on him by nominalism precisely because many Roman Catholic authors have laid
great stress on what they see as the pernicious influence of nominalism
at work in Luther's theology. The first important Catholic to develop
this view was Heinrich Denifle in his bitterly hostile biography of
Luther. [10] His thesis was taken up and developed even further by
Louis Bouyer. [11] Even Catholics relatively sympathetic to Luther such
as John Todd and Joseph Lortz highlight the same theme. [12] These
writers often begin by pointing out that nominalism represents decadent
scholasticism, even a theology no longer authentically Catholic. They

---

[8] Schmidt, *Leben*, 60; McNair, 122.

[9] Sturm reaches a similar judgement on Martyr and Thomism: 185-187, 114,
142, 147, 154, 190, 200, 217, 232, 253.

[10] Oberman, 425.

[11] *The Spirit and Forms of Protestantism*, trans. A. V. Littledale, (London:
1956), 162-165.

[12] John Todd, *Martin Luther: A Biographical Study*, (London: 1964), 53-56.
Joseph Lortz, *The Reformation in Germany*, trans. Ronald Walls, (New York,
1968), I, 195-200.

see Luther's theology partly as a direct result of his nominalist background, partly as a reaction against it, especially its Pelagianism. For these Catholic authors several of Luther's central teachings—justification by extrinsic imputation, *simul justus et peccator*, predestination, distrust of human reason—are rooted in nominalist presuppositions. In fact, none of these Catholic authors has an expert background in nominalist theology or philosophy. Recent research, especially that of Heiko Oberman, has revised their interpretation of nominalism, seeing it in a more favorable light, exploying more precise scholarship, and re-opening the question of Luther's relation to the whole Occamist tradition.[13] Yet because this older Catholic interpretation of the relation of Protestant theology to nominalism is so wide spread and because Peter Martyr's theological development runs counter to it, several typical examples of this older Catholic view should be presented.

Joseph Lortz writes:

> From the days of his youth, Luther's concept of the unknown God had been that of a wrathful judge. The doctrines of Occam now turned him into the God of caprice; for the basic thing in the Occamist concept of God is that God is and must be absolutely free from every possible norm or definition conceivable or expressible by man. This freedom amounts to utter caprice. This means that God calls one act good and another act bad, commands one to be done and forbids the other, because of 'interior' reasons; he could have made things quite the opposite. This is full blown nominalism, which makes the sacraments mere outward signs, and grace a mere gracious designation of the favored soul. It goes further and says that in the sheer arbitrariness of his sovereignty God predestines this man to heaven and that man to hell.[14]

Philip Hughes develops the same theme a bit differently (all italics his):

> The whole of Ockham's influence is the history of the disappearance of certitude; of the end of all grasp of reality, and of all clear, distinct

---

[13] Oberman, passim, especially 423-428. Several recent Catholic studies, independently of Oberman, have begun a reassessment of the relationship between nominalism and the Reformation, particularly McSorley, 183-215, and Francis Clark, *Eucharistic Sacrifice and the Reformation*, (London: 1960), 296-322. William J. Courtenay reviews the recent literature, "Nominalism and Late Medieval Religion," forthcoming in, Charles Trinkaus and Heiko A. Oberman, editors, *The Pursuit of Holiness in Late Medieval and Renaissance Religion*, (Leiden, 1974).

[14] Lortz, I, 195. Used with the permission of the McGraw-Hill Book Company.

thought. And it was from Ockham, also, that Luther derived one of the two elements of his own peculiar system, the idea, namely that the whole of grace and of salvation is something altogether external to man in cause and effect. It is, for Luther, wholly and purely the act of God. Man's actions can have no share in it, except in so far as God *accepts* that action as meritorious. As things are, so Ockham declares, such human acts must be acts of a personality united to God by a supernatural charity, acts of a soul possessed by sanctifying grace; but only *as things are*. For God could, in his omnipotence, just as well accept as meritorious acts done by his enemies, ... From Ockham the tradition had come down through a succession of masters. Gregory of Rimini has the same teaching, so has Peter d'Ailly, so has Gabriel Biel. It is not *inherently* impossible for man—so they all concur—to be accepted by God as meriting, even though he does not possess charity. . . . . for the whole basis of man's relation with God is God's arbitrary attitude of acceptance or non-acceptance of his acts.[15]

Hughes goes on to describe how Luther, under the pressure of his conviction of his own utter sinfulness and his anguished quest for a gracious God, took the short step of asserting that what the nominalists held possible in the *potentia absoluta* was in fact the human condition in the *potentia ordinata*: God did justify man even though he remained a sinner. *Simul justus et peccator.*

My purpose in dwelling on the connection between the theology of Occam and of Luther is not to question the fact of nominalism's influence on Luther's *personal* development, still less to become involved in controversy over the proper evaluation of nominalism as a philosophical or theological system. Rather it is to urge that the connection between nominalist thought and such distinctive Protestant doctrines as justification by imputation, extreme predestination, and emphasis on God's freedom and sovereignty is not as tight as the Roman Catholic historians cited above have assumed. The thesis that Occam is the foster father of Protestantism needs revision in the light of Peter Martyr's theology. Martyr's teachings on the sacraments, justification, predestination, and God's sovereignty yield little in vigor to Luther and Calvin. Yet Martyr came to these conclusions out of a generally Thomistic rather than Occamist background. The same applies *a fortiori* to Zanchi.[16] Martyr's teaching owes little to

---

[15] Philip Hughes, *A History of the Church*, III, *The Revolt against the Church: Aquinas to Luther*, (New York: 1947), 511.

[16] Gründler's thesis in the only modern book on Zanchi is that he returns to Aquinas for his doctrine of God. I expand this to other areas in Zanchi's theology in my "Calvinist Thomism" which will appear in *Viator* in 1976.

nominalism but flows from his interpretation of Paul and Augustine. In this light the alleged affinities between certain nominalist teachings and Protestant doctrines become less important than many historians of the Reformation suppose.

Although I suggest it only as a hypothesis for further investigation, I think the above point can be expanded. The influence of several currents within nominalism diminished greatly within Catholic circles after the middle of the sixteenth century, but it seems also to have played a diminishing role in Protestant circles too, especially in the development of Reformed scholasticism. Nominalism was flourishing in the first decades of the century. Many universities had chairs *in via moderna*. Several of the earliest Catholic critics of Luther, Johann Eck among them, have nominalist backgrounds.[17] Many factors contributed to the decline of nominalism, most importantly the Thomist revival of the sixteenth century. Another factor was geographical. Nominalism was particularly strong in many areas that became Protestant. It was particularly weak even early in the century in those countries, Spain and Italy, which took the lead in the Counter-Reformation. The Council of Trent gave an impetus to the Thomist revival, not least because the council fathers and theologians were overwhelmingly Italian and Spanish. Nominalism was under-represented at Trent because the countries north of the Alps, the heartland of nominalist strength, were under-represented.[18]

The decline of nominalism within Catholic Europe probably affected its lack of influence in the development of Protestantism later in the century, since Protestant scholasticism was partly linked to developments in Catholic Europe. The striking thing about the rise of Reformed scholasticism is that its roots in medieval scholasticism run heavily to Thomism, hardly at all to nominalism. The great vogue of Suarez in Germany and the Netherlands in the early seventeenth century has been mentioned already: Suarez considered himself a follower of St. Thomas, although he was surely a very independent one. Richard Hooker's debt to Thomas is well known. The index of books in the library of Calvin's Geneva academy is revealing: Thomas and Thomism are well represented—Cajetan alone by twelve

---

Bray (246, 253) finds Thomistic influences at work in Beza's theology, but these seem not to be so important as they were for Martyr and Zanchi.

[17] Oberman, 427.

[18] The importance of Thomism at Trent is sometimes overdrawn since the Scotist contingent was also very strong. See Hubert Jedin, *A History of the Council of Trent*, trans. Ernest Graf, (New York: 1957, 61), II, 194-95, 251, 288, 296.

works—but there is not a work by an Occamist.[19] As has been pointed out, the role attributed to reason within developed Protestant scholasticism was the antithesis of the teaching of nominalism. Although Hughes and Lortz would blanch at the suggestion, in the last decades of the sixteenth century does not Thomas play a role in the development of Protestant thought nearly as important as that of Occam in the first decades?

There remains one task: to relate Martyr's contribution to the origins of Reformed scholasticism to the contributions of those other pioneers, Zanchi and Beza. I have already argued that Zanchi was well grounded in Thomism before he came into contact with Martyr at Lucca, but Martyr was instrumental in his becoming a Protestant.[20] Martyr and Zanchi lived on most intimate terms during Zanchi's first years as a professor at Strasbourg. During these years Martyr's example showed Zanchi how a scholastic training could be utilized in the defense of Protestant doctrine. Zanchi's writings are not as extensive as Martyr's and did not enjoy quite so many editions, perhaps seventy printings in all. Still his contribution to the rise of Reformed scholasticism was immense since the scholastic character of his theology was far more pronounced than that of either Martyr or Beza.

Martyr's contacts with Beza were chiefly through correspondence, although they labored together at Poissy. Beza's letters make clear his respect and affection for Martyr; they are filled with phrases such as *mi pater, eximio servo Dei, alterum meum parantem*.[21] Beza had high regard for Martyr as a theologian; thus he urged Bullinger to get Martyr to publish "*thesauros illos suos*," and he first suggested the idea of the *Loci Communes*.[22] In several letters Martyr advises Beza on important theological points: on the Christian's union with Christ,

---

[19] Ganoczy, *Bibliothèque*, 95, 103, 107: "Et l'école occamienne? Son absence est totale! Pas le moindre extrait du "Venerabilis Inceptor" lui-même, qui pourtant, d'après une thèse largement répandue, aurait servi de pionnier lointain mais efficace aux penseurs de la Réforme. Quant à l'absence de tout représentant du nominalisme, elle fait un singulier contraste avec l'opinion selon laquelle Calvin avait été formé à cette école théologique dès jeunes années, au Collège Montaigu. Pas de Robert Holcot, ni de Nicolas d'Autrecourt, ni de Pierre d'Ailly ou de Gabriel Biel . . ." 107.

[20] Gründler, 12-13. Armstrong (p. 131) is wrong in suggesting that Zanchi's scholastic bent comes from his contact with Martyr at Lucca; Zanchi himself asserts just the opposite. See Zanchi's letter printed in McNair, 228.

[21] Beza *Correspondance*, I, 148; II, 172; III, 209.

[22] Beza *Correspondance*, II, 57; IV, 162.

Christ's presence in the Eucharist, and predestination.[23] In 1557 Beza tells Bullinger that he has read Martyr's Corinthians commentary and refers to a particular passage; two years later he writes to Bullinger and refers to passages in both Martyr's *Tractatio* and the Corinthians commentary and says his own views on the Eucharist do not vary a hair's width from Martyr's.[24] When Beza lost his copy of Martyr's *Dialogus*, he wrote Bullinger for another copy; in later letters he tells Bullinger that he has three times devoured ("voravi") the *Dialogus*.[25] In his attack on Brenz, Beza cites the *Dialogus* over a dozen times.[26] Before becoming a Huguenot, Beza was a young nobleman noted as a brilliant humanist and an accomplished neo-Latin poet, but his education included little contact with scholastic theology. His theological writings became increasingly scholastic during his long life, which suggests that the example of Martyr and Zanchi, as well as the polemical needs of the age, affected his theological method and style.[27]

In conclusion, Jerome Zanchi was the most thorough-going and influential in pioneering Calvinist scholasticism, Theodore Beza was the best known and most prolific, but Peter Martyr Vermigli was the first and the inspiration of all who came after.

---

[23] Beza *Correspondance*, I, 153, 155; II, 79.

[24] Beza *Correspondance*, II, 99; III, 36-38.

[25] Beza *Correspondance*, V, 46, 59.

[26] Theodore Beza, *Volumen Tractationum Theologicarum*, (Geneva: 1576), 544, 545, 547, 549, 557, 562, 578, 580, 581, 590, 592, 608, 619.

[27] Bray, 241-243, independently suggests that Martyr probably played an important role in the increasingly scholastic tone in Beza's thought. Kickel, 168, probably overstates the impact of Aristotelianism and the role of reason in theology on Beza's doctrine of predestination.

PETER MARTYR'S LIBRARY

There are few seminal thinkers in the history of ideas. Peter Martyr was not among them. Although he was not very original, he was among the most erudite men of his time. Although most of his ideas were borrowed from earlier or contemporary writers, his theology presents a personal synthesis, not merely an eclectic patchwork of ill-fitting pieces. The frequent citations and quotations in Martyr's writings are the best guide to the sources of his ideas, but a reconstruction of Martyr's library would supplement these citations. In two respects a reconstruction of Martyr's library would surpass the citations in his writings as a guide to the sources of his thought and intellectual development. Firstly, it would indicate which editions Martyr used of the many works he cites rather casually and would provide the student of Vermiliana with something like the hard data which the bibliography gives in a modern work. Secondly, the most elusive sources of Martyr's thinking are his contemporaries since he seldom refers to them or their writings by name, even when his debt to them is enormous. A reconstruction of his library throws considerable light on which contemporary writers, especially theologians, Martyr was reading.[1]

Martyr bequeathed his books to his servant Giulio Santerenziano, who put the library up for sale. Theodore Beza was a prospective buyer and wrote to Bullinger asking for a catalogue of the library and a suggested price. Unfortunately the catalogue has not survived. Another prospective buyer was Froschauer, the publisher of so many of Vermigli's works. But the eventual buyer was, in fact, the city of Geneva, which was seeking to build up the meager holdings in the library of the Geneva Academy. Three barrels of books weighing twenty-three quintals, somewhat over a thousand pounds, arrived in

---

[1] I doubt if Martyr had many books that he did not read, even among those volumes which carry no marginalia as proof of his assiduity. Books were relatively expensive in the sixteenth century. Martyr was not a rich man who could line the walls of a library with uncut volumes to impress guests. He was a genuine and profound scholar. He also had the great advantage over friends such as Bullinger and Calvin that practical, political and ministerial duties were not constantly interrupting his studies.

Geneva from Zurich in March, 1566. Freight charges ran to 210 Florins. Apparently the size of Vermigli's library took the city fathers a bit by surprise; in any event they decided to economize by sending back to Zurich those books that were considered useless for the Academy library.[2]

This decision has made anything like a complete list of Vermigli's library impossible, for there is no way of knowing which books were sent back. One can only surmise that the "useless" books were mainly duplicates of what the library already possessed. Probably the toll was especially high in rabbinic commentaries and scholastic works.[3] Of the books purchased, many have disappeared, whether lost, stolen, or simply worn out and discarded, who can say? Most of Vermigli's volumes retained at Geneva have survived the attrition of centuries and can still be studied at the Bibliothèque publique et universitaire de Genève.

Two able scholars have devoted their attentions to this task and have laid the foundation of a partial reconstruction of Martyr's library. Over fifty years ago Frederic Gardy published an article on Martyr's library which traced its acquisition by Geneva and gave the general outlines of Martyr's holdings.[4] Gardy did not publish a list of Martyr's books. He continued his research and compiled considerable additional notes on Martyr's library but left these unpublished at his death. Very recently Alexandre Ganoczy had devoted a whole volume to a careful study of the library of Calvin's academy at Geneva.

---

[2] Frédéric Gardy, "Les Livres de Pierre Martyr Vermigli conservés à la Bibliothèque de Genève." *Anzeiger für Schweizerische Geschichte*, N.F. XVII, 1919, 2, 3.

[3] Martyr's mastery of the rabbinic commentaries on the Old Testament and his use of them has already been pointed out, yet only a few elementary works of this sort have been identified as his in the Geneva collection, which is very rich in this category. Either his works escaped detection by Gardy and Ganoczy or they were shipped back to Zurich as duplicates. The only scholastic work of Vermigli's identified in the Geneva collection is St. Thomas' *Quaestiones Disputatae*. Given Martyr's fairly numerous and often precise references to scholastic writers, his library either originally possessed several such works or he had easy access to them. Even Martyr's remarkable memory cannot explain the precise references. Ganoczy (106-08) emphasizes the general lack of scholastic authors and suggests a conscious policy by those in charge to explain the lack.

[4] Gardy, "Les Livres." E. Rodocanachi also used Gardy's research to compile a list, although an incomplete one, of books in Martyr's library: *La Réforme en Italie*, (Paris: 1920), I, 444-48. These lists are sometimes overlooked, for instance by McLelland, 269, who claims that nothing is known about Martyr's library aside from the possession of a few works of the church fathers acquired while in England.

He makes very extensive use of the notes left by Gardy but has been able to go beyond them with his own research.[5]

This appendix is completely dependent upon the research of Gardy and Ganoczy. But neither gives a single list of all the books which they attribute to Martyr's library. In compiling and arranging such a list I only wish to make their research more accessible to future Vermigli scholars.

Some words of caution are necessary. The list that follows is inclusive, not exclusive. Not only were many of Martyr's books sent back to Zurich, not only have many books disappeared from the Geneva library, but also Martyr usually did not write his name in his books. In identifying Martyr's books Gardy and Ganoczy frequently had to rely on marginalia in Martyr's hand or on envoys, usually on the frontpiece by the author, which presents the book to Martyr and mentions his name. Ganoczy often prints these envoys; they are invariably respectful and indicate the high esteem of Calvin, Bullinger, Beza and others for Martyr. Some of the identifications are based on a very few marginal comments and therefore lack certainty. In some instances a book is identified as belonging to Martyr solely because it is bound together with another book or two which can be identified as his. In these instances there is the danger that the books may have been bound together after their acquisition by the Geneva library. Ganoczy is properly cautious about some attributions made on this basis in the notes of Gardy which he utilized.[6] In the list which follows I have placed a D after entries which seemed rather doubtful. For several Greek works, Ganoczy gives both the Greek and Latin titles; I give only the Latin in these instances. For Hebrew titles I repeat the transliterations into Roman type given by Ganoczy and identify the subject in English within parentheses when there is no Latin subtitle. I have arranged the books into six categories: classical literature, ancient philosophy, Old Testament scholarship, patristic and scholastic theology, contemporary theology (Protestant and Catholic), contemporary scholarship, and law. The books within each category are listed alphabetically by author.

---

[5] Ganoczy, *Bibliothèque*, 7, 20, 21.

[6] Ganoczy (20, 21) gives a discussion of the problems he and Gardy encountered in identifying Martyr's books. After each entry in his catalogue of the books in the Geneva library he indicates the evidence for concluding that the book once belonged to Martyr.

CLASSICAL LITERATURE [7]

Aristophanes: *Aristophanis comoediae novem, cum commentariis antiquis* . . . Florence: Heirs of F. Giunta, 1525.

Athenaeus: *Dipnosophistarum* . . . Basel: J. Valderus, 1535.

Cicero: *M. T. Ciceronis De Legibus Libri III. In eosdem commentarii* Andr. Turnebo autore . . ., Paris, A. Turnebre, 1552.

——: *Opera Marci Tullii Ciceronis* . . ., Basel: J. Hervagius, 1540. 4 vol. in 2.

——: *In omnes M. Tulli Ciceronis orationes, quot quidem extant, doctissimorum virorum enarrationes* . . ., Basel: J. Oporin, 1553.

Columella: *Libri De re rustica, M. Catonis, M. Terentii Varronis, L. Iunii Moderati Columellae, Palladii Rutilli* . . ., Paris: Josse Bade, 1529.

Demosthenes: *Demosthenis Graecorum oratorum* . . . *Orationes duae et sexaginta, et in easdem Ulpiani Commentarius* . . . *Libani Argumenta* . . ., Basel: J. Hervagius, 1532.

Livy: *T. Livii Patavini Latinae Historiae principis Decades tres* . . . Caeli Secundi Curionis industria . . . Beati Rhenani et Sigismundi Gelenii . . . in hunc autorem Annotationes . . ., Basel: J. Hervagius, 1549.

Lucian: *Luciani Samosatensis Pars Prima*, Haguenau: J. Sacerius, 1526.

Pindar: ΠΙΝΔΑΡΟΥ ΟΛΥΜΠΙΑ ΠΥΘΙΑ ΝΕΜΕΑ ΙΣΘΜΙΑ, Rome: Zacharias Calgerus Cretenais, n.d.

Polybius: *Polybii Megalopolitani Historiarum libri priores quinque*, Nicolao Perotto Sipontino interprete. *Item epitome sequentium librorum* . . . Wolfgango Musculo interprete, Basel: N. Episcopius, 1557.

——: *De Romanorum militia et castrorum metatione liber utilissimus ex Polybii historiis per A. Ianum Lascarem Rhyndacenum excerptus* . . ., Basel: B. Lasius and Th. Platter, 1537.

Priscian: *Prisciani Grammatici Caesariensis libri omnes* . . ., Cologne, Eucharius Cervicornus, 1528.

Sophocles: *Sophoclis Tragoediae septem, cum interpretationibus vetustis et valde utilibus* . . ., Florence: Heirs of F. Giunta, 1522.

Suetonius: Ex recognitione Des. Erasmi Roterodami. *C. Suetonius Tranquillus. Dioncassius Nicaeus* . . . (a dozen more names follow), Cologne: Eucharius Cervicornus, 1527.

ANCIENT PHILOSOPHY

Aristotle: *Aristotelis* . . . *Opera* . . . *omnia*. Per Des. Eras. Roterodamum, Basel: J. Bebel, 1531. (Greek edition)[8]

---

[7] Among the editions of Greek writers, only Martyr's copy of Polybius is a Latin translation. This is noteworthy since most sixteenth century scholars knew their Greek authors mainly through Latin translations.

[8] Jasper Ridley states that Martyr had to leave all his possessions behind when he left Marian England: *Knox*, 157. This cannot be correct. Martyr's Greek *Opera* editions of Aristotle and Plato, as well as his Lucian and Greek grammar by Lascaris all belonged to him as far back as his Italian days since all contain references to ownership by Martyr's dearest monastic friend, Benedetto Cusano de Vercelli, who died at Naples in 1540. See Ganoczy, 23. That Martyr took the trouble to have these books shipped indicates that he by no means saw his conversion to Protestantism as a rejection of philosophy. I doubt that many other books in Martyr's library date from his Italian career. On the basis of publication dates and places the most likely candidates would be his Hebrew Bibles, but the earlier of these has an inscription in English: "For Mast. D. Martyr." It therefore must have come to him while at Oxford or later.

——: *Aristotelis De natura lib. IX. Ejusdem De partibus animalium lib. IV. Ejusdem De generatione animalium lib. V. Theophrasti De historia plantarum . . . lib. IX. Et decimi principium duntaxat. Ejusdem de causis plantarum lib. VI . . .*, (Venice): Aldus, (1503).

——: *Aristotelis Poetica, per Alexandrum Paccium, patricium Florentinum in Latinum conversa . . .*, Basel: B. Lasius and Th. Platter, 1537.

——: *Problematum Aristotelis . . . Problematum Aphrodirici . . .*, Venice: Aldus, n.d.

Marcus Aurelius: *M. Antonini Imperatoris Romani et philosophi De se ipso seu Vita sua Libri XII* graece et latine nunc aediti Gulielmo Xylandro.

——: Augustano interprete, qui etiam annotationes adiecit, Zurich: A. Gesnerus, 1558. (i.e.: the *Meditations*).

Plato: *Omnia Platonis Opera*, (Venice): Aldus, 1513. (Greek edition).

——: *Omnia Divini Platonis Opera* tralatione Marsilii Ficini . . ., Venice: J. M. Bonellus, 1556.

Plutarch: *Plutarchi Chaeronei moralia opuscula . . .*, Basel: Froben, 1542. (Greek edition).

Porphyry: *Porphyrii Institutio. Aristotelis Categoriae . . .* Iacobo Lodoico Strebaeo interprete, Paris: Vascosan, 1550.

OLD TESTAMENT SCHOLARSHIP

Biblia Hebraea cum commentariis rabbinorum, Venice: Bomberg, 1524, 1527. 2 vol. (The real title is several rabbinic sentences in Hebrew; this is the second Bomberg edition of the rabbinic Bible).

Nebiy'îm 'aharônîm 'im ha-targûm, Venice: Bomberg, 1517, 1518, 2 vol. in 1. (This is Bomberg's first edition of the rabbinic Bible).

Elia Levita: *Pirqéy 'Eliyahû kiklalîm, Capitula cantici, specierum, proprietatum . . . de literis, punctis, et quibusdam accentibus . . .* per Sebastianum Munsterum Latine versum, Basel: Froben, 1527. D

——: *Séphèr ha-diqdûq, Grammatica Heb . . .* per Sebastianum Munsterum versa . . ., Basel: Froben, 1532.

Capito, Wolfgang: *Institutionum Hebraicarum libri duo . . .*, Strasbourg: Wolfus Cephalaeus, 1525.

Munsterus, Sebastianus: *Dictionarium Chaldaicum . . .*, Basel: Froben, 1527.

PATRISTIC AND SCHOLASTIC THEOLOGY [9]

Ambrose: *Omnia quotquot extant D. Ambrosii episcopi Mediolanensis Opera*, primum per Des Erasmum . . . mox per Sig. Gelenium castigata . . ., Basel: Froben, 1555. 2 vol. D

---

[9] The magnificent volumes of the Fathers are the most impressive part of Martyr's library. Many are in superb editions, especially those by Erasmus. Most noteworthy are the thirteen editions of the Greek Fathers. He had Justin, Clement of Alexandria, Athenaeus, Chrysostom, Gregory Nazianzen, Basil, and John Damascene in the original. There were Renaissance translations of Basil, Epiphanius, Theodoret and Eusebius (this last with a florilegium of church historians). The texts of Origen and Irenaeus were per force in Latin since most of the original has perished. His collection of Latin Fathers included Tertullian, Cyprian, Hilary, Ambrose, Leo I, and the massive editions of Jerome and Augustine. I feel quite confident that the works of a little known Father, Vigilius of Thapse, which are listed in the Geneva library catalogue but which disappeared before Gardy and Ganoczy began their research must have belonged to Martyr. There was a Cologne *editio princeps* in 1555. Martyr's *Dialogus* (f. 42r) quotes

Augustine: *Omnium operum D. Aurelii Augustini Hipponensis episcopi* . . ., Basel: Froben, 1543. 10 vol.

——: *Collectanea Sententiarum divi Aurelii Augustini* . . . per Magistrum Ioachim Westphalum . . ., Ratisbon: J. Carbo, 1555.

——: *Coacervatio Sententiarum aliquot* . . . *ex libris Divi Aurelii Augustini* . . . per Ioannem Tymannum . . ., Frankfort: P. Brubachius, 1555.

Basil: . . . *Operum, Catalogum et Erasmi Roterodami praefationem* . . ., Basel: Froben, 1532. (Greek edition).

——: *Omnia D. Basilii Magni Archepiscopi Caesareae Cappadociae Quae ad nos extant opera* . . . ab Iano Corrario interpretata . . ., Basel: Froben, 1552. (Latin translation). 4 vol. in 1.

Chrysostom: *Divi Ioannis Chrysostomi In omnes Pauli apostoli epistolas* . . ., Verona: Nicolinus a Sabio, 1529. (Greek edition). 3 vol.

Clement of Alexandria: *Clementis Alexandrini omnia quae quidem extant Opera* . . . Gentiano Herveto Aurelio interprete . . ., Florence: L. Torrentinus, 1551. (Greek edition). D

Cyprian: *Divi Caecilii Cypriani episcopi Carthaginensis et Martyris Opera* . . . repurgata per Des. Erasmum . . ., Basel: Hervagius, 1540.

Damascene: *Beati Ioannis Damasceni Orthodoxae fidei accurata explicatio* . . . Iacobo Fabro Stapulensi interprete . . ., Basel: Henric-Petri, 1548. (Greek edition).

Epiphanius: *D. Epiphanii episcopi Constantiae Cypri, Contra octoginta haereses opus, Panarium sive Arcula aut Capsula Medica appellatum* . . . Iano Cornario medico physico interprete . . ., Basel: R. Winterus, 1545.

Eusebius: *Ecclesiasticae historiae authore Eusebii Pamphili.* W. Musculo interprete . . ., Ruffini Presbyteri . . . Eusebii Pamphili . . . Socratis . . ., Basel: Froben, 1554.

Gregory Nazianzen: *Divi Gregorii* . . . *Opera* . . ., Basel: Hervagius, 1550. (Greek edition). 2 vol. in 1.

Hilary: *D. Hilarii Pictavorum episcopi Lucubrationes quotquot extant,* olim per Des. Erasmum . . ., Basel: Froben, 1550.

Irenaeus: *Opus eruditissimum Divi Irenaei episcopi Lugdunensis in quinque libros digestum* . . . Des. Erasmi . . . opera emendatum . . ., Basel: Froben, 1548.

Jerome: *Omnes quae extant D. Hieronymi Stridonensis lucubrationes* . . . per Des. Erasmum digestae . . . in novem tomos, Basel: Froben, 1553. 9 vol. in 5.

Justin Martyr: ΤΟΥ ΑΓΙΟΥ ΙΟΥΣΤΙΝΟΥ ΦΙΛΟΣΟΦΟΥ ΚΑΙ ΜΑΡΤΥΡΟΥ . . ., Paris: R. Estienne, 1551. D

Leo the Great: *D. Leonis huius nominis primi, qui summo iure Magni cognomentum iam olim obtinet, Opera* . . ., Cologne: Melch. Novesianus, 1546. D

Origen: *Origenis Adamantii eximii Scriptuarum interpretis Opera,* per Des. Erasmum partim versa . . ., Basel: Froben, 1545. 2 vol. D

Tertullian: *Q. Septimi Florentis Tertulliani Carthaginensis presbyteri* . . . *Scripta* . . . B. Rhenani annotationibus . . ., Basel: Froben, 1550.

Theodoret: *Theodoreti episcopi Cyri Eranistes seu Polymorphus* . . ., *Eiusden Haereticorum* . . . *nugarum ac fabularum compendium. Eiusdem Divinorum seu dogmatum epitome,* Venice: J. Farreus, 1548.

Thomas Aquinas: *Quaestiones Disputatae Sancti Thomae Aquinatis Doctoris Angelici...,* Venice: Hieronymus Scotus, 1555. D

Vigilius at length. Significantly it was bound with a copy of Smith's work (Louvain, 1550) on celibacy against Martyr, which is also lost. Martyr certainly had a copy of Smith's work since he devoted over six hundred pages to refuting it in his *Defensio de Coelibatu.* See Ganoczy, *Bibliothèque,* 177.

CONTEMPORARY THEOLOGY
Protestants

Artopoeus, Peter: *Vaticinium sacrum de Ecclesia* . . ., n.p.: 1556. D

Beza, Theodore: *De haereticis a civili magistratu puniendis adversus Martini Bellii farraginem*, Geneva: R. Estienne, 1554.

Bibliander, Theodore: *Temporum a condito mundo usque ad ultimam ipsius aetatem supputatio partitioque exactior* . . ., Basel: J. Oporin, 1558.

Brenz, Johann: *In Exodum Mosis commentarii*, Halle: P. Brubachius, 1544. D

——: *In librum Iudicum et Ruth commentarii* . . ., Halle: P. Brubachius, 1544. D

——: *Iob. Cum piis et eruditis Ioannis Brentii commentariis* . . ., Halle: P. Brubachius, 1546. D

——: *In Acta Apostolica Homiliae 122, Auctore Ioanne Brentio* . . ., Frankfort: P. Brubachius, 1546. D

——: *In Leviticum librum Mosis commentarius*, Frankfort: P. Brubachius, 1552. D

Bullinger, Heinrich: *De Gratia iustificante nos per Christum* . . . *lib. IV* . . ., Zurich: Froschover, 1554.

——: *Apologetica expositio, qua ostenditur Tigurinae Ecclesiae ministros nullum sequi dogma haereticum in Coena Domini* . . ., Zurich: A. and J. Gesner, 1556.

——: *De fine saeculi et iudicio venturo Domini* . . . *orationes duae* . . ., Basel: J. Oporin, 1557.

——: *In Apocalypsim* . . ., Basel: J. Oporin, 1557.

——: *De Coena Domini sermo* . . ., *recitatus in concione sacra Tiguri 19 Decemb. 1557* . . ., n.p.: 1558.

——: *In Ieremiae Prophetae Sermones* . . ., Zurich: Froschover, 1557.

——: *Sermones Ieremiae prophetae quatuor* . . ., Zurich: Froschover, 1558.

——: *Conciones XXXXIIII Heinrychi Bullingeri in Ieremiae capita XVI* . . ., Zurich: Froschover, 1559.

——: *Festorum dierum Domini et Servatoris nosti Jesu Christi sermones ecclesiastici* . . ., Zurich: Froschover, 1558.

——: *Tractatio verborum Domini In Domo Patris mei mansiones multae sunt etc* . . ., Zurich: Forschover, 1561.

Calvin, John: *In primum Mosis librum qui Genesis vulgo dicitur, commentarius* . . ., Geneva: R. Estienne, 1554. D

——: *Ultima admonitio Ioannis Calvini ad Ioachimum Westphalum* . . ., Geneva: J. Crespin, 1557.

——: *Ioannis Calvini Opuscula omnia in unum volumen collecta. Quibus accessit libellus nunc primum editus, De Aeterna Dei praedestinatione* . . ., Geneva: J. Gerard, 1552.

——: *Brevis responsio Ioannis Calvini ad diluendas nebulonis cuiusdam calumnias, quibus doctrinam de aeterna Dei praedestinatione foedare conatus est*, Geneva: J. Crespin, 1557. D

Capito, Wolfgang: *Responsio de Missa, Matrimonio et iure magistratus in Religionem*, Strasbourg: W. Rihelius, 1540. D

Draconites, Johann: *In Obadiam prophetam et Psalmum 137 commentariolus ad inclitum Senatum Francofortensem*, Strasbourg: W. Cephalaeus, 1538. D

Flacius Illyricus, Matthias: *Albini seu Alcuini, Caroli Magni praeceptoris Confessio aut doctrina de Deo, compendio exposita, et numquam antea impressa. Confessio M. Flac. Illyrici de sacrosancta Trinitate contra Servetianos, Stencfeldianos et alios.* No place, publisher, or date. D

Gualther, Rudolph: *In Acta Apostolorum* . . . *Homeliae* . . ., Zurich: Froschover, 1557.

Hotman, Francis: Francisci Vilerii, *De statu primitivae Ecclesiae* . . ., Geneva: J. Crespin, 1554.

à Lasco, John: *Forma ac Ratio tota ecclesiastici ministerii in peregrinorum, potissimum vero Germanorum Ecclesia, instituta Londini in Anglia* . . . No place, publisher, or date.

———: *Epistolae tres lectu dignissimae, de recta et legitima Ecclesiarum bene instituendarum ratione ac modo* . . ., Basel: J. Oporin, 1556.

Luther, Martin: *Contra Henricum Regem Angliae* . . ., Wittemberg: 1522. D

———: *Ein Sermon von den Heyltumen und gezierdt mit überflusz vom heyligen Creatz in den Kirchen* . . ., 1523. D

Melanchthon, Philip: *Operum Philippi Melancthonis tomi quinque* . . ., Basel: J. Hervagius, 1541. D

———: *Reverendi et clarissimi viri D. Philippi Melanthonis de Coena Domini ex scriptis collecta per Joachimum Westphalum*, Nuremberg: J. Montanus and U. Neuberus, 1557. D

Oecolampadius, John: *Quod non sit onerosa Christiana Confessio, Paradoxon* . . ., Augsburg: S. G. Medici and M. Wyrsung, 1521. D

Regius, Urban: *Wider den newen irrsal Doctor Andreas von Carlstadt des Sacraments halb Warnung*. 1524. D

Scalichius, Paul: *Dialogus Pauli Scalichii de Lika, comitis Hunorum et Baronis Zkaradini S.T. Doct. de Missa* . . ., Tubingen, 1558. D

Sylvius, Bartholomew: *De Eucharistia tractatulus D. Barptolomaei Sylvii Cremonensis* . . ., 1551. D

Vadian, Joachim: *D. Ioachimi Vadiani Cos. Sangallensis ad Ioan. Zviccium Constantien. Eccelesiae Pastorem Epistola, in qua post explicatas in Christo naturas diversas. . . . Accessit huic eodem authore Angologia, ad clarissimi viri D. Gasparis Schvenckfeldii argumenta* . . ., Zurich: Froschover, n.d.

Vergerio, Peter Paul, editor: *Articuli contra Cardinalem Moronum, de Lutheranismo accusatum et in carcere coniectum.* No place, publisher or date. D

Westphal, Joachim: *Epistola Joachimi Westphali* . . . *ad* . . . *Ioannis Calvini.* . . . No place, publisher or date.

———: *Adversus cuiusdam Sacramentarii falsam criminationem iusta defensio Ioachimi Westphali* . . ., Frankfort: P. Brubachius, 1555. D

———: *Apologia Confessionis de Coena Domini contra corruptelas et calumnias Ioanni Calvini* . . ., Oberursel: N. Henricus, 1558. D

Zwingli, Huldreich: *Von erkiesen und Freiheit der Speisen* . . . Zurich: 1523. D

Francoforto Anglorum ad Amplissimum Senatum Francofor. Oratio, sive gratiarum actio, Frankfort: 1559.

Liturgia sacra seu ritus Ministerii in Ecclesia Peregrinorum Frankfordias ad Moenum . . . Editio Secunda. . . . Frankfort: 1555.

Responsio Christianorum iurisconsultorum ad Fr. Duareni Commentarios de ministeriis Ecclesiae. . . . Strasbourg: C. Mylius, 1556.

In hoc libello gravissimis . . . *rationibus variis probatur Apostolum Petrum Rhomam non venisse* . . . 1520. D

Scriptum Collocutorum Augustanae Confessionis qui in urbe Vangonum fuerunt . . . Anno 1557. . . . Strasbourg: S. Emmel, 1557. D

Vera expositio disputationis institutae mandato D. Mariae Reginae . . . *in Synodo ecclesiastica Londini* . . . 1554. D

Catholics

Erasmus, Desiderius: *Omnia Opera Des. Erasmi Roterodami quaecumque ipse autor suis agnovit.* . . . Basel: Froben, 1540. 9 vol. in 8.

———: *In Novum Testamentum Annotationes,* Basel: Froben, 1540.

Gardiner, Stephen: *Confutatio Cavillationum, quibus sacrosanctum, ab impiis Caper-*

naitis impeti solet, authore Marco Antonio Constantio, Theologo Lovaniensi. . . .
Paris: J. de Roigny, 1552.

Hosius, Stanislaus: *Verae, christianae catholicaeque doctrinae solida propugnatio.* . . .
Cologne: M. Cholinus, 1558. D

Longdail, Alban: *Catholica Confutatio impiae cuiusdam determinationis D. Nicolai
Ridlei* . . ., *post disputationem de Eucharistia in Academia Cantabrigiensi habitae.* . . .
Paris: M. Vascosan, 1556. D

Pole, Reginald: *Pro ecclesiasticae unitatis defensione.* . . . Strasbourg: W. Rihelius,
1555. (Pole's is the first of several works for and against papal primacy
gathered in this volume by P. P. Vergerio.)

Confessio catholicae fidei christiana . . . *in Synodo* . . . *quae habita est Petrikoviae* . . .
(1541) . . . Poznam: J. Patruus, 1557. (Printed at Mainz by Franciscus Behem).

CONTEMPORARY SCHOLARSHIP

Acontius, Jacobus: *De Methodo, hoc est de recta investigandarum tradendarum scien-
tiarum ratione.* Basel: P. Perna, 1558. D

Bembo, Pietro: . . . *Opera in Unum corpus collecta.* . . . Basel: M. Isegrin, 1556. 3 vol.

Beroaldo, Philippus: *Commentarii questionum Tusculanarum.* . . . Paris: J. Petit,
1509. D

Betti, Francesco: *Lettera all'illustriss. et excellentiss. Marchese di Pescara* . . . 1557. D

Budé, Guillaume: *Omnia Opera.* . . . Basel: Nicolaus Episcopius, 1556-57. 4 vol.
in 3. D

Camerarius, Joachim: *Commentariorum in M. T. Ciceronis Tusculanam primam
. . . super Apollonii Tynaei de Imitatione.* . . . Basel: J. Oporinus, 1538. D

Corrado, Sebastianus: *Commentarius, in quo M.T. Ciceronis de claris oratoribus
liber, qui dicitur Brutus* . . ., Florence: L. Torrentinus, 1552.

Grataroli, Gulielmus: *De Literorum et eorum qui magistratibus funguntur conservanda
perseverandaque valetudine* . . ., Basel: Henric-Petri, 1555.

Lascaris, Constantinus: *De octo partibus orationis Lib. I* . . . *liber secundus* . . . *Eiusdem
De constructione* . . ., Venice: Aldus, 1512.

Linacre, Thomas: *De emendata structura latini sermonis libri VI, cum Praefatione
Philippi Melanchthonis.* . . . Cologne: J. Gymnicus, 1539. D

Manutius, Paulus: *Commentarius Pauli Manutii in Epistolas M. Tulli Ciceronis
ad I. Brutum et ad Q. Ciceronem fratrem.* Venice: Aldus, 1557. D

——: *In Epistolas Ciceronis ad Atticum Pauli Minutii Commentarius.* Venice: Aldus,
1557.

Melanchthon, Philip: *Initia Doctrinae Physicae dictata in Academia Witebergensi,*
Philip. Melanth. iterum edita. . . . Wittemberg: Heirs of P. Seitzius, 1553. D

Pierius, Giovanni: *Hieroglyphica sive De sacris Aegyptiorum literis commentarii.* . . .
Basel: M. Isengrin, 1556.

Pius, Ioannes Baptista: *In Carum Lucretium poetam Commentarii.* . . . Paris: Josse
Bade and J. Petit, n.d. D

Rhodigini, Luigi: *Lectionum antiquarum libri XVI.* . . . Basel: Froben, 1517. D

Gardi, Alessandro: De moribus ac ritibus gentium. . . . Venice: J. Zilletus, 1557.

Strebaeus, Iacobus: *In tres priores libros Aristotelis* ΗΘΙΚΩΝ ΝΙΚΟΜΑΧΕΙΩΝ
commentaria. Paris: Vascosan, 1549. D

Streinnius, Richardus: *Gentium et familiarum Romanorum stemmata.* . . . Geneva:
H. Estienne, 1559.

Varennius, Ioannes: *Syntaxis linguae graecae.* . . . Basel: B. Lasius and T. Platter,
1536.

Vives, Juan Luis: *Rhetoricae, sive de recte dicendi ratione libri tres. Eiusdem De con-
sultatione liber I.* Basel: B. Lasius and T. Platter, 1536-37.

——: *De anima et vita libri tres.* . . . Basel: R. Winter, 1538.

LAW

Codicis D. N. Iustiniani Sacratissimi principis principis ex repetita praelectione libri XII . . ., Paris: C. Guillard and G. Desbois, 1550. 3 vol. in 2.

Digestorum seu Pandectarum tomus primus . . . *Antonii Augustini emendationibus* . . . *tomus alter* . . . *Iuris civilis tomus tertius.* . . . Paris: C. Guillard and G. Desbois, 1548-50.

Azo, Portius: *Aurea Summa.* . . . Lyons: M. Bonhomme, 1550. D

Balduinus, Franciscus: *Constantinus Magnus, sive De Constantini Imp. legibus ecclesiasticis atque civilibus Commentariorum libri duo.* . . . Basel: J. Oporin, 1556.

Hotman, Franciscus: *De legibus populi Romani liber.* Basel: N. Episcopius, 1557.

BIBLIOGRAPHY

I. PRIMARY SOURCES

A. The Works of Peter Martyr Vermigli
(Listed in the order of their first editions)

Una Simplice Dichiaratione sopra gli XII articoli della fede christiana. Basel: 1544.

Tractatio de Sacramento Eucharistiae, . . . (and) *Disputatio de eodem Eucharistiae Sacramento. . . .* Zurich: Andr. Gesner, 1557.

An Epistle unto the Right Honorable and Christian Prince, the Duke of Somerset. . . . London: Walter Lynne, 1550.

In Selectissimam S. Pauli Priorem ad Corinthios Epistolam . . . Commentarii . . . Zurich: Froschoverus, 1551.

In Epistolam S. Pauli Apostoli ad Romanos . . . Commentarii. . . . Basel: P. Perna, 1558.

Defensio Doctrinae Veteris et Apostolicae de Sacrosancto Eucharistiae Sacramento. . . . Zurich: Froschoverus, 1559.

Defensio . . . de Caelibatu. . . . Basel: P. Perna, 1559.

In Librum Iudicum . . . Commentarii. . . . Zurich: Froschoverus, 1565.

Dialogus de Utraque in Christo Natura, . . . Zurich: Froschoverus, August, 1562.

In Primum, Secundum, et Initium Tertii Libri Ethicorum Aristotelis ad Nicomachum. . . . Zurich: Froschoverus, 1563.

Preces Sacrae ex Psalmis Davidis Desumptae. . . . Zurich: Froschoverus, 1566.

In Duos Libros Samuelis Prophetae . . . Commentarii. . . . Zurich: Froschoverus, 1567.

Melachim Id Est, Regum Libri Duo Posteriores cum Commentariis. Zurich: Froschoverus, 1571.

In Primum Librum Mosis Qui Vulgo Genesis Dicitur Commentarii. . . . Heidelberg: Johann Lancellot, 1606.

Trattato della vera Chiesa catholica, et della necessita di viver in essa. N.P.: 1573.

Loci Communes, . . . Edited by Robert Masson. London: Thomas Vautrollerius, 1583.

In Lamentationes Sanctissimi Ieremiae Prophetae . . . Commentarium. Zurich: J. J. Bodmer, 1629.

B. Documents and the Works of other Theologians

Aquinas, Thomas. *Summa Theologiae.* 5 vols. Ottawa: Studium Generale O. P., 1951.

Beza, Theodore. *Icones, id est Verae Imaginis virorum doctrina simul pietate illustrium.* Geneva: J. Laonius, 1580.

——. *Volumen Tractationum Theologicarum.* Geneva: Eustathius Vignon, 1576.

——. *Correspondance de Theodore de Bèze,* Edited by F. Aubert, H. Meylan et al. Geneva: Droz, 1960ff.

Der Briefwechsel der Schweizer mit den Polen. Edited by Theodore Wotschke. Leipzig: M. Heinsius Nachfolger, 1908.

Bucer, Martin. *Opera Latina,* XV, *De Regno Christi.* Edited by François Wendel. Paris: Presses Universitaires de France, 1955.

——. *In Sacra Quatuor Evangelia, Enarrationes. . . .* N. P.: Robertus Stephanus, 1553.

——. *Psalmorum libri quinque . . . enarrati.* N. P.: Robertus Stephanus, 1554.

——. *Martin Bucer: Études sur la correspondance*, Edited by J. V. Pollet. Paris: Presses Universitaires de France, 1958.

Calfhill, James, et al. *De Katherinae . . . Vermilii exhumatione . . . Carmina.* London: John Day, 1561.

Calvin, John. *Opera quae supersunt omnia.* 59 vols. Edited by Wm. Baum, Edward Cunitz and E. Reuss. Brunswick: C. A. Schwetschke, 1863-1900.

Cranmer, Thomas. *The Works of Thomas Cranmer.* Edited by G. E. Duffield. Philadelphia: Fortress Press, 1965.

Erastus, Thomas. *Explicatio Gravissimae Quaestionis utrum excommunicationis. . . .* (London): 1589.

Jewel, John. *The Works of John Jewel.* 4 vols. Edited for the Parker Society by John Ayre. Cambridge: Cambridge University Press, 1845-50.

Luther, Martin. *D. Martin Luthers Werke. Kritische Gesammtausgabe.* Weimar: H. Bohlau, 1883ff.

Melanchthon, Philip. *Philippi Melanthonis Opera quae supersunt omnia.* XIII. Edited by Karl Bretschneider. Halle: C. A. Schwetschke, 1864.

——. *Melanchthon on Christian Doctrine: Loci Communes 1555.* Translated and edited by Clyde Manschreck. New York: Oxford University Press, 1965.

Original Letters Relative to the English Reformation, 1531-58. 2 vols. Edited for the Parker Society by Hastings Robinson. Cambridge: Cambridge University Press, 1846-47.

Perkins, William. *A Golden Chain. . . .* Translated by R. H. Here. Cambridge: John Legat, 1600.

Pomponazzi, Pietro. *Libri Quinque de Fato, De Libero Arbitrio et De Praedestinatione.* Edited by Richard Lemay. Lucca: Thesaurus Mundi, 1957.

——. *Les Causes de merveilles de la nature, ou les enchantements.* Edited and translated by Henri Busson. Paris: Edition Rieder, 1930.

Reformed Dogmatics. Edited and translated by John W. Bearslee. New York: Oxford University Press, 1965. (J. Wollebius, G. Voetius, and F. Turretin)

Schulting, Cornelius. *Bibliotheca catholica contra . . . Locis Communibus Petri Matyris. . . .* Cologne, S. Hemmerden, 1602.

Ursinus, Zacharias. *Commentary on the Heidelberg Catechism.* Translated by G. W. Willard. Grand Rapids: Eerdmans, 1956.

Vives, Juan Luis. *De Anima et Vita Libri Tres.* Basel: R. Winter, 1538.

Zanchi, Girolamo. *Operum Theologicorum . . .* 8 tomes. Geneva: Gamonetus, 1605.

The Zurich Letters. 4 vols. in 2. Edited for the Parker Society by Hastings Robinson. Cambridge: Cambridge University Press, 1842-45.

Zwingli, Hulderic. *Opera*, IV. Edited by M. Schuler and J. Schulthess. Zurich: F. Schulthess, 1841.

——. *Sämtliche Werke.* Edited by E. Egli, G. Finsler, and W. Kohler. Leipzig: M. Heinsius Nachfolger, 1914ff.

II. SECONDARY STUDIES

A. Books

Adam, Gottfried. *Der Streit um die Prädestination im ausgehenden 16. Jahrhundert: Eine Untersuchung zu den Entwürfen von Samuel Huber und Aegidius Hunnius.* Neukirchen: Neukirchener Verlag, 1970.

Allen, Don Cameron. *Mysteriously Meant: The Rediscovery of Pagan Symbolism and Allegorical Interpretation in the Renaissance.* Baltimore: Johns Hopkins University Press, 1970.

Althaus, Paul. *Die Prinzipien der deutschen reformierten Dogmatik im Zeitalter der aristotelischen Scholastik.* Darmstadt: Wissenschaftliche Buchgesellschaft, 1967.

——. *The Theology of Martin Luther*. Translated by Robert Schultz. Philadelphia: Fortress Press, 1966.

Armstrong, Brian G. *Calvinism and the Amyraut Heresy: Protestant Scholasticism and Humanism in Seventeenth Century France*. Madison: University of Wisconsin Press, 1969.

Beck, Lewis White. *Early German Philosophy*. Cambridge, Mass.: Harvard University Press 1969.

Béné, Charles. *Erasme et saint Augustin, ou influence de saint Augustin sur l'humanisme d'Erasme*. Geneva: Droz, 1969.

Bennett, H. S. *English Books and Readers, 1558-1603*. Cambridge: Cambridge University Press, 1965.

Berkouwer, G. C. *Faith and Perseverance*. Grand Rapids: Eerdmans, 1958.

Bietenholz, Peter. *Der Italienische Humanismus und die Blütezeit des Buchdrucks in Basel*. Basel: Verlag von Helbing und Lichtenhahn, 1959.

Bizer, Ernst. *Frühorthodoxie und Rationalismus*. Zurich: Evz-Verlag, 1963.

Blench, J. W. *Preaching in England in the Late Fifteenth and Sixteenth Century*. Oxford: Basil Blackwell, 1964.

Bohatec, Josef. *Die Cartesianische Scholastik in der Philosophie und reformierten Dogmatik des 14. Jahrhunderts*. Hildesheim: Georg Olms, 1966.

Boisset, Jean. *Sagesse et sainteté dans la pensée de Jean Calvin: Essai sur l'humanisme du réformateur français*. Paris: Presses Universitaires de France, 1959.

Bourke, Vernon J. *Augustine's Quest of Wisdom: Life and Philosophy of the Bishop of Hippo*. Milwaukee: Bruce, 1945.

Bouvier, André. *Henri Bullinger: le successeur de Zwingli*. Paris: Droz, 1960.

Bouyer, Louis. *The Spirit and Forms of Protestantism*. Translated by A. V. Littledale. London: Harvill Press, 1956.

Breen, Quirinus. *John Calvin: A Study in French Humanism*. 2nd edition. New York: Archon Press, 1968.

Bromiley, G. W. *Thomas Cranmer, Theologian*. London: Lutterworth, 1956.

Brook, V. J. K. *Whitgift and the English Church*. London: Hodder and Stoughton, 1964.

Burnet, Gilbert. *The History of the Reformation of the Church of England*. Revised by E. Nares. New York: Appleton, 1842.

Calvetti, Carla. *La filosofia di Giovanni Calvino*. Milano: Vita e Pensiero, 1955.

Cantimori, Delio. *Eretici italiani del Cinquecento*. Florence: Sansoni, 1967.

——. *Prospettive di storia ereticale italiana del Cinquecento*. Bari: Laterza, 1960.

Cantù, Cesare. *Gli eretici d'italia: discorsi storici*. Turino: Unione tipografico-editrice, 1865-67. 4 vols. in 2.

Cassirer, Ernst. *The Individual and the Cosmos in Renaissance Philosophy*. Translated by Mario Domandi. Oxford: B. Blackwell, 1963.

Cassirer, Ernst, Randall, John H., Jr., and Kristeller, Paul O., editors. *The Renaissance Philosophy of Man*. Chicago: University of Chicago Press, 1948.

Chenu, M-D. *Toward Understanding St. Thomas*. Translated by A. M. Henry and D. Hughes. Chicago: Regnery, 1964.

Chrisman, Miriam Usher. *Strasbourg and the Reform: A Study in the Process of Change*. New Haven: Yale University Press, 1967.

Church, Frederic C. *The Italian Reformers, 1534-1564*. New York: Columbia University Press, 1932.

Clark, Francis. *Eucharistic Sacrifice and the Reformation*. Westminster, Md.: Newman Press 1960.

Clasen, Claus Peter. *The Palatinate in European History, 1559-1660*. Oxford: Basil Blackwell, 1963.

Collinson, Patrick. *The Elizabethan Puritan Movement*. London: Jonathan Cape, 1967.

Congar, Yves M.-J. *A History of Theology*. Translated and edited by Hunter Guthrie. Garden City, N.Y.: Doubleday, 1968.

Copleston, Frederick. *A History of Philosophy*. Westminster, Md.: Newman Press, 1953ff.

Costello, William T. *The Scholastic Curriculum at Early Seventeenth Century Cambridge*. Cambridge: Harvard University Press, 1958.

Courvoisier, Jacques. *Zwingli: A Reformed Theologian*. Richmond, Va.: John Knox Press, 1963.

Cremeans, Charles Davis. *The Reception of Calvinist Thought in England*. Urbana: University of Illinois Press, 1949.

Croce, Benedetto. *Vite di avventure di fede e di passione*. Bari: Laterza, 1936.

Curtis, Mark. *Oxford and Cambridge in Transition 1558-1642*. Oxford: Oxford University Press 1959.

Denzinger, Henricus, and Schönmetzer, Adolphus. *Enchiridion Symbolorum, Definitionum, et Declarationum de Rebus Fidei et Morum*. Barcelona: Herder, 1963.

Davies, Horton. *Worship and Theology in England from Cranmer to Hooker, 1543-1603*. Princeton: Princeton University Press, 1970.

Dibon, Paul. *La Philosophie néerlandaise au siècle d'or, I, L'Enseignement philosophiques dans les universités à l'époque précartésienne*. Paris: Elsevier, 1954.

Dominigo de Santa Teresa. *Juan De Valdes*. Rome: Universitas Gregoriana, 1957.

Dugmore, C. W. *The Mass and the English Reformers*. London: Macmillan, 1958.

Dowey, Edward A. *The Knowledge of God in Calvin's Theology*. New York: Columbia University Press, 1952.

Eells, Hastings. *Martin Bucer*. New Haven: Yale University Press, 1931.

Evennett, Henry Outram. *The Cardinal of Lorraine and the Council of Trent*. Cambridge: Cambridge University Press, 1930.

Febvre, Lucien. *Le Problème de l'incroyance au XVIe siècle*. Paris: Albin Michel, 1942.

Fenlon, Dermot. *Heresy and Obedience in Tridentine Italy: Cardinal Pole and the Counter Reformation*. Cambridge: Cambridge University Press 1972.

Fraenkel, Peter. *Testimonia Patrum: the Function of the Patristic Argument in the Theology of Philip Melanchthon*. Geneva: Droz, 1961.

Fraenkel, Peter, and Greschat, Martin. *Fünfzehn Jahre Melanchthonforschung: Sechs Literaturberichte (1945-1965)*. Geneva: Droz, 1967.

Ganoczy, Alexandre. *La Bibliothèque de l'académie de Calvin*. Geneva: Droz, 1969.

——. *Le Jeune Calvin: Genèse et évolution de sa vocation réformatrice*. Wiesbaden: Franz Steiner Verlag, 1966.

Gardy, Frederic. *Bibliographie des œuvres théologiques, littéraires, historiques, et juridiques de Théodore de Bèze*. Geneva: Droz, 1960.

Garrett, Christina H. *The Marian Exiles: A Study in the Origins of the Elizabethan Puritanism*. Cambridge: Cambridge University Press, 1938.

Gerdes, Daniel. *Scrinium Antiquarum sive Miscellanea Groningana, III, II*. Groningen: Barlinkhof, 1753.

Gerrish, Brian A. *Grace and Reason: A Study in the Theology of Luther*. Oxford: Clarendon Press, 1962.

Gilbert, Neal W. *Renaissance Concepts of Method*. New York: Columbia University Press, 1960.

Gilson, Etienne. *The Christian Philosophy of Saint Augustine*. Translated by L. Lynch. New York: Vintage Books, Random House, 1967.

——. *History of Christian Philosophy in the Middle Ages*. New York: Random House, 1955.

Ginzburg, Carlo. *Il nicodemismo: Simulazione e dissimulazione religiosa nell' Europa del'500*. Turin: G. Einaudi, 1970.

Gorham, George Cornelius. *Gleanings of a Few Scattered Ears During the Reformation in England and the Times Immediately Succeeding A.D. 1533-A.D. 1589.* London: Bell and Daldy, 1857.

Grabmann, Martin. *Die Geschichte der scholastischen Methode.* Berlin: Akademie-Verlag, 1957.

Greenslade, S. L., editor. *The Cambridge History of the Bible, III, The West from the Reformation to the Present Day.* Cambridge: Cambridge University Press, 1969.

Gründler, Otto. *Die Gotteslehre Girolami Zanchi und ihre Bedeutung für seine Lehre von der Prädestination.* Neukirchen: Neukirchener Verlag, 1965.

Haw, Reginald. *The State of Matrimony.* London: S.P.C.K., 1952.

Haydn, Hiram. *The Counter-Renaissance.* New York: Scribner's, 1950.

Heppe, Heinrich. *Die Dogmatik der evangelisch-reformierten Kirche.* Neukirchen: Neukirchener Verlag, 1958.

Hughes, Philip. *A History of the Church, III, The Revolt Against the Church: Aquinas to Luther.* New York: Sheed and Ward, 1947.

Jahier, Augusto. *Reformatori e reformati italiani dei secoli XV° e XVI°.* Florence: Società Editrice Claudiana, 1925.

Jedin, Hubert. *A History of the Council of Trent.* Translated by Ernest Graf. New York: Nelson, 1957, 1961.

——. *Studien über die Schriftstellertätigkeit Albert Pigges.* Münster i. W.: Aschendorffsche Verlagsbuchhandlung, 1931.

Jordan, W. K. *Edward VI: The Young King.* Cambridge: Harvard University Press, 1968.

——. *Edward VI: The Threshold of Power.* Cambridge: Harvard University Press, 1970.

Kickel, Walter. *Vernuft und Offenbarung bei Theodor Beza.* Neukirchen: Neukirchener Verlag, 1967.

Klibansky, Raymond. *The Continuity of the Platonic Tradition during the Middle Ages.* London: Warburg Institute, 1939.

Knappen, M. M. *Tudor Puritanism.* Chicago: University of Chicago Press, 1939.

Knowles, David. *The Evolution of the Medieval Mind.* New York: Vintage Books, Random House, 1962.

Kristeller. *Eight Philosophers of the Renaissance.* Stanford: Stanford University Press, 1964.

——. *Iter Italicum.* London: Warburg Institute, 1963-67. 2 vols.

——. *Renaissance Thought: The Classic, Scholastic, and Humanist Strains.* New York: Harper Torchbooks, 1961.

——. *Le Thomisme et la pensée italienne de la renaissance.* Paris: J. Vrin, 1967.

Leff, Gordon. *Gregory of Rimini: Tradition and Innovation in Fourteenth Century Thought.* New York: Barnes and Noble, 1961.

Leonard, Emile G. *A History of Protestantism, I, The Reformation.* Translated by J. Reid. II, *The Establishment.* Translated by R. M. Bethell. London: Nelson, 1965, 67.

Liedtke, Helmut, *Pädagogik der werdenden Orthodoxie: Ein Beitrag zur Bestimmung des Verhältnisses von Reformation und Humanismus.* Königsdorf: Hans Reykers, 1968.

Locher, Gottfried. *Huldrych Zwingli in neuer Sicht.* Zurich: Zwingli Verlag, 1969.

Lortz, Joseph. *The Reformation in Germany.* Translated by Ronald Walls. New York: Herder and Herder, 1968 .2 vols.

Maddison, Carol. *Marcantonio Flaminio: Poet, Humanist, and Reformer.* Chapel Hill: University of North Carolina Press, 1965.

Mallet, Charles Edward. *A History of the University of Oxford, II, The Sixteenth and Seventeenth Centuries,* London: Methuen, 1924.

McKenzie, John L. *Dictionary of the Bible*. Milwaukee: Bruce, 1965.

McLelland, Joseph C. *The Visible Words of God: An Exposition of the Sacramental Theology of Peter Martyr Vermigli*. Grand Rapids: Eerdmans, 1957.

McNair, Philip. *Peter Martyr in Italy: An Anatomy of Apostasy*. Oxford: Clarendon Press, 1967.

McNeill, John T. *The History and Character of Calvinism*. New York: Oxford University Press, 1954.

McSorley, Harry J. *Luther: Right or Wrong? An Ecumenical-Theological Study of Luther's Major Works, The Bondage of the Will*. New York: Newman Press; Minneapolis: Augsburg Publishing House, 1969.

Meyer, Gerhard. *Die Entwicklung der Strassburger Universität aus dem Gymnasium und Akademie des Johann Sturm*. Frankfurt a. M.: Selbstverlag des Institutes, 1926.

Miller, Perry. *The New England Mind: The Seventeenth Century*. Cambridge: Harvard University Press, 1963.

Milner, Benjamin Charles. *Calvin's Doctrine of the Church*. Leiden: E. J. Brill, 1970.

Moltmann, Jürgen. *Prädestination und Perseveranz: Geschichte und Bedeutung der reformierten Lehre "de perseverantia sanctorum."* Neukirchen: Neukirchener Verlag, 1961.

Morison, Samuel Eliot. *Harvard College in the Seventeenth Century*. Cambridge: Harvard University Press, 1936. 2 vols.

Muller, James Arthur. *Stephen Gardiner and the Tudor Reaction*. New York: Octagon Books, 1970.

Nardi, Bruno. *Saggi sull' aristotelismo padovano dal secolo XIV al XVI*. Florence: Sansoni, 1958.

——. *Studi su Pietro Pomponazzi*. Florence: Felice Le Monnier, 1965.

New, John F. H. *Anglican and Puritan: The Basis of their Opposition, 1558-1640*. Stanford: Stanford University Press, 1964.

Niesel, Wilhelm. *The Theology of Calvin*. Translated by Harold Knight. London: Lutterworth Press, 1956.

Nieto, Jose C. *Juan de Valdes and the Origins of the Spanish and Italian Reformation*. Geneva: Droz, 1970.

Oberman, Heiko Augustinus. *The Harvest of Medieval Theology: Gabriel Biel and Late Medieval Nominalism*. Cambridge: Harvard University Press, 1963.

O'Malley, John W. *Giles of Viterbo on Church and Reform*. Leiden: E. J. Brill, 1968.

Ong, Walter. *Ramus: Method and the Decay of Dialogue*. Cambridge: Harvard University Press, 1958.

Ozment, Steven, ed. *The Reformation in Medieval Perspective*. Chicago: Quadrangle Books 1971.

Pelikan, Jaroslav. *From Luther to Kierkegaard: A Study in the History of Theology*. St. Louis: Concordia, 1950.

Petersen, Peter. *Geschichte der aristotelischen Philosophie im Protestantischen Deutschland*. Leipzig: Verlag von Felix Meiner, 1921.

Popkin, Richard H. *The History of Scepticism from Erasmus to Descartes*. New York: Harper Torchbooks, 1964.

Poppi, Antonio. *Saggi sul pensiero inedite di Pietro Pomponazzi*. Padua: Antenore, 1970.

——. *Introduzione all' aristotelismo padovano*. Padua: Antenore, 1970.

Porter, Harry C. *Reformation and Reaction in Tudor Cambridge*. Cambridge: Cambridge University Press, 1958.

Preus, Robert D. *The Theology of Post-Reformation Lutheranism: a Study of Theological Prolegomena*. St. Louis: Concordia Publishing House, 1970.

Powell, Chilton. *English Domestic Relations, 1487-1653*. New York: Columbia University Press, 1917.

Procter, Francis, and Frere, H. H. *A New History of the Book of Common Prayer*. London: Macmillan, 1902.

Raitt, Jill. *The Eucharistic Theology of Theodore Beza: Development of the Reformed Doctrine*. AAR. Studies in Religion, No. 4, Chambersburg Pa. 1972.

Randall, John Herman, Jr. *The Career of Philosophy*, I, *From the Middle Ages to the Enlightenment*. New York: Columbia University Press, 1970.

——. *The School of Padua and the Emergence of Modern Science*. Padua: Antenore, 1961.

Rex, Walter. *Essays on Pierre Bayle and Religious Controversy*. The Hague: Martinus Nijhoff, 1965.

Ridley, Jasper. *John Knox*. Oxford: Clarendon Press, 1968.

——. *Thomas Cranmer*. Oxford: Clarendon Press, 1962.

Ritschl, Otto. *Dogmengeschichte des Protestantismus*, III. Göttingen: Vandenhoeck und Ruprecht, 1927.

Rodocanachi, E. *La Réforme en italie*. 2 vols. Paris: A. Picard, 1920.

Rondet, Henri. *The Grace of Christ: A Brief History of the Theology of Grace*. Translated by Tad Guzie. Westminster, Md.: Newman Press, 1967.

Ruffini, Francesco. *Studi sui riformatori italiani*. Turin: Ramella, 1955.

Santini, Luigi. *La comunità evangelica di Bergamo: Vicende storiche*. Torre Pellice: Claudiana, 1960.

Scharlemann, Robert. *Thomas Aquinas and John Gerhard*. New Haven: Yale University Press, 1964.

Schenk, W. *Reginald Pole, Cardinal of England*. London: Longmans, Green and Co. 1950.

Schlosser, Friedrich Christoph. *Leben des Theodore de Beza und des Peter Martyr Vermili*. Heidelberg: Mohr und Zimmer, 1809.

Schmidt, Charles. *Peter Martyr Vermigli: Leben und ausgewählte Schriften*. Elberfeld: R. L. Friderichs, 1858.

——. *Vie de Pierre Martyr Vermigli*. Strasbourg: Silbermann, 1834.

Seeberg, Reinhold. *Textbook of the History of Doctrines*. Translated by Charles Hay. Grand Rapids: Baker Book House, 1966.

Simler, Josiah. *Oratio de vita et obitu viri optimi, praestantissimi Theologi D. Petri Martyris Vermilii. . . .* Zurich: Froschoverus, 1562. Also printed in Martyr's *Loci Communes*.

Simon, Joan. *Education and Society in Tudor England*. Cambridge: Cambridge University Press, 1966.

Smiths, Luchesius. *Saint Augustin dans l'œuvre de Jean Calvin*. 2 vols. Assen: Van Gorcum, 1957-58.

Smyth, Charles H. *Cranmer and the Reformation under Edward VI*. Cambridge: Cambridge University Press, 1926.

Sohm, Walter. *Die Schule Johann Sturms und die Kirche Strassburgs in ihren gegenseitigen Verhältnissen, 1530-1581*. Munich: R. Oldenbourg, 1912.

Southgate, W. M. *John Jewel and the Problem of Doctrinal Authority*. Cambridge: Harvard University Press, 1962.

Steinmetz, David C. *Reformers in the Wings*. Philadelphia: Fortress Press, 1971.

Stephens, W. P. *The Holy Spirit in the Theology of Martin Bucer*. Cambridge: Cambridge University Press, 1970.

Sturm, Edmann K. *Der junge Zacharias Ursin*. Neukirchen: Neukirchener Verlag, 1972.

Sturm, Klaus. *Die Theologie Peter Martyr Vermiglis während seines ersten Aufenthalts in Strassburg 1542-1547*. Neukirchen: Neukirchener Verlag, 1971.

Strype, John. *Ecclesiastical Memorials*. 2 vols. Oxford: Clarendon Press, 1822.

Sudhoff, Karl. *C. Olevianus und Z. Ursinus: Leben und ausgewählte Schriften*. Elberfeld: R. L. Friderichs, 1857.

Thorndike, Lynn. *A History of Magic and Experimental Science*, V. New York: Columbia University Press, 1959.

Todd, John M. *Martin Luther: A Biographical Study*. London: Burns and Oates, 1964.

Torrance, T. F. *Calvin's Doctrine of Man*. London: Lutterworth, 1949.

Trinkaus, Charles. *In Our Image and Likeness: Humanity and Divinity in Italian Humanist Thought*. 2 vols. Chicago: University of Chicago Press, 1970.

Trinterud, Leonard J., editor, *Elizabethan Puritanism*. New York: Oxford University Press, 1971.

Waddington, Charles. *Ramus, sa vie, ses écrits et ses opinions*. Paris: Meyrueis, 1855.

Walser, Peter. *Die Prädestination bei Heinrich Bullinger im Zusammenhang mit seiner Gotteslehre*. Zurich: Zwingli Verlag, 1957.

Weber, E. *Der Einfluss der Protestantischen Schulphilosophie auf die orthodox-lutherische Dogmatik*. Leipzig: A. Deichert'sche Verlagsbuchhandlung, 1908.

Weber, Hans Emil. *Reformation, Orthodoxie, und Rationalismus*. Gütersloh: Gerd Mohn, 1940.

Wendel, François. *Calvin: The Origins and Development of His Religious Thought*. Translated by Philip Mairet. New York: Harper and Row, 1963.

Wesel-Roth, Ruth. *Thomas Erastus*. Lahr, Baden: Verlag Moritz Schauenburg, 1954.

Williams, George Huntston. *The Radical Reformation*. Philadelphia: Westminster Press, 1962.

Willis, E. David. *Calvin's Catholic Christology: the Function of the So-Called Extra Calvinisticum in Calvin's Theology*. Leiden: E. J. Brill, 1966.

de Wulf, Maurice. *History of Medieval Philosophy*. 3 vols. Translated by Ernest Messenger. London: Thomas Nelson, 1951ff.

Wundt, Max. *Die deutsche Schulmetaphysik des 17. Jahrhunderts:*. Tübingen: J. C. B. Mohr, 1939.

Yates, Frances A. *Giordano Bruno and the Hermetic Tradition*. New York: Vintage Books, Random House, 1964.

Young, M. *The Life and Times of Aonio Paleario, or the History of the Italian Reformers of the Sixteenth Century*. 2 vols. London: Bell and Daldy, 1860.

B. ARTICLES

Anderson, Marvin W. "Word and Spirit in Exile (1542-61): the Biblical Writings of Peter Martyr Vermigli," *Journal of Ecclesiastical History*, XXI, 1970, 193-201.

Anderson, Marvin. "Peter Martyr, Reformed Theologian (1542-1562): His Letters to Heinrich Bullinger and John Calvin." *Sixteenth Century Journal*, IV, 1973, 41-64.

——. "Peter Martyr on Romans," *Scottish Journal of Theology*, XXVI, 1973, 401-20.

——. "Pietro Martyre Vermigli on the Scope and Clarity of Scripture". *Theologische Zeitschrift*. forthcoming, Fall, 1974.

Ashton, J. W. "Peter Martyr on the Function and Character of Literature," *Philological Quarterly*, XVIII, 1939, 311-314.

Battenhouse, Roy W. "The Doctrine of Man in Calvin and in Renaissance Platonism," *Journal of the History of Ideas*, IX, 1948, 447-71.

Beesley, Alan. "An Unpublished Source of the Book of Common Prayer: Peter Martyr Vermigli's *Adhortatio ad Coenam Domini Mysticam*," *Journal of Ecclesiastical History*, XIX, 1968, 83-88.

Boesch, Paul. "Julius Terentianus, Factotum des Petrus Martyr Vermilius und Korrector der Offizin Froschauer," *Zwingliana*, VIII, 1948, 587-601.

Brassel, Thomas. "Drei umstrittene Traktate Peter Martyr Vermiglis," *Zwingliana*, XI, 1962, 476.

Courtenay, William J. "Covenant and Causality in Pierre D'Ailly," *Speculum*, XLVI, 1971, 94-119.

Gardy, F. "Les livres de Pierre Martyr Vermigli conservés à la Bibliothèque de Genève," *Anzeiger für Schweizerische Geschichte*, L, 1919, 1-6.

Gray, Hanna. "Renaissance Humanism: the Pursuit of Eloquence," *Journal of The History of Ideas*, XXIV, 1963, 497-514.

Gilson, Etienne. "Autour de Pomponazzi: Problématique de l'immortalité de l'âme en Italie au début du XVIe siècle," *Archives d'histoire doctrinale et littéraire du moyen age*, XXVIII, 1961, 163-279.

——. L'Affaire de l'immortalité de l'âme à Venise au début du XVIe siècle, in *Umanismo Europeo e Umanismo Veneziano*. Edited by V. Branca, Florence, 1963.

Guellury, R. "L'Evolution des méthodes théologiques à Louvain d'Erasme à Jensenius," *Revue d'histoire ecclésiastique*, XXXVII, 1941, 31-144.

Hall, Basil. "Calvin against the Calvinists" in *John Calvin: Courtenay Studiae in Reformation Theology*, edited by Gervase Duffield. Grand Rapids: Eerdmans 1966. 19-37.

Hotze, M. A. "Scholastic Theology," *The New Catholic Encyclopedia*, New York: McGraw Hill, 1967. XII, 1153.

Hugelshofer, W. "Zum Porträt des Petrus Martyr Vermilius," *Zwingliana*, V, 1930, 127-29.

Jung, Eva Maria. "On the Nature of Evangelism in Sixteenth Century Italy," *Journal of the History of Ideas*, XIV, 1953, 511-27.

Logan, O. M. T. "Grace and Justification: Some Italian Views in the Sixteenth and Early Seventeenth Century," *Journal of Ecclesiastical History*, XX, 1969, 67-78.

Lohr, Charles H. "Aristotle in the West: Some Recent Books," *Traditio*, XXV, 1969, 417-31.

McLelland, Joseph. "The Reformed Doctrine of Predestination according to Peter Martyr." *Scottish Journal of Theology*, VIII, 1955, 255-271.

Mesnard, Pierre. "The Pedagogy of Johann Sturm (1507-1589) and its Evangelical Inspiration," *Studies in the Renaissance*, Translated by Evelyn Hartman. XIII, 1966, 200-19.

Monter, E. William. "The Italians in Geneva, 1550-1600: A New Look," in *Genève et l'Italie*, Edited by Luc Monnier. Geneva: Droz, 1969.

Nauert, Charles G. "The Clash of Humanists and Scholastics: An Approach to Pre Reformation Controversies," *Sixteenth Century Journal*, IV, 1973, 1-18.

Ong, Walter J. "Ramist Method and the Commercial Mind," *Studies in the Renaissance*, VIII, 1961, 155-72.

Paist, Benjamin F. "Peter Martyr and the Colloquy of Poissy," *Princeton Theological Review*, XX, 1922, 212-31; 418-47; 616-46.

Pirotti, Umberto. "Aristotelian Philosophy and the Popularization of Learning: Benedetto Varchi and Renaissance Aristotelianism," in *The Late Italian Renaissance*. Edited and translated by Eric Cochrane. New York: Harper Torchbooks, 1970. 168-208.

Rist, Gilbert. "Modernité de la methode théologique de Calvin." *Revue de théologie et de philosophie*, XVIII, 1968, 19-33.

Ristori, Renzo. "Le Origini della riforma a Lucca," *Rinascimento*, III, 1952, 269-91.

Santini, Luigi. "Appunti sulla ecclesiologia di P. M. Vermigli e la edificazione della Chiesa," *Bolletino della società di studi valdesi*, CIV, 1958, 69-75.

——. " 'Scisma' e 'eresia' nel pensiero di P. M. Vermigli," *Bolletino della società di studi valdesi*, CXXV, 1969, 27-43.

Schmidt, Charles B. "Aristotle as a Cuttlefish: the Origin and Development of a Renaissance Image," *Studies in the Renaissance*, XII, 1965, 60-72.

Spalding, James. "The Reformatio Legum Ecclesiasticarum of 1552 and the Furthering of Discipline in England," *Church History*, XXXIX, 1970, 162-71.

Spini, Giogio. "Riforma italiana e mediazioni ginevrine nella nuova Inghilterra puritana," in *Ginevra e l'Italia*. Edited by Delio Cantimori et al. Florence: Sansoni, 1959. 451-89.

Staedtke, Joachim. "Der Züricher Prädestinationsstreit von 1560," *Zwingliana*, IX, 1953, 536-46.

——. "Drei umstrittene Traktate Peter Martyr Vermiglis", *Zwingliana*, XI, 1962, 553-554.

Starr, G. A. "Antedatings from Nicholas Udall's Translation of Peter Martyr's *Discourse*," *Notes and Queries*, new series, XIII, 1966, 9-12.

Trinkaus, Charles. "The Problem of Free Will in the Renaissance and the Reformation," *Journal of the History of Ideas*, X, 1949, 51-62.

Vander Molen, R. J., "Anglican against Puritan: Ideological Origins during the Marian Exile." *Church History*, XIIL, 1973, 45-57.

Wallace, Dewey D., Jr., "The Doctrine of Predestination in the Early English Reformation," *Church History*, XIIIL, 1974, 201-215.

Williams, Arnold. "Milton and the Renaissance Commentaries on Genesis," *Modern Philology*, XXXVII, 1939, 263-78.

Williams, George H. "Camillo Renato," in *Italian Reformation Studies in Honor of Laelius Socinus*. Edited by John A. Tedeschi. Florence: Felice Le Monnier, 1965. 103-83.

——. "The Two Social Strands in Italian Anabaptism ca. 1526-ca. 1565" in *The Social History of the Reformation*. Edited by L. P. Buck and J. W. Zophy. Columbus: Ohio State Press, 1972.

C. Unpublished Material

Bray, John Stanley. "Theodore Beza's Doctrine of Predestination." unpublished Ph. D. dissertation. Department of History, Stanford University, 1972.

Huelin, Gordon. "Peter Martyr and the English Reformation." Unpublished Ph. D. dissertation, University of London, 1955.

Toft, Daniel John. "Shadows of Kings: The Political Thought of David Pareus, 1548-1622." Unpublished Ph. D. dissertation, Department of History, University of Wisconsin, 1970.

——. "Zacharias Ursinus: A Study in the Development of Calvinism." Unpublished Master's thesis, Department of History, University of Wisconsin, 1962.

INDEX OF NAMES

INDEX OF SUBJECTS